poetic
obligation

poetic
obligation

ETHICS IN EXPERIMENTAL
AMERICAN POETRY AFTER
1945 **G. MATTHEW JENKINS**

University of Iowa Press IOWA CITY

TC P

University of Iowa Press, Iowa City 52242
Copyright © 2008 by the University of Iowa Press
www.uiowapress.org
All rights reserved
Printed in the United States of America
Design by Rich Hendel

The University of Iowa Press is a member of Green Press
Initiative and is committed to preserving natural resources.

Printed on acid-free paper

LCCN: 2007907339
ISBN-13: 978-1-58729-635-2
ISBN-10: 1-58729-635-7

08 09 10 11 12 C 5 4 3 2 1

for Logan

Contents

Preface

AUDREY. I do not know what 'poetical' is. Is it honest in deed and
word? Is it a true thing?
TOUCHSTONE. No, truly; for the truest poetry is the most
feigning, and lovers are given to poetry; and what they
swear in poetry may be said as lovers they do feign.
(*As You Like It*, III.iii)

In Plato's *Republic,* Socrates famously perpetuates what he calls
"the ancient quarrel between philosophy and poetry" by banishing imitative
poetry from the real work of society—the pursuit of the True, the Just, and
the Good. These values, of course, are best pursued by philosophers who
by all means should rule the new State. In that text, Socrates essentially
lays claim to ethics and justice as the sole propriety of philosophy, which
unfailingly avoids the emotionalism and ruse inherent in other forms of discourse.[1] Poetry, he argues, is the worst of any of the arts because it is too far
removed from truth to do any good in the polis, unless that be singing the
epic tales of military heroes who bring glory to the State and to higher truth.
In fact, poetry distracts from the pursuit of justice and virtue.[2] For many
centuries, as Shakespeare's satire of Touchstone's position above indicates,
this interpretation of Plato's rejection of poetry has dominated not only the
theory and criticism of poetry but its public perception as well.

But beginning with the likes of Friedrich Nietzsche and Martin Heidegger, philosophy increasingly draws, particularly after World War II, on art
and literature for its inspiration and models for new ways of thinking. For
Heidegger, it is Rainer Maria Rilke and Heinrich Heine, for Jacques Derrida
it is Francis Ponge, for Gilles Deleuze and Félix Guattari, it is Franz Kafka
and Samuel Beckett, for Julia Kristeva it is James Joyce and Stéphane Mallarmé. In conjunction with many avant-garde American poets' penchant for
theory, the new respect for the critical power of creative discourse within
twentieth-century philosophy is a key condition in the possibility of a new
ethics and poetics.[3]

To chart this changing relation between poetry and philosophy, this project explores a "double-double turn" in writing and thought circa 1960 that

includes both the infamous "linguistic turn" and what Peter Baker calls "the ethical turn" in the fields of poetry, theory, and criticism. Not only are there two ostensible "turns" in the second half of the twentieth century, ethical and linguistic, but these turns occur both in philosophy and poetry on two continents roughly at the same time. Beginning with this historical event and focusing on one side of each turn (the philosophy of Europe and the poetry of the United States—the examination of the philosophy of the United States with the poetry of France would require another separate work), this project locates in the poetry and poetics of experimental or avant-garde American poetry a different relationship between poetry and ethics than what has been imagined since Plato. In fact, the various turns on both sides of the Atlantic show the shared historical, cultural, and social conditions that fostered such reconsiderations of ethics and poetics. But rather than revealing some model of influence where philosophy would again be king of the Republic and poetry its shamed handmaiden, I attempt to show a parallel discovery by both sides of a new approach to ethics. No doubt these American poets were conditioned by the growing ethical concerns of French existential and poststructuralist thought, but their poetic tradition was already enacting many of the ethical principles that the philosophers were merely describing. Drawing on the formal lessons learned from their Modernists predecessors, including Gertrude Stein, Ezra Pound, and William Carlos Williams, this tradition of poets—often called *avant-garde, experimental, innovative,* or *postmodern*—spans several generations starting with George Oppen and ending with the likes of Susan Howe. One purpose of this work is to investigate the involvement of these three generations of experimental poets to this ethical-linguistic turn and to show that this ethical concern continues through the second half of the twentieth century. Living in the shadow of the devastation of two world wars and one cold one, these poets and philosophers question many of the assumptions about ethics and language that inform philosophy from Plato through Hegel. Namely, these twentieth-century writers question a stable notion of truth, the certainty of reason, the unity of the rational subject, the antagonism toward the Other, and the possibility of ethics (and poetics) after Auschwitz. This is why it is important to study the avant-garde poetics of America and the theoretical works coming out of the continent at this time: they can change our notion of philosophy and truth, a change that necessarily conditions the emerging rapprochement between poetry and ethics.

In addition to these three historical contexts—the question of the relation between poetry and philosophy, the evolution of avant-garde American poetry, and the emergence of postmodern ethical theory—my project participates in a recent critical development that Lawrence Buell calls *the new ethical inquiry* (12). Beginning perhaps in 1978 with the translation into English of Derrida's *Writing and Difference*, which introduced English-speaking audiences to Emmanuel Levinas's ethical thought,[4] this mode of criticism takes seriously the implications of postmodern ethical theory for the reading of literature. Among the writers that Buell outlines in his introduction to the 1999 issue of *PMLA* that announced this trend, I include the significant number of texts that address the work of Levinas for considerations of language, linguistics, art, and literature. A prime example is Jill Robbins's *Altered Reading* that shows both the limits and possibilities of Levinas's thought for literary studies.

This renewed interest in ethics—which had often been discounted in early postmodern thought as a "grand narrative" along with science, religion, capitalism, communism, psychoanalysis, and philosophy—is conditioned by a hostile cultural environment. The charges against postmodern ethics come from both sides of the political spectrum. From the right in Western popular culture and mass media, the criticisms include nihilism and relativism, while from the philosophical left the likes of Jurgen Habermas claim that postmodern thought and art cannot address our serious historical and moral crises. Similarly, this current ethical inquiry is conditioned by a globalized economy and new technological advancements that put us face-to-face with others around the world and challenge our ethical interactions with them. Although I do not fully explore these historical conditions for the new ethical inquiry as the focus of my project, I bring them up in the interest of self-disclosure and situating my perspective *as a perspective.*

Another important critical context for my study, perhaps the most important guiding issue, is the changing use during the period in question of the term *the Other,* which plays a central role in my reconsideration of poetry and ethics. In the introduction and subsequent chapters, I distinguish my use of the terms *Other, otherness,* and *alterity* from those employed frequently in postcolonial, multicultural, psychoanalytic, and feminist theory. By *the Other,* I mean what Levinas would describe as a person who manifests as a face that speaks but who cannot be reduced to knowledge or theme. The synonymous terms, *otherness* and *alterity,* refer to that quality the Other exudes of being beyond knowledge. Because language embodies this ethical relationship for Levinas, his notion of alterity gives us a new way to think of the ethical implications of poetic form. Once we begin to notice these

implications, I argue, we can also see that the poetry has already been enacting what the philosophers were merely theorizing.

My book, oriented within those critical contexts, follows a line of inquiry
recently begun by the likes of Joan Retallack, Peter Baker, Krzysztof Ziarek,
and Tim Woods into the ethical valence of postmodern American poetry.
My inquiry, however, attempts to do things that I think are particularly lacking in the previous: (1) locate the "ethical turn" in the three generations of
this experimental poetry historically;[5] (2) argue for hermeneutical and phenomenological "close-reading" as a way to seek the invitation to ethical relations with alterity in writing; and (3) consider poetry as a "way of thinking
ethically" that takes poetic form into consideration as bearing ethical meaning that philosophy negates in, as Levinas would say, its drive to "speak
without a stop" ("Servant" 153). Ultimately, the question I want to ask is, what
can this experimental poetry and poetics teach us about ethics in a postmodern world? To begin answering this question, I focus primarily on ethical theory, particularly Levinas's, and the formal elements of a tradition of
poetry that reconsiders the way we relate to the Other.

As to the scope of my project, I examine three closely related generations
of American poets who all take the ethical turn in their poetry and poetics
starting approximately around 1960. George Oppen and Charles Reznikoff
are the oldest of my poets, though slightly younger than their Modernist
contemporaries, and have been associated with the Objectivist poetics of
Louis Zukofsky beginning in the 1920s. Both of their careers, however, do
not truly "take off" until after World War II when their poetry deals with
ethical issues uniquely in both form and content. In the first part of the
book, I begin with their rejection of Modernist totality and chart the development of a poetics of obligation that involves an infinite responsibility for
and nonjudgment of the Other. In Part II of the book, I look at the work
of two poets, Robert Duncan and Edward Dorn, who arguably reach their
prime during the 1950s and 1960s, the height of the so-called ethical turn.
These two poets knew each other from their time at the experimental Black
Mountain College and through their shared network of fellow poets and
friends, including poets Charles Olson, Denise Levertov, and Robert Creeley.
Their ethics involve the issues of community and embodiment that marked
the social change attributed to this time period. Finally, I end with two poets
who began writing poetry after 1960 but who are probably the most steeped
in the postmodern context of philosophy and the historical context of the
social upheaval of the time, particularly the women's movement. Both poets,
Lyn Hejinian and, to a lesser extent, Susan Howe, are associated with the

avant-garde group of Language poets, who began corresponding and working together in the late 1960s and early 1970s and continuing into the twenty-first century.

I choose American poetry coming out of Modernism after World War II because it more boldly invites otherness, or alterity, into its content and, especially, its form. The formal experiments of these poets imply new understandings of language far beyond the mimetic vehicle that Plato did (and most of philosophy until the nineteenth century). The new understandings of language, found in these writers' poetry and poetics, range from seeing language as embodying unconscious energies to reflecting corresponding social and political orders. Such ideas, though unique in their own right, are best illuminated in the context of the concomitant rise of discussions of ethics and language in continental philosophy, namely the poststructuralism of psychoanalysis, deconstruction, feminism, neo-Marxism, and phenomenology. Therefore, I place each poet in dialogue with specific philosophers who are addressing some of the same ethical issues as each poet (e.g., in the 1940s and 1950s Maurice Merleau-Ponty is dealing with the role of the body and sexuality in ethical relations, as is Robert Duncan). More importantly, though, these poets were concerned with language as an obligation to others always already, to use a common poststructuralist phrase, immersed in a complex social network. The poets conceive of that interrelation as the necessary condition for ethics, law, morality, and goodness traditionally defined. In many ways, the poetry anticipates and extends (by way of form) the developments of the philosophy, but this possibility has rarely been considered in the ascension of theory in the academy since the early 1980s.

These writers, by shunning the platonic demand that poetry serve a dialectical, mimetic form of truth, follow a more uncertain and circuitous route to unlock poetry's ethical power. At the same time, both poets and philosophers reject the idea that philosophy must be propositional, dialectical, prosaic, and have nothing to do with poetry or poetic form. Instead of writing poetry that seeks to represent some singular and limited reality and therefore capture truth, these poets explore the ambiguities, uncertainties, and aporias in language that lead us past truth and to what lets truth itself arise—the ethical, social relationship with the Other.

In short, the poetics and poetry of these experimental American writers demonstrates that poetry can be *more* ethical than philosophy because it speaks with a language that does not try to control, judge, know, or totalize the Other. The poetry of the writers in my project indicates a broader posture in American verse that welcomes the Other into language—both through

intentional artistic choice and through demands that override and over-
whelm intention—and faces us with the obligation that the Other always
demands of us. This courage to accept the ethical obligation for the Other
separates this experimental poetics from other forms of poetry and writing
and offers an example of how to read humanity's cultural and linguistic production in a new, ethical way.

As many of my colleagues in ethical criticism have acknowledged, academic work is always beholden to the Other for its existence, and it is no different with this inquiry. I would first like to thank my friends and mentors
who gave me inspiration for and invaluable feedback on drafts of the manuscript: Joan Retallack, Joseph Kronick, Marjorie Perloff, Toril Moi, Burt
Hatlen, David Goldstein, Ann Vickery, Krzysztof Ziarek, Stephen Fredman,
Jacqueline Brogan, and Gerald Bruns. This project would have not been
possible without the financial and technical support of the following organizations: The University of Tulsa, especially the Department of English Language and Literature, the Office of Research, and the Dean of Arts and
Sciences, D. Thomas Benediktson; the Department of English at the University of Notre Dame, particularly Ewa Ziarek; the Notre Dame Graduate
School, including the Zahm Travel Grant and the GSU Travel Grant Committee; the Charlotte Newcombe Fellowship Foundation; and the Friends
of the University of California, San Diego. Thanks for the ongoing support
of Lars Engle and my colleagues in the English Department at Tulsa, most
particularly Sandra Vice whose expertise with paper and people makes my
life much easier. Special thanks as well to Holly Laird—without her encouragement this project would have never seen its fruition. To the staff and
faculty at Old Dominion University English Department, including Charles
Wilson, Joyce Neff, David Metzger, and David Pagano who believed in me
and provided me with a much needed stepping-stone on the road to com-
pleting this project. Most importantly, I'd like to thank Aaron Jenkins,
Marcia Spencer, Herbert Jenkins, Laura Newcomber, Melanie Logan, Brian
Riley, Jeffrey Roessner, Erich Hertz, and Christy Rieger whose camaraderie,
laughter, and renewing encouragement nurtured my spirit as well as my
mind—my obligation to them could never be fulfilled.

For permission to include materials published by them, I am grateful to
the following: the Mandeville Special Collections Library, University of California at San Diego (hereinafter UCSD), for portions of the Lyn Hejinian and
Susan Howe papers housed there; to Lyn Hejinian for use of excerpts from
her archives at UCSD and her book, *The Cell;* to Susan Howe for excerpts
from *The Nonconformist's Memorial* and her papers at UCSD; and to the Lit-

erary Estate of Robert Duncan for permission to reproduce Duncan's drawing from *Play Time: Pseudo Stein.* Parts of this book appeared previously in the following journals. Chapter 3 appeared as "*Gunslinger*'s Ethics of Excess: Subjectivity, Community, and the Politics of the *Could Be.*" *Sagetrieb* 15 (Winter 1996): 207–42, while chapter 1 appeared as "Saying Obligation: The Ethics of George Oppen's Objectivist Poetry." *Journal of American Studies* 37.3 (2003): 407–33.

poetic
obligation

Introduction The Double-Double Turn

HORATIO: O day and night, but this is wondrous strange!
HAMLET: And therefore as a stranger give it welcome
    There are more things in heaven and earth, Horatio,
    Than are dreamt of in your philosophy. (II.i)

If the experimental tradition of American poetry has rarely been read for its ethics, it is not for lack of interest on the part of the poets. In her journal dated May 1986 to December 1988, during the time she was writing her long poem, *The Cell,* Lyn Hejinian describes herself enigmatically as a "moral philosopher" (Lyn Hejinian Papers, UCSD 74.47.7). But if one had a conventional notion of what this phrase, "moral philosopher," has meant in the history of philosophy, then one might have a difficult time seeing what she means by it in her poetry:

With irony and recourse, head
    and case
I can say that I
    do not intend to be
    the end result of anything
Still the city is enticing
    and angles for the psyche
So which is the more
    personal, expectation or repose
The psyche uncertain and humane
Mineral is a mental category
It is a moral category
    in a certain metaphor
When we suggest we'll speak
    of sex, sex is everywhere
The psyche is lagging and
    inaccurate in its head
We cannot help but run
    sex gently over the word

head
The open mind
The bending of the head
    to see better
Spectacles to improve the eye
The eye to improve the
    psyche (*The Cell* 51–52)

The form of this poem, with line breaks and lack of punctuation that tangle
syntax, make it difficult to read at all, let alone as moral philosophy. The
phrase, "Mineral . . . is a mental category," certainly does not sound like typical moral philosophy because it lacks the rational, propositional quality of
philosophy in general and moral philosophy, specifically. But the phrase
does set a certain tone of philosophical inquiry into the basic conditions
of morality, a tone that is picked up again and again throughout the rest of
the poem. Clearly, there is a moral imperative in this poem, particularly in
regards to Hejinian's statements to "improve" or to correct a view of sexual
difference, but what could she mean by this improvement? Not only does
she, in the first five lines, resist a determining telos (the end result) that
would guide moral improvement, but she also undercuts intention as *the*
moral mechanism: "I / do not intend to be / the end result of anything." The
phrases "in a certain metaphor" and "over the word" self-consciously call
attention to the language of morality, not to the poet's inherent moral message itself. Rather than providing the correct moral answer, the poem instead shows that being (a woman, especially) does not matter as much as
objectification of (or ironic distance from) the language of morality and
moral philosophy. But in what sense is this self-awareness of and resistance
to moral language an ethical inquiry? What, then, could ethics mean for formally experimental poets like Hejinian?

   Some avant-garde Modernist poets, such as Ezra Pound, certainly saw
their poetic work as distinctly moral. In the case of Pound, right poetics
would lead to right action, as delineated in *The Cantos* and elsewhere.[1] But
his interest in fascism and his complex anti-Semitism render his didactic
approach, at best, questionable. Despite the fact that some of these poets
saw themselves as "moral," the critical consideration of avant-garde American poetry as ethical did not systematically begin until the 1960s. Even then,
only a handful of poets and critics took seriously the ethical challenge being
stoked by innovative poetics, while most in the poetry world who even knew
such poetry existed dismissed it as "arcane" and therefore having nothing to

say about how human beings might better live together (Kenner, *Homemade* 168–75). However, all of the poets in this study have identified ethical projects within their own writing. For example, George Oppen's poetry, as well as his life, keenly examines the very nature of ethics as a structure of relationship between self and others, as well as language's key role in that ethics. As a matter of fact, Tim Woods has done remarkable archival work to uncover the ethics of alterity in Oppen's conception of his own poetics (215–33). However, I don't think we need look to an author's life writings or theoretical writings only to find out what ethics means for them, as if the poetry were again merely adjunct, as in Plato, to what is properly a prosaic philosophical concern. The elucidation of these ethical tendencies *within the poetry itself* preoccupies the chapters of my study.

Since around 1990, new understandings of ethics and poetics have sparked what Lawrence Buell calls "a new ethical inquiry" in literary criticism that extends beyond generic and historical categories (12). But as Hejinian's poem shows, this inquiry begins much earlier in creative literature itself. In the field of avant-garde American poetry, this inquiry in both the literature and the criticism has been around since at least 1960 and was kindled by the compatibility between new philosophical movements and new poetics arising out of Modernism that both value uncertainty over certainty, undecidability over rational judgment, and Other over self. The central argument of this work is that what binds many of the writers in the United States after Modernism that might be called *experimental* is not merely their aesthetic concerns but their ethical fire as well. In fact, the poets in this study ignite an entirely new reconsideration of ethics from one that is essentially rule-based or self-directed (such as those found in universal or situational ethics) to one that is oriented through formal experimentation toward what is other, toward *the* Other.[2]

The American Avant-Garde

The confluence of ethics and poetics, addressed explicitly in Hejinian's 1988 poem, occurs much earlier in the twentieth century. Not until the second generation of Modernists, particularly the Objectivist poets who began writing in the 1930s, does the relation between ethics and poetry within the avant-garde American tradition move beyond didacticism or pronouncement toward the kind of indirect ethical inquiry that Hejinian is practicing in *The Cell*. By the 1960s, this ethics achieves its fullest articulation.

This new strain of poetry and poetics concerned with nonproscriptive, linguistically self-conscious ethics begins with a group of friends who started writing mostly in New York in the 1920s whose common link was Louis Zukofsky. Mediating between the older, more established Modernists like Pound and William Carlos Williams and younger writers like George Oppen, Lorine Niedecker, Basil Bunting, and Carl Rakosi, Zukofsky was already beginning to imagine a new breed of experimental poets coming out of Modernism who combine the fragmented, Imagist style of Pound with the emphasis on the American vernacular of Williams and the wordplay of Stein. This new poetry would be minimal, austere, sensual, historical, linguistically oriented, and more comfortable than its predecessors with addressing the disjointed modern world of urban America. Zukofsky began articulating this poetics in the late 1920s through his prose and poems, particularly "Poem Beginning 'The,'" which was published by Pound in the 1928 issue of *The Exile*. Aside from this publication, his efforts remained in relative obscurity.

Before long, Zukofsky would have the chance to make his vision a bit more concrete and public. Allegedly in 1931, Harriet Monroe, then the editor of *Poetry* magazine, pressured young Zukofsky to come up with a name, like Imagism, that would make the February issue, which he was guest editing, more attractive to its readership in that age of "-isms."[3] Agreeing to this condition because Monroe had given him the editing opportunity only at the request of Pound, Zukofsky unilaterally coined the term Objectivist. But because the members of the association, which critics Peter Quartermain and Rachel Blau DuPlessis aptly call a "nexus," did not agree on a central aesthetic, let alone the one Zukofsky articulates in his "manifesto," the Objectivists could hardly be called a school or movement. Zukofsky's essay, however, has served often as a critical gateway into Objectivist poetry and, as revealed in Part 1 of this book, provides clues into the ethical concerns of all its writers.

Even if we don't consider the Objectivists a school with their own manifesto, there are other ties among these writers that make them an important group when thinking about the ethical aspect of American poetry. With the exception of Bunting, who is British, and Niedecker, who is from Wisconsin, most lived in New York City and share the experience of being children of immigrants. In terms of conditions for their moral and ethical viewpoints, the fact that Zukofsky, Rakosi, Reznikoff, and Oppen are Jewish and share a moral and religious cultural heritage is not of small consequence.[4] It's also interesting to note that many of the philosophers working out of the linguistic and ethical turns in Europe, such as Emmanuel Levinas and Jacques

Derrida, are also Jewish—this tradition provides some of the vocabulary and forms employed by both the poets and the philosophers.

In the 1930s, after the 1931 Objectivist issue of *Poetry*, the Objectivists continued to work together. Most of them contributed to an anthology that was edited by Zukofsky and published by TO Publishers, formed when Oppen and his wife, Mary, moved to France to escape the moral indignation of U.S. Customs officials for the cheaper and more accessible paperback books that they were producing by poets such as Williams. Keeping in touch mostly through correspondence and occasional visits, all of them wrote in relative obscurity throughout the 1940s and 1950s, as the war and other social and personal concerns intervened. Oppen, for instance, stopped writing during the Depression to work as a labor organizer and then served in the army during World War II. He was injured during the Battle of the Bulge and likes to recount his famous story of how reciting a poem by Reznikoff kept him alive. After his return to the States, he was harassed by the FBI during the McCarthy era for his participation in the Communist Party in the 1930s. To escape the witch hunt, the Oppens moved to Mexico for almost ten years, returning to New York only a few times, which meant they were out of touch with the thriving poetry scene there. Although many of these poets like Oppen were out of the business of publishing, their impact was most greatly felt in the lives and work of other poets working in the experimental, Modernist vein in the United States. Slightly younger poets, such as Robert Duncan and William Bronk, looked to the Objectivist writers as major influences. Even much younger poets like Rachel Blau DuPlessis and Lyn Hejinian wrote and visited Oppen as early as the 1960s. By then, the Objectivists began garnering critical attention beyond their circle of influence. For instance, Oppen won the Pulitzer Prize in 1969 for *Of Being Numerous*, the same year Zukofsky was nominated for the National Book Award for parts of "A," which the two previous years had won him the National Endowment for the Arts American Literary Anthology awards ("Louis Zukofsky"). By the mid-1970s, there were several book-length studies dedicated to the work of the Objectivists.

Meanwhile in the 1950s and 1960s, two other groups of writers began to emerge with an avant-garde aesthetic rooted in high Modernism. Although many of these poets were connected through Donald M. Allen's 1960 anthology, *The New American Poetry*, they had previous ties as well. In North Carolina, poets such as Charles Olson, Robert Duncan, Robert Creeley, Edward Dorn, and Denise Levertov served on the faculty and were published by or took classes at the alternative arts school, Black Mountain College. They began working with the ideas of so-called projective verse, once articulated in a famous essay by Olson of that title, and the closely related open-field poetics. Duncan was also part of what has been called The San Francisco Renaissance, which saw the coalescence of the Beat poets in the Bay Area along with Jack Spicer, Robin Blaser, Madeline Gleason, and Kenneth Rexroth. Coming into their own during the conflict in Vietnam, these poets grapple with such ethical issues as the responsibility of the individual (poet) within society and the state. Also in San Francisco, a younger scene of poets, including the likes of Hejinian, began to read and write together at the end of the turbulent 1960s and by the early 1970s began to produce such magazines as *Poetics Journal* and *L=A=N=G=U=A=G=E,* from which the group has received the moniker, "Language poetry." Reacting against what they saw as an overemphasis on the lyric subject as a unified voice, these poets drew on ideas such as Ron Silliman's "new sentence" and Michel Foucault's "author function" to break normal frames of discourse and to reveal how meaning, political to poetic, is constructed in language. In his anthology, *In the American Tree,* Silliman identifies another coast of Language poets, in the East, which included Clark Coolidge, Charles Bernstein, and Susan Howe, among others, to compliment the vibrant scene in California. Both groups take their focus on language itself and apply it to the language of ethics and morality that they find in the discourse around them.

These three "generations" of poets are bound not only by the time of the 1960s and the places of New York and San Francisco but also by their concerns for ethics and for language. They are an essential part of the "double-double turn" in philosophy and poetry in both America and Europe. A brief examination of the contexts implied in these two turns—one ethical, the other linguistic—is crucial to understanding what the poetry is doing both formally and ethically.

The Double-Double Turn: Ethics

As I mentioned in the preface, what reunites philosophy with poetry in this period in the early 1960s is the parallel *double turn* both make toward ethics and language as primary issues. About the time Oppen returns from exile in Mexico in 1958 to again writing poetry, writers in Europe and America begin simultaneously to evince an epistemological shift. First, the linguistic turn, about which much more has been said, makes language, or discourse, itself the study of all social sciences. Since all experience, perception, and thus reality is mediated by language, as the postmodern position goes, then by understanding the problems in language itself we can better arrive at the limitations of our knowledge and understanding of reality, including our ethical relations with others. Second, what Peter Baker calls *the ethical turn* demarks a shift in poetics and philosophy from aesthetics, epistemology, or ontology to ethics (*Deconstruction* 1). Distinct from morality or politics, this ethics addresses what gives rise to our religious, moral, legal, and ethical systems as they are. Because it is less well known, I'll begin with the ethical turn.

Even before deconstruction, French Jewish philosopher Emmanuel Levinas was grounding his analysis of the phenomenology of ethics in language before World War II. His first major work on ethics, *Totality and Infinity*, which was first published in France in 1961 and translated into English in 1969, predates the "linguistic turn" of poststructuralism by a few years. Thus, the ethical turn is at least coexstensive, if not older than, the linguistic turn that has gotten so much more attention in the field of literary theory and criticism. I should also mention that other philosophers extend Levinas's notion of alterity into contexts that he himself does not really address but that the poetry makes evident. The story of this ethical turn goes something like this: In reaction to the prevalent structuralist, essentialist, pragmatist, and situational ethics inherited in the twentieth century from modern thinkers such as Immanuel Kant and John Stuart Mill, these postmodern thinkers question the rational assumptions underlying such systems. Rather than seeking new-and-improved moral systems that would give us rules of how to behave properly, these writers examine the holes, or aporia, that inhabit all moral systems and instead seek there the nonrational, nonsystematizable Other who demands ethics in the first place. Throughout this book, I will refer to the latter understanding as "ethics" and to the rational or legalistic systems as "morality." In addition to the distinction between morality and ethics, the epistemological shift of the ethical turn also includes an explicit separation of ethics from politics. Ethics in this context is not reducible to politics, for one, because ethics does not involve the just distribution of resources or even a choice between two evils. Secondly, ethics does not coincide with what poststructuralists would call *the political* either because ethics for them is in essence the limit of power, not the archaeology of its workings (Levinas, *Totality* 21–23, 46–47, 87).

Blossoming concomitantly in experimental American poetry and in continental philosophy (and only later in poetry criticism), concern for ethics as a relation with the Other has been fueled by myriad historical and cultural developments after World War II. Such events include the Holocaust, Hiroshima, and the beginning of the nuclear age; the revelations of horrors behind Stalinism, the subsequent resurgence of a New Left, the cold war and the not-so-cold wars against communism in Korea and Vietnam; the end of colonial imperialism and the rise of third world democracies; the civil rights and women's movements, revolutions in social and sexual relations, the evolution of mass media and popular culture, the emergence of homosexuality out of the proverbial closet; advancements in technology, such as the transistor and microprocessor that build on the modern inventions of the locomotive, electric lighting, the telephone, automobile, and airplane, which connected the world in an ever-shrinking network of movement, information, and language, and the potentially disastrous effects of that technology on the global ecosystem sustaining all life. Of course, this is a brief and overly general list, but it gives a sense to the range, type, and severity of ethical situations out of which these poets are writing.

By the late 1950s and early 1960s, these conditions ignited new and profound questions about the nature of "the good" and the human ability to achieve and sustain it, not to mention relating with each other through justice and peace. Experimental American poetry during this period, from the Objectivists like Oppen to the incipient Language poetry of Hejinian, question language's ability to capture total meaning and thus to fully convey the rational, moral message of an orderly society bent on social control for the sake of a peaceful marketplace and compliant population. On the opposite side of the Atlantic, postmodern continental philosophy—in the forms of existentialism, psychoanalysis, Marxism, phenomenology, feminism, and, most importantly, poststructuralism—argued that the "master narratives" (e.g., Christianity, science, enlightenment, rationality, etc.) that have supported the ethical systems of the West had failed. Without these *grands recits,* as Jean-François Lyotard calls them, the question of what can then found ethics becomes tantamount. One answer to this question within the ethical turn in poetry and philosophy in the 1960s is the term, *the Other.*

What I mean by the terms *the Other* or *otherness* (or any of its cognates— *alterity, strangeness,* etc.) is not what is commonly understood in most critical approaches to literature, from feminism to postcolonial theory. Concurrent with the change in experimental poetics toward otherness in the 1950s and 1960s, was a movement among French philosophy, deeply influenced by existentialism and German phenomenology, which begins to theorize this new consideration of the Other. These new developments can be distinguished along two axes: The first is whether the use of the term is "positive" or "negative." The second, as Ewa Ziarek has succinctly pointed out, is between understandings of alterity as either the "other of language" or the "other of the subject" (8).[5] I see Ziarek's diad more in terms of a tension, a continuum along in which different accounts of alterity can be mapped with the full understanding that the complete effacement of one for the other is impossible. Using these two axes, positive/negative and language/subject, we can get a brief outline of understandings of alterity since 1945.

The negative use of the term *other* is as old as philosophy itself. In the philosophical tradition since Plato, many uses of the word involve a logical relationship of identity, where the other signifies what is not the same and thus can be identified negatively: what is not one is the other. Hegel's philosophy is the fulfillment par excellence of this dialectical definition of the other. For Hegel, morality is the sublation, or overcoming, of oppositions—such as reason/sensuality, home/foreign, freedom/duty, duty/actuality—through synthesis in the historical progress of the Concept. This overcoming of otherness is what Hegel calls *Spirit,* which is ultimately "God appearing in the midst of those who know themselves as pure knowing" (158).[6] Thus, the moral telos of history is the totality of Spirit via the dialectical sublation of all that is other. According to most poststructuralist renderings, Hegel's discussion of this relationship between same and other is the culmination of a tradition since Plato that posits the other as negative, thinkable, and ultimately inferior. This use of "other" is far from obsolete.

Existential or phenomenological thinkers—including Maurice Merleau-Ponty, Simone de Beauvoir, Franz Fanon, and Jean-Paul Sartre—seem to portray alterity as the other of the subject, a person who exists to some degree in opposition to the subject. Sartre's famous line from *No Exit,* "Hell is other people," is indicative of this oppositional conception, and in this way some are the inheritors of Hegel. But not all in this group see alterity negatively. For Merleau-Ponty, a person is essentially other to himself because of the ambiguity of the sexual body—this is not a state to be avoided because it simply is. This notion of sexual ambiguity is also explored, as we will see' in chapter 4, by Duncan in his poetry that expresses not only homosexual desire but also the ethical exigency of remaining other to oneself. Such thinking about the subject as an other, according to Jean-Luc Nancy in his reinterpretations of Heidegger in the 1980s, allows us to reconsider how we understand "community," a project that preoccupies Dorn's mock-epic, *Gunslinger.* Likewise, much feminist, Marxist, racial, and cultural criticism has also appropriated this dialectical definition of alterity in order to expose the real-life consequences of logical hierarchies on actual human beings in particular historical moments. In postcolonial or feminist theory, for example, "the Other" often refers to peoples who have been "othered," colonized

THE DOUBLE-DOUBLE TURN   9

and thus marginalized, in the global expansion of nation-states. Edward Said's *Orientalism* is a good example of this application. Consequently, in this context the term has taken a negative valence in order to document the oppression and pain experienced by real human beings in political situations. These views seek to end the oppression of some politically defined minority group that has been traditionally labeled as "other," and this word is often capitalized in these contexts to refer to people. Though it may achieve a narrow political goal, this use does nothing to challenge the label of "otherness" as negative and thus remains dependent upon the identity of the subject.

In poststructuralist thinking, the term *other* assumes, for lack of a better phrase, a "positive" valence. In the work of thinkers from Levinas to Jacques Derrida and Julia Kristeva, the historical hierarchy of the One over the Other comes into question because of its correlation to linguistic systems of domination and violence, such as fascism or patriarchy. In psychoanalytic or deconstructive discourse from this period, such as Kristeva's work from the 1960s and 1970s, alterity becomes a linguistic effect, a result of the inadequacy or failure of language to represent events or reality. To identify with this other of language—or *kora*, as Kristeva calls the pre-semantic feminine source that is excluded from but gives rise to all philosophy—is the raison d'être of critical theory. Innovative American poetics more closely resembles this poststructuralist project to responsibly respond to the Other in any aesthetic, philosophical, moral, religious, or legal system. Both poetry and philosophy share a desire to think the relation with alterity otherwise than as opposition, while at the same time aware that many social and political structures in our society still see the *Other* as inimical. Both Susan Howe and Charles Reznikoff, as the most indicative examples, seek to inscribe the social mechanisms by which people are othered and thus excluded from power; this aim does not, however, prevent them from inviting otherness *as strangeness* into their texts as the possibility of ethics. Many contemporary thinkers have similarly searched for a way to articulate an otherness or alterity not based in logic.

Not surprisingly, Derrida's negotiations of alterity fall elusively between these two axes. One the one hand, his work seems to avoid employing the negative understanding of the Other based on identity, while he obviously values the merit of looking for alterity within a text. On the other hand, he seems to focus primarily on "the trace" as the textual trace of the Other in language, while leaving open the possibility of a concrete, material, human Other, particularly in his later texts on DeMan, Levinas, and others. In his famous 1968 essay, "*Différance*," which was first published in the United States in 1973, Derrida notes how this trace evokes both the Other of the subject but also of the inscription of writing: "Always differing and deferring, the trace is never as it is in the presentation of itself. It erases itself in presenting itself, muffles itself in resonating, like the *a* writing itself, inscribing its pyramid in *différance*" (*Margins* 23). In Derrida's work we see that both versions of alterity alert us to what might lie outside of the tradition of philosophy focused on the subject, its constitution and its functioning, particularly in ethical contexts. His example also teaches us that the two versions of the Other, of language or subject, are not so readily distinguished in continental thought.

What Levinas adds to this discussion are the vast consequences to Derrida's coincidence, as in the accidental elision, of the two approaches to alterity. Unique in the philosophy of ethics is Levinas's definition of the Other, which he develops after the end of World War I through the 1970s and that can help us understand the ethics behind experimental poetics. Neither oppositional nor dialectical, Levinas's "Other" explicitly avoids a negative definition because he sees this "allergy" as the source of a deeply unethical strain in Western philosophy that seeks totality. Instead, he defines subjectivity as "welcoming the Other, as hospitality" (*Totality* 47, 27). His notion of the Other is marked by an alterity that cannot be captured by thought or category because it is a relation with infinity (*Totality* 48–50). Such a notion of everyday contact with infinity resonates nicely with Oppen's statement in *Of Being Numerous* that "[s]urely infiniteness is the most evident thing in the world" (*New Collected* 184) and will help us read a similar failure of identification in the poetry. Although often figured in everyday metaphors such as "the neighbor," "the widow, the orphan, and the Stranger," the Other for Levinas cannot be completely identified as a "human being" by traits or qualities because the Other, as infinite, exceeds all possible identification. When referring to the Other, I prefer to use the term *person* to *human*. I purposefully choose this term to invoke the genderless anonymity in the French word, *personne* (no one). Language poet Lyn Hejinian makes a similar lexical move when she writes in her essay "The Person and Description" that "there is no self undefiled by experience, no self unmediated in the epistemological situation, but a person instead" (*Cold* 167). The Other for Levinas is not simply an unknowable person who is the other of the subject because the Other is always announced in language. The Other is the one who reveals herself to me in a face, a face that speaks, as a student who questions a teacher (*Totality* 50–51). The key difference between Levinas and his philosophical contemporaries is that alterity necessitates responsibility from the self. The face of the Other, which manifests itself as language as well as flesh, calls my autonomy as a subject into question and obligates me to respond (*Totality* 82–84; "Trace" 350–353). In Levinas's estimation, I am literally sub-ject to the Other (*Totality* 235; *Otherwise* 116). This obligation, however, does not happen to me after the fact of the encounter with the Other, as in conventional definitions of ethics; instead, obligation is an ontological structure of human being, the very "curvature of the intersubjective space," as Levinas puts it (*Totality* 291). Notably, because ethics does not begin with my decision, it is not simply a matter of duty, political decision, or legality. Obligation happens, as Levinas puts it, "despite oneself" (*Otherwise* 51). Thus, my relationship with the Other as a person is always already linguistic and prior to moral judgment. Because this definition intertwines both strands of otherness, the relationship with this face of the Other through language, according to Levinas, becomes the foundationless foundation for all conventional ethics, laws, politics, and morality.

Such a rhetorical move—the paradoxical foundationless foundation— evokes the poetics of our experimental American authors who, through their textual practices, attempt to shoot the gap between the other of language and the other of the subject in order to bring ethics into their poetry. This invitation is offered under the risk of bringing alterity into being and therefore denuding it of its very otherness, while at the same time acknowledging the failure of any representational system to totalize that otherness.

The Double-Double Turn: Language

Aside from the issue of alterity, the foremost issue raised in avant-garde American poetics is the centrality of language to ethics. This integration of language, poetics, and ethics begins in American poetry with the Objectivists. Tellingly, Oppen in an interview responds to the interviewer's sentence, "You seem to establish an ethical criticism in terms of . . . ," by finishing it himself: "Language. Right. Yes, I think I do" (Schiffer, "Interview" 15). In fact, the issues are so integral that Joan Retallack and Gerald Bruns independently arrived at the neologism, "poethics," to describe the phenomenon.[7] In their work, both Retallack and Bruns draw on a major philosophical development in the twentieth century that places language's mediating function at the center of the study and production of all human knowledge. Referred to often as the linguistic turn of postmodernism, this movement begins with Martin Heidegger, Ludwig Wittgenstein, J. L. Austin, and Emmanuel Levinas who see the linguistic means of philosophy as integral to its ends and eventually involves the works of thinkers like Jacques Derrida, Michel Foucault,

Julia Kristeva, Jacques Lacan, Jean-François Lyotard, Jean Baudrillard, and Stanley Cavel. From this movement emerges new definitions of language that deemphasizes its structural and communicative features and emphasizes its deferring, obfuscating, equivocating, and social qualities. Many of these writers, furthermore, engage the intersection of language, literature, and ethics to show that aesthetic works, because their medium is language, can offer alternative views of ethics other than the normative.

Influenced by the linguistic turn of postmodern thought, American Language poet Bruce Andrews, in his essay, "Writing Social Work and Practice," concisely summarizes three models of language that are crucial to the poetry and poetics of the writers in this book. The first model is what Andrews identifies as the capitalistic belief that language is a transparent medium of communication founded on the correspondence of word to thing. In this model, meaning is an exchange of commodities between subjects who consume but have little say in the production of meaning (those word-object correspondences), which is objectified, commodified, and taken for granted as natural. The second model is the structuralist view, based on the work of Ferdinand de Saussure and subsequent poststructuralist thinkers, which sees the relation between word (signifier) and thing (signified) as arbitrary. Meaning is dependent on the *difference between* rather than the *reference of* words. Akin to a state of anarchy or fascism, this free-flowing system unanchored by essential or necessary relationship between words and objects liberates "libidinal" desires that can force repressed or novel juxtaposition of words, but the meaning of these formations tends toward a "homogenized meaninglessness." Andrews calls the third model "practice," which is essentially a socialist view of language, in that meaning arises from the relationship between reader and text and from the contextual or social discourses involved. (De)constructive rather than simply destructive, reading then is a form of writing and vice versa that is incapable of a wholesale rejection of consensus or socially imposed norms (19). This third method does not destroy but puts the means of production of meaning in the hand of anyone and everyone. As Ron Silliman observes, it marks "the return of the poem to the people" ("Open Letter," 93). In other words, this last idea of language is socialist and democratic and based in the act of writing.[8]

But in addition to these three models of language—capitalistic, anarchistic, and democratic—the poets of this experimental strain fashion and rely on a fourth understanding of language after the 1950s. Thus, to Andrews's categories, I would add the *ethical* model of language, which pervades and perverts each of the other three categories. This fourth version remains on their hither side and fuses the other models with alterity that is both the other of the subject and the other of language, which are congruent as far as experimental American poetics is concerned. Rather than relying on reason and syntax like the first model, ethical language welcomes the uncategoriz-able, unforseeable, inescapable *saying* of language that becomes legible once we acknowledge the failure of referential language. This saying, which is contentless and full of desire for the Other, like the second model, does not merely institute free play but also burdens the subject with an obligation that conditions and pervades all action and discourse. Slightly different still from the third model that through labor returns the means of production to the hands of the excluded and oppressed, the ethical model reminds us that language is always already social and that we are born into a world peopled with others. Others to whom we are obligated in the very fact of being in human relationships. This notion of sociality—an (in)expressible experience of a relationship with the Other who is beyond all categorization and who demands obligation—is at the heart of any demystification or change of social production and illuminates the ethical resonance of every politics.

I see the poets interacting and negotiating with these four models in various ways: The referential relationship between word and object, which Williams and Zukofsky endorse (Zukofsky, *Prepositions* 14), becomes prob-lematic when the importance of desire is taken into consideration in their work, as revealed in the beginning of Part I. Reznikoff, much less convinced in the referential power of language but nevertheless depending on it, uses that mode of language against itself to hold a mirror, as it were, up to the very phenomenon of reading/writing as judgment. His ethics of nonjudgment is the topic of chapter 2. Oppen, who was less sure of this correspondence and equally uncertain about the ability of words (or poets) to invoke presence or control meaning, embraces this problem and turns the failure that desire for the Other causes in the commodified system of reference into an ethics of poetic responsibility. In this poetics, I outlined in chapter 1, Oppen elevates the passive and the unforseeable to a status unlike any poet before. Follow-ing Oppen's lead, Duncan and Dorn harness the excess libidinal energy re-leased by the valorization of desire in poetry when they rely on the arbitrary and contingent relationship between the material of the body and (social) meaning. In Andrews's terms, Duncan and Dorn draw on the differential or structuralist view of language for what I call respectively, their ethics of excess and Eros. Although the relationship between word and object is arbitrary for these poets, such difference does not inhibit play and the free envision-ing of new social forms. Dorn and Duncan simply do not legislate what those new forms can and can't be. In this poetics of openness and multiplicity, which I detail in chapters 3 and 4, new possibilities proliferate for the way we may live, as both embodied subjects and as members of a community.

Drawing on the third, socialist understanding of language, Language poets Susan Howe and Lyn Hejinian bring to our attention in Part III to the regulating and oppressive mechanisms that were resisted by the rebellious forms utilized in the Black Mountain poetry. The controlling discourses of society, the targets of the poetics of excess, did not simply disappear when challenged by poetry, as the aftermath of 1960s' idealism has shown. In addition to rebellion, these women poets endorse a poetics that puts the means of production in the hands of the readers and subjects of the poems. By making the production of meaning, especially in terms of sexual difference, a social phenomenon, Howe and Hejinian reveal to us the way those socially instituted and regulated definitions of sex exclude and control women. When the workings of such naturalized discourses are demystified, they believe, then they may be changed and redirected. In the context of these women writers—who accept the arbitrary relationship between language and determinations of sex but do not want to deny their sexed being—this redirection is what I call *sexual alterity* to refer to the "transcendence" of gender, as the exposing of social norms once thought in natural and essential relation to sex. As these poets show us, we are not determined by traditional understandings of our bodies. More important, the meaning of those bodies is linguistic, and the means to (change such tyrannical) meaning are at our disposal. In other words, we are free to challenge and change those norms, and in fact are obliged by the Other to do so.

As the writers of this postwar period understood it, language is first and foremost *uttering* and *writing*, as verbs rather than nouns. All other models of language begin and end in innovative American poetry with this twofold notion of ethical language that emphasizes the very saying of language, not just what is said. Because each of the poets employs and invites this fourth model of language differently, my task is to show how the fourth model works in their writing. Allow me first to briefly sketch out the philosophical context that lends ethical weight to this bifurcated language practice.

In *Otherwise Than Being*, originally published in 1974, Levinas reworks his ethics by tying responsibility directly to this twofold notion of ethical language. Drawing on Heidegger's later notions of poetic language, Levinas describes language as doubled and diachronous in order to emphasize the role the Other plays in language.[9] By bifurcating language into *le dire* (the saying) and *le dit* (the said), Levinas is able to show that there is a precinct of language that signifies my responsibility to the Other *above and beyond any content assigned to the words themselves.* Basically, the said becomes the totality of what is spoken or written—the text, the play of the signifier, representation, and thus any existent that can said to have being—including all three of Andrews's models of language. Additionally, structuralist divisions of language, such as signifier/signified or langue/parole, would fall within the purview of this notion of the said. Out of phase with the said, the saying constantly accompanies the totality of the said on its "hither side," which is the inarticulate aspect of language that can never come into being in a text. Instead of being partner to what is said, the saying disrupts the totality of a text's autonomy and is responsible for a certain sense of anarchy in its logic.[10] Otherness requires a place or being to disrupt/inhabit. In philosophical terms, every "an-archy" needs its *arché,* or origin/order. The saying demands a said, and where these two meet is, to borrow a word from the first poem of Oppen's *Of Being Numerous,* an "occurrence," an ethical situation from the start. But this anarchy is not merely the libidinal force of Andrews's second model of language; it instead makes time/space for the Other to enter language. In this sense, an object, a word, is not purely autonomous; it is vulnerable to an alterity that marks its relation to the Other. The poem also is vulnerable to the trace of the Other.

Aside from its disruptive feature, the saying has a certain integrity and cannot be described as simply parasitic on what is said. Although it does not belong to Being, the saying traces itself in the said and in Being. According to Levinas in *Otherwise Than Being,* this saying presupposes a relation to the Other—this is its "content": "Antecedent to the verbal signs it conjugates, to the linguistic systems and the semantic glimmerings, a foreword preceding languages, it is the proximity of one to the other, the commitment of an approach, the one for the other, the very signifyingness of signification" (5). This trace, found in all language according to many poststructuralist thinkers, in turn obligates the subject.[11] The saying says nothing but that one is obligated—this is what makes it ethical—language constantly reminds us that our lives are burdened with responsibility, even before we accept our duties and even before we can signify these responsibilities (*Otherwise* 6). The saying, then, becomes the condition for all language because it presupposes a relation with an Other who exists only as a trace in language. Thus, language, no matter what is said, is always already the call to be responsible to the Other. In fact, my responsibility gives occasion to make a said (a representation, a poem, a story, a response):

But the relationship with a past [*le dire*] that is on the hither side of every present and every re-presentable, for not belonging to the order of presence, is included in the extraordinary and everyday event of my responsibility for the faults or the misfortune of others, in my responsibility that answers for the freedom of another, in the astonishing human fraternity in which fraternity, conceived with Cain's sober coldness, would not by itself explain the responsibility between separated beings it calls for. (*Otherwise* 10)

This unexplainable saying can be thought of as an obligation to the Other that is beyond all order, anything that can be said. In a sense, the saying is to the said as ethics is to morality, with the anarchy of the former giving rise to the order of the latter.

This innovation of Levinas's will allow us to expose a different sense of responsibility underlying the avant-garde tradition in American poetry whose main impetus is the disruption of the said and thus of totality. This responsibility is why, for example, Oppen must say, "I cannot even now / Altogether disengage myself / From those men" (*New Collected* 171). As I demonstrate in chapter 1, his language is attuned to the saying. But this responsibility cannot be merely thematic, it is poetic.

Poethical Form

In poststructuralist thought during this period, poetry comes to embody what is most ethical about language, contrary to Plato's ancient banishment. In his work in the late 1960s and early 1970s, Levinas connects the saying with poetry as the exit from philosophical totalization, as do many writers such as Blanchot, Kristeva, and Derrida. This idea of poetry as an ethical remedy to rhetoric continues well into the next century in both philosophy and literary theory. As Retallack states in the introduction to *Poethical Wager*, "Everything in mass culture is designed to deliver space-time in a continuous drone. One writes poetry and essays to disrupt that fatal momentum" (5). The idea that poetry stops the vertigo of language and gets off the carousel of totality persists throughout this book, but the idea relies on something other than logic for its ends. "Language is closed like that bedroom," Levinas says referring to the claustrophobic setting of Blanchot's 1962 novel *L'attente, l'oubli*. But poetry, which is not required to conform to the order of logic, speaks of its own impossibility of meaning: "Poetic language gives sign without the sign being a bearer of signification through relinquishing signification" ("Servant" 156). The *giving* of language, the saying, is stressed in poetry because it is a relinquishing—the giving up of intentional representation that might totalize the Other—not a grasping, which characterizes the said. Because signs contain the saying, each word breaks ethically with the one before in a constant interrupting of continuity and order. Here, Levinas qualifies poetry as contradictory—it opens itself to betrayal in that it runs the risk of totalizing the Other—but it is contradictory only in the said. The saying gives language its sincere ethical bearings.

By focusing on the way the saying infects poetic language and returns us to the trace of the Other in the text, Levinas changes the focus of the interpretation of poetry, a change that the avant-garde American poets of this postwar period share. Rather than emphasize the said, one must seek the saying. What is primary in Levinas's work, by the time he first publishes his piece on Celan in French (1972), is a responsibility prior to the consideration of aesthetics, which arises in/as poetry:

> Will the centrifugal movement of the "one-for-the-other" be the mobile axis of being? or its rupture? or its meaning? The fact of speech to the other—the poem—precedes all thematization; it is in that act that qualities gather themselves into things. But the poem thus leaves the real its alterity, which pure imagination tears away from it; the poem "lets otherness's ownmost also speak: the time of the other." (*Proper,* 44)

The word *poème* is doubled in Levinas's analysis: Poetry refers to a particular form and to the disruption (*arrache*) to which all form is prone. The interruption of form and meaning, according to Blanchot, is necessary for understanding, but an understanding that is always ambiguous (*Infinite* 76–79). That ambiguity renders impossible the critical paraphrasing of the said of the poem. Thus, the poetic, as Levinas and Blanchot define it, simultaneously underwrites and breaks with aesthetic considerations of poetry. The poem may be words on a page in a specific form, a sonnet perhaps, but the saying is what gives it meaning and prevents that meaning from being reduced simply to a scientific treatise "or the minutes of board meetings of Limited Companies" ("Servant" 157). Furthermore, the poetic saying is what allows for that said-form (e.g., the sonnet) to arise as such. In this view, the poem is "a language without words" ("Servant" 157) or "a saying without a said" (*Proper* 40), and thus before thematics and poetics, the poem allows for the return to the self in responsibility. In other words, "The tracking down dedicating itself in the poem to the Other: a song rises in the giving, in the one-for-the-other, in the signifying before signification" (*Noms* 56, translation mine).[12] The inability of Levinas to distinguish a form for poetry reflects the incertitude that brings about an epiphany of my responsibility.[13] The poetic, Blanchot writes at the end of his discussion of Levinas in *The Infinite Conversation* (1993, *L'entretien Infini*, 1969), is the "[n]aming of the possible, responding to the impossible" (*Infinite* 48). Poetry responds to the "impossible" because the saying, the obligation of the one-for-the-Other, occurs where form *de-forms* and is impossible to read as a said. Thus, in a poetic form that is open to the impossible—discontinuity, disruption, interruption—we should be more likely to trace the trace of the saying and its poetic obligation.

As several recent commentators on Levinas such as Jill Robbins have pointed out, there are many pitfalls that confront this kind of ethical reading of poetry.[14] Foremost of these problems is to find a method that seeks to take into account the ineffable quality of the Other in the poetry without, as Simon Critchley warns, trying to name and reduce that alterity to a rational description through criticism (48). But it is precisely this kind of grasping incorporation, typical of reason and law, not to mention dichotomizing, that difficult poetic forms attempt to avoid. Alterity in and through language blurs the distinction between form and content, so it becomes imperative to find a way to "read" form, not just content. As Levinas articulates it, "the first content of expression is the expression itself" because the proximity of the Other "breaks through all the envelopings and generalities of Being to spread out in its 'form' the totality of its 'content,' finally abolishing the distinction between form and content" (*Totality* 51). Because avant-garde work, by its very definition, engages what is Other—unfamiliar, new, unseen, or unknowable—what most new readers of this kind of poetry most often have trouble with is its formal strangeness, particularly considering that the thematic content or subject matter is often completely quotidian. My method seeks to address the centrality of experimental poetic form to new ways of thinking about ethics and attempts to remedy what I diagnose as a lack of detailed and convincing reading strategies in the current texts engaged in the so-called new ethical inquiry of literary criticism. I offer a concrete version of what Levinas's notion of ethical responsibility in poetry might look like while at the same time elucidating some of the issues to be confronted when giving a Levinasian interpretation of any literary text. I assert through my method of close reading that we can glimpse the traces of *le dire* (the saying) in postmodern poetic form, traces that give rise to a new kind of ethics. As chapters progress, I raise additional ethical imperatives in the context of other philosophers, to show how orientation toward alterity in this poetry takes many forms.

In addition to the formally challenging, I have purposely chosen some of the longer poetry in the American experimental strain—Oppen's *Of Being Numerous,* Reznikoff's *Holocaust,* Dorn's *Gunslinger,* Duncan's *Passages* poems, Howe's *The Nonconformist's Memorial,* and Hejinian's *The Cell*—because, like their Modernist predecessors—Pound's *Cantos* and Williams's *Paterson*—they provide a canvas where the most pressing ethical issues of the time can be writ large. As Alan Golding has argued, the fusion of moments of lyrical conviction in the long serial poem—unintelligible to many models of epic verse—has often been couched in ethical terms (90). But unlike the Modernists who preferred the coherence and order of the epic scale in order to wrest virtue and myth from history, what is legible in this postwar strain of long poem is the disruptive call of alterity within the structure and technique of their poetics, what Golding refers to as the postmodern privilege of the "possible" over the "perfect" (103). In Baker's terms, "modernist and postmodern poets are in fact seeking to achieve the level of ethicity present in the successful epic poems of the past, but in the absence of the traditional epic hero and without centering on their own internal feelings or experiences." For Baker, this "outward orientation" that "challenges the unity of the presumed poetic speaker" is the main parallel between the long poems and ethical theory of the twentieth century (*Obdurate* 2, 11).

Last, and most important, the focus on the materiality of the poem, in terms of its shape and construction, as well as of its context, reveals a common belief most of the poets share with the thinkers of the ethical turn such as Levinas. For Levinas, it is impossible to consider the dynamic of the ethical relation without taking into account the relation between what he calls, echoing Heidegger, the *existence of existents* and the transcendent otherness that coincides with them. In other words, there is no ethical content or possibility without the material form.

In undertaking an ethical interpretation of poetry, I have formulated a set of questions, derived from the contexts discussed in the introduction, that I raise with each of my selected poets:

The Ethical Turn: How does each poet conceive of ethics and how is that ethics enacted in the poetry?

The Other: In the context of continental theories of otherness, how does each poet characterize alterity or otherness in the poetry? In what ways does that alterity ethically obligate us to the Other?

Language: In what ways does language mediate the ethical charge of the poetry? How does each poet imagine the ethical aspect of language?

How does the language of the poetry foreground ethics as responsibility
to the Other, if at all?

Form: How do the poets' uses of poetic form enhance or inhibit the ethical
responsibility embodied in the poetry? How does the form of the long
poem or series condition the ethical possibilities of the poetry? How
do formal choices work beyond the intention of the poet, if at all, to
address what is beyond control, judgment, authority, and definitions
of body and gender?

These questions allow me to have a unified field of study while paying attention to the subtle variations each poet has in the relationship between
poetic form and ethical responsibility.

Contrary to much mainstream criticism, this poetry is not intentionally
arcane or difficult, as if there were a moral secret the poets were hiding from
us. Instead, the writing forces, invites, and obliges us to face the strangeness
that pervades everything around us, particularly the work and relations between people in language. A critical understanding of our ethical responsibilities to others in the world depends on it. We must, as Derek Attridge
points out, continually develop reading strategies to evolve with the ever-
mutating edge of formal experimentation in order to face the strangeness
and give it meaning (21–26).[15] In our reading, we can learn to welcome the
Other, as this poetry does.

part 1

OBJECTIVIST POETHICS

JULIET: And yet I wish but for the thing I have.
My bounty is as boundless as the sea,
My love as deep; the more I give to thee,
The more I have, for both are infinite. (*Romeo and Juliet* II.ii)

In his seminal 1931 essay, "Sincerity and Objectification: With Special Reference to the Work of Charles Reznikoff," Louis Zukofsky defines the terms through which Objectivist poetry, the movement he inaugurated that year in *Poetry* magazine, has come to be judged and interpreted. It has also provided the genesis of ethical approaches to avant-garde poetry since 1945, which is why the essay deserves some introductory examination, despite the fact that I do not include a separate chapter on Zukofsky for reasons that should become clear. Although more than mere literary criticism, Zukofsky's essay is not a manifesto (none of the other contributors had a say in its contents and only later a few actually endorsed its claims), but it seems to function like one, at least in terms of the way it was later received by critics eager for some hermeneutic with which to read this mysterious poetry. If not a manifesto, it certainly can be read as a statement of poetics, one that exhibits the unmistakable penchant for the elegance of totality fancied by many Modernists at the time. For example, in a 1932 issue of *Contact,* William Carlos Williams writes, "I cannot swallow the half-alive poetry which knows nothing of totality," a sentiment echoed in other totalizing Modernist gestures, such as Pound's Imagist dicta from his essay "A Retrospect."[1] To clear the ground for poetry's new objective, Zukofsky begins his essay in *Poetry* by advocating a total correspondence between poetry and historical, existential reality:

An Objective: (Optics)—The lens bringing the rays from an object to a focus. That which is aimed at. (Use extended to poetry)—Desire for what is objectively perfect, inextricably the direction of historic and contemporary particulars. ("Sincerity" 269)

Using a visual analogy, Zukofsky implies a totalizing aesthetic: the poem is to be written in such a way as to focus on an object or particular, defined as "a thing or things as well as an event or a chain of events," in order to achieve a "desire for what is objectively perfect," perhaps as total as one can get (*Prepositions* 12; "Sincerity" 269). Through the rest of the essay, this aesthetic develops into one of completion and totality, perhaps the two ideas furthest from the turn toward alterity that I'm arguing distinguishes the ethics of the American avant-garde tradition.

Full of such clear and totalizing indications, the young poet's short document has not always been appreciated for its complexity. First, there were three versions of it: the 1931 *Poetry* version, an earlier, unpublished version that Zukofsky submitted to the Jewish intellectual magazine *Menorah Journal* in 1929, and a much later revised version that Zukofsky included in a collection of essays titled *Prepositions* (1967).[2] Between 1931 and 1967, Zukofsky removed most of the references to Reznikoff and foregrounded his critical method, which at first seems like a consolidation consonant with the idea of totality. However, the mutable texture of this document reveals that Zukofsky's poetics is much less complete than the stated quest for totality would require. Although the changes made between the versions are subtle and significant, what is more important to my reading is that Zukofsky's form and diction in the essay are multifarious and do not deliver a clearly totalizing vision of objectification and sincerity, as usually thought. Though I do not argue that Zukofsky completely embraces a nontotalizing ethics of alterity in "Sincerity and Objectification," such a current does run through his work in a productive tension between totality and desire. By briefly revisiting the essay we can see that it not only proposes a poetics of totality but also a contrary poetics of desire, much like what Levinas and other poststructuralists were describing in the decades after World War II, for an alterity that introduces an ethical failure in the process of objectification by the subject. As Peter Baker points out, Zukofsky's interest in poetic form involved a concomitant "lifelong questioning of identity" (124), and Tim Woods, in his book *The Poetics of the Limit* (2002), writes that American Modernism, particularly the Objectivist strain, "was deeply concerned with the problem of how ethics manifests itself as linguistic representation in poetic form" (2).

Zukofsky, in my estimation, never solves this problem. Though Woods has rightly sensed that Zukofsky's poetry gestures toward an ethics of responsibility to the other and that "Objectivist poetics disrupts totality" (2–11), Woods elides the fact that Zukofsky's interest in totality persists throughout his career, when most American writers had moved toward a more open-ended poetics. Zukofsky cannot divorce himself enough from the need for totality in his criticism or his epic work "A." At most, Zukofsky's is a failed ethics of desire, not a full-fledged poetics of obligation. But his failure is nonetheless instructive of how other poets in this tradition do negotiate the problem of ethics and poetic form. And since the Objectivist strain has largely been read in terms of Zukofsky's process, by redefining his terms, we can begin to redefine experimental poethics from its manifestation in George Oppen and Charles Reznikoff through Language poetry.

After defining poetry's "Objective" in the opening, Zukofsky defines his two primary terms, *sincerity* and *objectification. Sincerity,* as a shape in the form of a combination of words, "is the detail, not mirage, of seeing, of thinking with things as they exist, and of directing them along the line of melody" (*Prepositions* 12). In other words, sincerity in writing does not shape reality but follows the shape of an existence outside the poem, such as a melody follows the rise and fall of pitch, evoking a certain trueness to reality in the seeing of particulars. Similar to Andrews's capitalistic model of language, this staying true to reality would seem to foreclose on any alterity (here in the form of "mirage" or losing direction) coming in between the poem and its representation of the world. *Objectification,* even more overtly, involves the "objectively perfect" through the achievement of "rested totality." This rest, defined in terms of a mental state, is a "perfect rest, complete appreciation" and is "the resolving of words and their ideation into structure," conceivably the placement of words and the concepts to which they refer into the structure of a poem (*Prepositions* 13). As Stephen Fredman has pointed out, the relation between the two terms is that of part and whole (*Menorah* 136–37), which reinforces the weight of totality that Zukofsky seeks in objectification itself. The whole, the "rested totality" of objectification, is comprised of parts, sincere particulars, fused "into one apprehended unit, or minor units of sincerity" (Zukofsky, *Prepositions* 13). So, in a properly structured poem, units of sincerity, which are observations of details that can be expressed in simply a few lines or even a word, cohere into a poetic object when objectification has been reached. In the 1967 version of his essay, Zukofsky clearly intends these terms, in addition to a method of composition, as a method of criticism by which poems can be judged according to their success or failure at the objectifying process. Indeed, in the years since Zukofsky last revised his essay, it has spawned political, aesthetic, and ontological approaches to Objectivist ethics that actually reinforce his value on totality.[3] In searching for ways to understand the ethics of Objectivist poetry, much earlier criticism has followed Zukofsky's cue by making morality a matter of determining a set of aesthetic rules, plumbing the poet's politics, or foregrounding the ontological trueness of the poems.[4]

Moving beyond these approaches, Woods pushes this ontological reading into the realm of ethics by arguing that Zukofsky "sets up a stance to the world that situates the subject/reader in an ethical relation to the world" (6). But in order to make his argument, Woods elides the residues of totality in Zukofsky's corpus. Even in the disappearance of the subject/object distinction that Woods convincingly attributes to Zukofsky, there is no room left for otherness in Zukofsky's poetry; the relation is a complete adequation. A passage from the second half of Zukofsky's "A"-9 (1948–50)—a series of sonnets often taken to exemplify Zukofsky's poetics of immanence and totality— highlights this problem of measure as a relation of adequation between word and object, poem and subject matter, subject and world:

> An eye to action sees love bear the semblance
> Of things, related is equated, — values
> The measure all use who conceive love, labor
> Men see, abstraction they feel, the resemblance. ("A" 108)

Seemingly based on a relational notion of existence, this passage purports to make measure a feeling/seeing of resemblance, which is an act of love, and that act is consummated in the sentence as a whole and in the balance of the stanza as a quatrain. There is also symmetry in the form of "A"-9. On the larger level, the poem is divided in half, with each half, though written a decade apart, mirroring the other composed of five sonnets plus a five-lined stanza. We see the same reflective structure in the above passage as well in almost every part of the whole: the nouns in the last two lines are an inversion of the nouns in the first two, with "values" playing off "measure," "things" matched with "labor," and "eye" tied with "resemblance," each fulfilling its counterpart. "Measure" in this passage thus exemplifies the totality of values, while "values" as a verb makes "measure" the ultimate goal of action. Unmistakably, "measure" here in Zukofsky is contextualized with words that imply closure and adequation: "all" is universalizing and totalizing, while "semblance," "resemblance," "equated," and "see" all imply the adequation of (visual) representation to thing.[5] In fact, the poem states quite clearly that "related is equated." In other words, the measure (of the poem) conceives and bears the labor of things—the measure is equal to what is measured. Almost literally, the poem is sealed within its own enclosure.

If we are to consider Woods's claim that Zukofsky creates "the conditions for a new ethical poetics to emerge," then we must locate the source of those conditions. One possible approach involves *desire*'s role in objectification; after all, Zukofsky writes that it is the "*Desire* for what is objectively perfect" not necessarily its completion (*Prepositions* 12, emphasis mine). Every so often in Zukofsky criticism, the discussion of this term, *desire*, returns to haunt Zukofsky's poetics of totality, a poetics that by his own definition requires the adequation of subjective measuring to the world and the completion of the desire for poetic perfection.[6] So how are we to understand Zukofsky's *desire*? On the other side of the Atlantic, at the beginning of the ethical turn, Levinas published his first major book, *Existence and Existents*, which gives us insight into how some people in the 1930s and 1940s may have understood the word *desire*. Begun in 1935 but not published until 1947 because of Levinas's imprisonment during the war, *Existence and Existents* ties desire intimately with the emergence of ethics and justice in "the proximity with another" (ix, xxvii, 98). As opposed to other notions of desire, perhaps that found in Freudian psychoanalysis, defined as need, Levinas understands desire as intending beyond the given world:

> The burning bush that feeds the flames is not consumed. The trouble one feels before the beloved does not only precede what we call, in economic terms, possession, but is felt in the possession too. In the random agitation of caresses there is the admission that access is impossible, violence fails, possession is refused. There is also the ridiculous and tragic simulation of devouring in kissing and love-bites. It is as though one had made a mistake about the nature of one's desire and had confused it with hunger which aims at something, but which one later found out was a hunger for nothing. The *other* is precisely this objectless dimension. (35)

To translate this into Zukofsky's terms, desire would not necessarily lead the apprehension of totality; instead, it may lead us to what is not graspable about "historic and contemporary particulars."

Though still mired in ideas of totality, the desire for what is other is present in Zukofsky's poetics from the start and is amplified as his career matures. The first visible cracks in totality in Zukofsky's writing may be glimpsed in a small but extremely important equivocation in Zukofsky's manifesto, that between "the Ineffable" and "the infinite." Like the term *desire,* these terms survive the various revisions of the essay, and in their context the ethical import of desire achieves full force. Although the terms *ineffable* and *infinite* seem like synonyms—they both signify something that escapes language— Zukofsky employs these terms in opposing contexts. In defense of his "faith" in the total connection of words to referents out in the world, Zukofsky argues that "[t]he revolutionary word if it must revolve cannot escape having a reference. It is not infinite. Even the infinite is a term" (*Prepositions* 16).[7] In other words, the word *infinite* is not a special category of word because it too must have a referent, or thing, that it marks. It is "*impossible,*" Zukofsky emphasizes, "to communicate anything but particulars," and that category of particulars includes the infinite, the totality of the word *infinite* with its referent.

However, when he uses "Ineffable," he seems to place the term in a privileged place, to use Ferdinand de Saussure's terms (to which Zukofsky is perhaps responding), as a signifier without a signified:

> A poem. A poem as object—And yet certainly it arose in the veins and capillaries, if only in the intelligence—Experienced—(every word can't be overdefined) experienced as an object—Perfect rest—Or nature as creator, existing perfect, experience perfecting activity of existence, making it—theologically, perhaps—like the Ineffable—. (*Prepositions* 15)

Again, this passage's emphasis on "intelligence" illustrates why most readings of Objectivist poetics gravitate toward the cognitive judgment of the subject as the basis for poetics, ethics, and politics. Yet there is more in this passage than mere mental experience. The "veins and capillaries," where the poem arises, show the importance Zukofsky places on the body, a priority that, as I show later in the book, is very important for poets such as Robert Duncan and Susan Howe. In seeming contrast to the centrality of the body, this passage also suggests a paradoxical existence of a perfection that appears simultaneously in the poem/body/mind, yet beyond them, too. Something in the perfect poem-as-object is beyond experience, "theologically, perhaps—like the Ineffable—." Something about the poem remains unspeakable, like the divine who resides in the burning, but not consumed, bush in Levinas's figure. This Other lies beyond the referential power of language and beyond the subject's power to totalize and include everything into an adequate reference. Zukofsky's line tellingly ends with a long dash trailing off into silence, as if to signal typographically that ineffability. The question becomes, then, how can a word or poem be both total (as union of sign-referent) and ineffable (as beyond experience and signification)? The answer to the paradox implied in this question is not Reason, to which paradox and contradiction is anathema. It must be something else.

The tension between the infinite and the ineffable, which we see as early as in the 1931 manifesto, operates again in *"A"-12* in the 1950s. On the very first page we see a desire that provides an alternative to the pre-Socratic totality of the dialectic between being and non-being:

> Before the void there was neither
> Being nor non-being;
> Desire, came warmth,
> Or which, first? ("*A*", 126)

Although he does not claim for certain that it comes first, Zukofsky associates this desire closely throughout "*A*"-*12* with what is hidden and untouched (172), singular and unrepeatable (172), infinite (168), uncertain (180), and incomplete (181). In a word, desire implies the Other. As infinite other of the subject, this desire remains insatiable, as Zukofsky suggests in echoing Shakespeare's Juliet: "Desire you but to / Thirst what you have —" (136) and, as the other of language, does not have a proper object, as suggested again by the long dash. It simply desires what cannot be spoken, what cannot be thought.

A few more examples from other Objectivist poets before 1950 might suffice to illustrate this proto-ethics of desire in American avant-garde poetry after Modernism. In the following selection, from Charles Reznikoff's poem "Autobiography: New York" in *Going To and Fro and Walking Up and Down* (1941), the typical aim of Objectivist poetics, objectification that results in rested totality, falters and is displaced by attention to relations with others:

> Walking along the highway,
> I smell the yellow flowers of a shrub,
> watch the starlings on the lawn, perhaps—
> but why are all these
> speeding away in automobiles,
> where are they off to
> in such a hurry?
> They must be going to hear wise men
> and to look at beautiful women,
> and I am just a fool
> to be loitering here alone. (*Poems* II 26–27)

The vision (and scent) of objects gives way to a desire for others, the "these" that Reznikoff refuses to name except through deixis. Rather than leading to the dissolution of the subject, this experience, even as he describes the objectifying projects of these "these" ("to look at beautiful women"), meets with the limit of a failure ("I am just a fool") that evokes the paradox of a desire growing though separation:

> I like the sound of the street—
> but I, apart and alone,
> beside an open window
> and behind a closed door. (27)

Reznikoff marks the subject not only by its (in)ability to totalize and objectify others because of its separated or deferred status (the closed door), but by its desire for others (the open window). Thus, the poetry dramatizes the subject's desire rather than the power or disappearance of the subject. The eye is not totalizing, but in Michael Heller's words, it is "an eye desirous" (*Convictions* 11).

Likewise, the language of "troubling" desire, as Levinas calls it above, in sensual enjoyment may be seen in George Oppen's earlier work, particularly his 1934 *Discrete Series,* which is the first and last book of poetry he published before his twenty-four-year hiatus:

> Near your eyes——
> Love at the pelvis
> Reaches the generic, gratuitous
> (Your eyes like snail-tracks)
>
> Parallel emotions,
> We slide in separate hard grooves
> Bowstrings to bent loins,
> Self moving
> Moon, mid-air. (*New Collected* 26)

Oppen describes the act here as "generic" yet "gratuitous." The possession of the sexual object is prevented by the enjoyment that slides "in separate hard grooves / Bowstrings" and that ties the tension up, never to be resolved. The last line captures this sense of mutability: "Self moving / Moon, mid-air." Such movement renders as inconsistent a reading of this poem as "a rested totality." In a sense, the poem does not try to totalize the sexual enjoyment alluded to but never mentioned. Instead, the relation happens "outside" the poem itself. This poem not only describes the joys of sex but rather the joy of language, which has its own pleasures not found in the logical description of thought. Thought must be suspended for enjoyment or, as Oppen calls it in *Of Being Numerous,* "the pure joy / Of the mineral fact" (*New Collected* 164). In other words, desire for another displaces and disturbs totality.

In this 1930s manifestation, the concept of desire works against totality at the same time it seeks it, and this is the crack, so to speak, through which alterity seeps. This desire—both motivation for seeking totality to begin with and simultaneously the impetus to move beyond totality—is inseparable from the very foundation of Zukofsky's sincerity and objectification. Although critics such as Michael Davidson and Peter Quartermain seek totalizing remedies for the deforming influence of desire, I am arguing that we should embrace such deformation because it always portends an inevitable failure. This failure of totality leads us to what is most ethical about Zukofsky's poetics. But not until after 1958, the year that marks George Oppen's return to writing poetry after years of exile in Mexico, does American poetry, coming out of Zukofsky and the other Modernists, begin to fully question this valuation of totality. Even then, only the more innovative and experimental writers begin to shape their poetics along a new line (not system) of value, a value of what cannot be totalized or even known, that is, the Other. Furthermore, this new poetics embraces the ethical turn that acknowledges a foundational, primal *obligation* to the Other that gives rise to desire and informs language. The following two chapters follow the emergence of a poetics of obligation in two Objectivist writers, Oppen and Reznikoff.

Saying Obligation
George Oppen's *Of Being Numerous*

MACBETH: Come, seeling night,
    Scarf up the tender eye of pitiful day,
    And with thy bloody hand
    Cancel and tear to pieces that great bond
    Which keeps me pale! (III.ii)

After publishing his first book, *Discrete Series,* in 1934 at the age of twenty-one, George Oppen would remain poetically "silent," not writing, let alone publishing, a single poem until 1958, over twenty-four years later. When he comments in retrospect that "there are situations that cannot honorably be met by art," Oppen is referring to how he got involved in the ethical problems he saw around him by joining the Communist Party, organizing strikes, and fighting fascism in Europe during World War II in the U.S. Army ("Mind's Own Place" 136). As Mary Oppen explains this hiatus, "a life had to be lived out of which to write" (qt in DuPlessis, "When" 20). Because of his chosen silence, along with his work in the 1930s with tenant and labor organizations, his lifelong struggle against totalitarianism, and his lyrical critique of the consequences of modern technological progress, Oppen and his poetry have always been labeled as uniquely "moral" or "ethical" by his closest readers and critics.[1] His collections of poems such as *The Materials* (1962) and the Pulitzer Prize–winning *Of Being Numerous* (1968) minimalistically present us with the social and material reality of markedly twentieth-century issues, including urban experience, nuclear apocalypse, and the persistence of poverty amid widespread wealth. And this thematic concern with ethical issues has been one of the main impetuses behind many of the studies of Oppen's ethics.

In this long line of discussion, Peter Nicholls examines the contextual conditions—historical, biographical, philosophical, and literary—that make Oppen's work so attractive to ethical readings. Additionally, Nicholls inaugurates a new line of reading Oppen via Emmanuel Levinas's ethical philosophy. Nicholls ends his essay, "Of Being Ethical," by suggesting that Levinas's "way of understanding ethics may help to elucidate Oppen's evolving poetic. Levinas's sense of a relation to the Other as the quintessential expression of the ethical may define something in Oppen's writing that has strong social motivation but which is not, in his terms, 'political' as such" (251). Because Levinas's work focuses on the very sociality that underpins all political discourse and action, Nicholls suggests, Levinas allows us a much more dynamic and profound view of Oppen's ethics, one that is unique perhaps in American poetry.[2]

In this chapter, beginning with the notion that Oppen's poetry emerges out of a trend shared by the Objectivists for the desire for what is other, I propose a way of tracing Oppen's ethical response to the Other in the form, as well as the content, of his poetry. Using Levinas's notion of obligation and *le dire* (the saying) as a relevant historical context, I want to examine how Oppen engages both the Other of the subject in the themes of his work and the Other of language through formal choices and vulnerabilities. In doing so, I want to reveal a poetics that is in many ways "more" ethical than any other form of discourse, particularly that of moral philosophy or judgment. Oppen's poetics and its ethics, its poethics, not only asks us to redefine what we conventionally think of as ethics, but reveals to us the obligation to others, the Other, inhabiting the very interstices of language that makes all moral, political, and social action possible. In Oppen's poetry we come, to use Levinas's phrase, face-to-face with the Other.

Oppen, Levinas, and the Failure of Totality

Oppen's ethics are most often read within the context of Objectivist poetics, which has in some ways been a limitation. Objectivist poetics, against what Oppen calls "romanticism or even the quaintness of the imagist position," no longer sought to shape the world but rather to encounter the world and allow poetry to be shaped by historical particularity (Dembo 160). But Oppen was never fully comfortable with Louis Zukofsky's definitions that Oppen saw as too totalizing and perhaps totalitarian.[3] Although critics like Tim Woods have begun to reread Zukofsky against these terms, the qualification of totality is much more readily identified in Oppen's work, and, by examining that departure from the thinking of totality in Oppen, we can arrive at a clearer picture of his ethics. One illustration of this departure from the accomplished perfection of objectification occurs in a 1968 interview, where Oppen revises Zukofsky's notion of objectification not as the achievement of totality but as "the making an object of the poem" (Dembo 160). Instead of totality, Oppen often focuses in his own poetry on instances of "Failure and the guilt / Of failure," particularly in aesthetic (and everyday) language

(*New Collected* 174). Take this passage from section 10 of "Of Being Numerous," a series from the book of the same title:

> Or, in that light, New arts! Dithyrambic, audience-as-artists!
> But I will listen to a man, I will listen to a man, and when I
> speak I will speak, tho he will fail and I will fail. But I will
> listen to him speak. The shuffling of a crowd is nothing—
> well, nothing but the many that we are, but nothing.
>   (*New Collected* 167–68)

What Oppen ultimately returns to again and again in his writing is the "fact" of language, *that* we say anything at all, not its ability to capture a totality, whether in the communicative form of signifier capturing its signified or in the form of creating a proper aesthetic object. The content and meaning of the words "will fail," leaving bare the ethical relation that underpins all language: "But I will / listen to him speak."

This posture of engaging the other face-to-face without emphasizing success or total communication most resembles the ethical formulations coming from the continent around the time Oppen emerges from his hiatus. Like the poststructuralists, Oppen refuses the certainty of language and embraces its ambiguity, inordinateness, and ultimately its failure to represent truth and objectivity. His resulting humility, his distrust of poetry's ability to capture right reason, ethical certainty, or political necessity, perhaps ultimately separates Oppen from his contemporaries, particularly William Carlos Williams and Ezra Pound, who seem to have had the loudest voices in defining a Modernist ethics. What distinguishes Oppen is his attention to poetry not mainly as a tool for achieving a moral or political end but as a way "we are carried into the incalculable" (*New Collected* 201).

Words, especially the "little nouns," as Oppen called them in his 1965 poem, "Psalm," stand out not simply for their communicative or representational power, but for what is not recognizable, what is *other*, in them. The poem's theme bears this out. Through the slant homonym "woods / words," Oppen compares the wild deer with their "alien small teeth" hidden in the "strange woods" to the strangeness in the poem (and language) itself (*New Collected* 99). This sense that something is beyond words also haunts Oppen's "Of Being Numerous" (1968), a long series poem that resounds with the difficulties of language. "Speak," Oppen writes, "If you can / Speak," where the line breaks emphasize the imperative and conditional qualities of the sentence (168). Yet, as the poem progresses, "a ferocious mumbling, in public /

Of rootless speech" (173) begins to give way to an impression that this inarticulateness leads not to alienation and despair, but to a relationship with something transcendent: "Surely infiniteness is the most evident thing in the world" (184). In other words, Oppen's poetry with its concern for the "infinite" and "unforseeable" (185) is attuned to what Levinas would call *alterity*. In fact, his poetry could be described, in contradistinction to the usual definition of the lyric, as not focusing on the self but as uniquely *other-oriented*.

Unlike most notions of "the Other" formulated since Hegel, which are defined dialectically in relation to the self, Oppen's poetics expresses the radicalness of alterity not in the form of opposition but in figures of speech that resist logic. For example, paradoxes abound in both Levinas's and Oppen's writings. Note this one Levinas uses in *Totality and Infinity*: "[the relation with the Other is] a relation in which the terms *absolve* themselves from the relation, remain absolute within the relation" (64). Designated by paradox, the Other overflows any thought or statement I can have of him or her (48–52). In addition to paradox, Levinas and Oppen figure this radical alterity using hyperbole: *transcendence, destitution, height, remoteness, exteriority, absence,* and *void* are terms common to both writers. The paradoxical and hyperbolic alterity in their work makes the Other, although human, so radically different or separate from me that we are not "in" difference at all, what Levinas terms "non-in-difference" (*Ethics* 106, 52).[4] All conjunctions are inordinate to this relationship, as are all names, but both writers continue to try to bring it into language despite inevitable failure. In "Of Being Numerous," Oppen uses the phrase "the shipwreck of the singular" at the same time he writes of "being numerous" to capture the distance we often feel even when in proximity to others. In Oppen's verse, I am neither opposed to nor part of the crowd. Refusing the dialectical, Levinas's alterity, like Oppen's notion of singular-numerous humanity, thwarts the ultimate intention of Western philosophy to reabsorb the Other "into my own identity as a thinker and possessor" (*Totality* 33). As opposed to the disabled or oppressed Other of some dialectical theory, Levinas's and Oppen's decentering alterity places the Other completely beyond my power, or any power for that matter. Because of the absolute separation implied in alterity, the objective subject, the poet, cannot ever fully objectify an object or the Other. To be sure, alterity disturbs any objective, rational sense of language, the kind we might see in conventional readings of Objectivist objectification.

In an interview (one of the few public forums Oppen used to discuss his poetics), he describes his ethics as "the search for a morality of altruism" that would justify human life (Dembo 164). Unlike more traditional definitions of ethics as moral judgment, Oppen sees this altruistic obligation as a state of being, rather than as a duty one accepts. Nor is this altruism caught up in self-congratulation. The feeling we have that something exists beyond objective reality, Oppen might say, does not serve simply as a sublime experience; instead, it obligates the self to what is other. As we will see in the next section, the theme of responsibility to others will crop up again and again in Oppen's writing, particularly in his work after *The Materials* (1962). Oppen's poetry, more than any of the other original Objectivists, foregrounds the question of obligations to other human beings to the point that the social bond takes precedent over principle or proscription. Indeed, Levinas's in-depth phenomenology of the responsibility the subject bears the Other is reciprocally illuminated in the context of Oppen's preoccupation with this theme from 1958 until his death in 1984.

The Themes of Obligation and Vulnerability

Oppen's poetry is often read as ethical not only because of his life choices but because of its subject matter that engages with political and ethical situations. In short, Oppen concerns himself with ethical obligations to the other of the subject. However, in the context of Levinas's work from the late 1950s and early 1960s, which explicitly reframes how ethical obligations to others work, the possible meaning of Oppen's poeticizing of the ethical take on deeper, more profound implications. Even on this thematic level, Oppen's poetry is replete with an inescapable sense of obligation of self for others that arises out of the desire for the Other we find in Zukofsky and earlier Objectivist poetics. In short, Oppen's poetics is an exploration of how alterity evinces obligation from a subject.

A brilliant example of this sense of obligation in Oppen's oeuvre—and the instance that first interested me in Oppen from an ethical perspective—may be found in the relation between sections 13 and 14 in his 1968 "Of Being Numerous." At first reading, assigning a nonjudgmental ethical responsibility to section 13 seems unfitting because it indicts Americans as harshly as the writings of many high Modernists such as Pound:

    unable to begin
 At the beginning, the fortunate
 Find everything already here. They are shoppers,
 Choosers, judges; . . . And here the brutal
 is without issue, a dead end.

                    They develop
Argument in order to speak, they become
unreal, unreal, life loses
solidity, loses extent, baseball's their game
because baseball is not a game
but an argument and difference of opinion
makes the horse races. They are ghosts that endanger

One's soul. There is change
In an air
That smells stale, they will come to the end
Of an era
First of all peoples
And one may honorably keep

His distance
If he can. (*New Collected* 170–71)

Even in the middle of this indictment, the form of the poem suggests complicity on Oppen's part, which prevents the poem from being purely judgmental. Oppen is himself one of those who is "unable to begin at the beginning"; and he too is one of the "fortunate" whom he is indicting. The indentation and lack of beginning capitalization reinforce his complicity and suggest that Oppen is beginning this poem in medias res, therefore "unable to begin at the beginning" just like the objects of his poetic measure. Including himself is a way of responding to the problems and dangers of the "dead end" without judgment. Such a response consists of what Levinas would call responsibility.

The next section, almost a continuation of the previous one yet also its qualification, proves less judgmental and opens with a characteristic response of humility:

I cannot even now
Altogether disengage myself
From those men

Considering the supposed condemnation of the prior poem, this statement of humility captures the essence of Objectivist desire of the Other, the non-in-difference of not being able to disengage. But Oppen cannot rest there. The poem thematizes the very inescapability of responsibility to others that marks Oppen's ethics. The equivocal phrase "those men," set off in its own stanza, bonds the speaker both to the men in the previous poem and the more sympathetic ones that follow:

> With whom I stood in emplacements, in mess tents,
> In hospitals and sheds and hid in the gullies
> Of blasted roads in a ruined country,
>
> Among them many men
> More capable than I—
>
> Muykut and a sergeant
> Named Healy,
> That lieutenant also—
>
> How forget that? How talk
> Distantly of 'The People'
>
> Who are that force
> Within the walls
> Of cities
>
> Wherein their cars
>
> Echo like history
> Down walled avenues
> In which one cannot speak. (*New Collected* 171)

Critics have hotly contested the ethical import of this passage, partially because it has not been considered for its *lack* of moral judgment. Marjorie Perloff thinks that this pair of poems fails to solidify any sincere stance toward the men to whom Oppen claims to be so indebted: "But their only significance for him seems to be that he was with them. Aside from the two proper names, Muykut and Healy, and two designations of rank, he does not provide us with a single identifying feature of his fellow soldiers" ("Shipwreck" 200). Equating identification and sincere detail with ethics, Perloff sees as uncaring Oppen's overgeneralization, but this reticence to specify can also be read as an attempt not to judge, not to reduce them to Zukofskian "historic particulars," not to totalize these men who are remarkable for the way they transcend Oppen's previous judgment of them. Even though the poem prior to this one, section 13, could be said to characterize those same American men, as "brutal," "judges," "shoppers," " who must use "argument in order to speak," the speaker is still beholden to them (*New Collected* 170). He cannot "disengage."

In discussing the contemporary trend in the 1960s of a certain "apocalyptic poetry," Lévinas describes the kind of sincere poet Oppen is: "In these significations, far from any game and more strictly than in being itself, men stand who have never been more moved (whether in holiness or in guilt) than by other men in whom they recognize an identity even in the indiscerniblility of their mass presence, and before whom they find themselves irreplaceable and unique in responsibility" (*Otherwise* 58). This paradox and contradiction, which Oppen's poem shares, signal the failure of any judgment or politically determined morality. How can Oppen forget men like Muykut and Healy, who may be the two men who died in the foxhole in France where Oppen was injured (*New Collected* xx). Although Oppen both does and does not count himself as one of these "fortunate" who "Find everything already here," he is unable to "honorably keep / His distance / If he can" and "unable to begin / At the beginning." In other words, in the face of others he is humbled through his failure, his inability, to morally condemn such people with certainty.

Oppen's two poems and Lévinas's philosophy both evince a notion of responsibility that allows for the kind of distinction that I am making above between judgment and engagement. For Lévinas, responsibility is not reducible to the usual metaphors that signal the Judeo-Christian, or better yet, the Greek, understanding of the term: Responsibility is not a political duty that can either be executed *or* an account of transgression that can be repaid; neither is it a mode of cognitive reflection on action or a dependence upon grace. Responsibility, instead, demands the subject's engagement and thus undergirds the fabric of human existence. The subject cannot escape or be saved from responsibility. Oppen's work concurs with this perspective. In his poem on Thomas Hardy, for example, Oppen ends with what seems like a despair at the impossibility of salvation, but it can also be read as a statement about the way things are: "We might half-hope to find the animals / In the sheds of a nation / Kneeling at midnight," which would mean the world has been redeemed. But for Oppen it has not been redeemed because "we do not altogether matter" (*New Collected* 175). Not relying on a self-centered vision of salvation, Oppen resigns himself to this state that only we are responsible for cutting our own throats, as he phrases it in the previous poem (173).

For Lévinas this state of continual obligation is, for lack of better terminology, more primal than any law or morality. Obligation to the Other arises "before" or "above and beyond" duties such as the prohibition against murder, the burden of being a parent, and the loyalty to a state. These specific moral codes are always already anticipated as results of the very bonds created in community between self and Other. As a kind of gravity, in every sense of the word, responsibility is the very "curvature of intersubjective space" and, like Einstein's theory of relativity from which Levinas most likely draws this metaphor, is as such inescapable (Levinas, *Totality* 291). Even though unavoidable, this responsibility cannot be codified or made manifest because it allows for the manifestation of responsibility in the ordinary sense, as law, morality, and so forth; in other words, Levinas tropes "responsibility" and "obligation" to make a distinction between "ethics" and "morality." Ethics is the relationship with (responsibility for, obligation to) another that calls for morality (duty, law, code). "Of Being Numerous" sections 13 and 14 testify as well that ethical responsibility cannot fully be brought into the poem as a theme that would provide a moral by which the reader could lead a good life, yet the responsibility is somehow invested in language, a language in which "one cannot speak."

As the indecision and complicity of "Of Being Numerous" sections 13 and 14 demonstrate, ethics in Oppen's poetry resides closer to passivity and vulnerability than to action. Often ethics is thought of, certainly by many Modernist poets, as hardness and impenetrability to the corrupting influences of modern life, but Oppen's poetry takes the opposite posture (as does Reznikoff's, which we'll see in more detail in the next chapter). Ethics happens to one as much as it is something that one does, and the same can be said for poetry. In section 34 of "Of Being Numerous," Oppen employs gender to portray women neither as victims nor as moral deadweight (as Otto Weininger does in *Sex and Character* or as Ezra Pound and Wyndham Lewis do in *Blast,* for example) but to show how these particular women respond to the Other from the space of their own vulnerability and alterity:

Is it the courage of women
To assume every burden of blindness themselves

Intruders
Carrying life, the young women

Carrying life
Unaided in their arms

In the streets, weakened by too much need
Of too little

And life seeming to depend on women, burdened and
desperate
As they are (*New Collected* 184–85)

The mode of being of these women, "unaided in their arms," aspires not
to the militaristic heroism of Modernism, from which Oppen distances
himself when he states in an interview that "Pound's ego system, Pound's
organization of the world around a character, a kind of masculine energy,
is extremely foreign to me" (Dembo 170). What Oppen venerates is that
the women "assume every burden" themselves, even though (and possibly,
because) they are "weakened," needy, and "desperate." Although this image
seems to perpetuate representations of women as weak and as maternal nur-
turers of mankind, they are, paradoxically, powerful in their vulnerability
and impotence. After all, they "[carry] life" but do not act out of certain
knowledge that what they do is "right." The exact way or code by which they
respond and deal with these problems is not at issue—it is *that* they respond. Although this passage resists easy interpretation, my point here is that
the theme of obligation does not exist in Oppen's poetry as one of power,
control, and rationality.

What most critics of Oppen's work, as well as most critics of poetics as
a field, miss is the possibility that poetry does not resist uncertainty or fulfill
its obligation to the Other by imposing a rational system of judgment and
decision; rather, poetry strives to encourage uncertainty, disruption, and
otherness through a sort of "passivity more passive than all passivity," to use
a phrase of Levinas's (*Otherwise* 15). Critics perhaps overlook this vulnerable
responsibility in Oppen's writing because such passivity does not serve the
proper activism needed for a materialist understanding of social change. As
Rachel Blau DuPlessis (a critic, fellow poet, and valued friend of Oppen) remarks, "To gloss Oppen, one must speak of some model less purely political,
although part of Oppen's terror is the sense that he is taking responsibility
for the world of matter via poetry" ("When" 31). To most critics, accustomed
to believe, due to the prevailing understanding of ethics as right action, that
active strength is somehow superior to passive vulnerability, this type of responsibility *is* terrifying, as it was terrifying for Macbeth.[5] To say that a poet,
like some defender of alterity, makes choices that "disrupt" or "allow" is to
again retrieve subjective agency as the beginning of ethics. For Oppen, however, ethics becomes something to which the poetry is vulnerable, before
one can choose to "respect" or "let the other be." There is no need to fear this
vulnerability, for it signals the irruption of responsibility as inescapable

relation to the Other. My use of the passive voice in this chapter is often strategic, for responsibility is demanded of me by the Other *before* I choose it (and even this temporal metaphor of "before" is inadequate, though I employ it because it also implies the space where the Other faces me). Only an approach that closely examines the unintended effects of form, in addition to intentional themes, can allow us to read against the critical penchant for action and agency and come to a deeper understanding of the profundity of Levinas's and Oppen's ethics.

The Trace of Obligation in Poetry

As I suggested in the introduction, Oppen's poetry reveals the relevance of language to ethical relations by exploring it as a medium and making that medium opaquely visible. More precisely, Oppen's poetry asks not only *how should we* relate to each other, a conventionally ethical question, but also asks *how ethics is a problem of poetic language.* This poem from *Of Being Numerous* explicitly lays out these connections:

> The emotions are engaged
> Entering the city
> As entering any city.
>
> We are not coeval
> With a locality
> But we imagine that others are,
>
> We encounter them. Actually
> A populace flows
> Thru the city.

> This is a language, therefore, of New York (*New Collected* 164)

There is a marked shift in this poem not only in the historical conception of the poet's relation to the objects in the world but also in his relations with other people. They engage the emotions (as did Muykut and Healy in section 14) as we encounter them, but this engagement is "a language." The passive voice enacts this shift: "emotions are engaged," as passive and vulnerable encounter with the Other.

To read Oppen's sense of obligation, therefore, as only a thematic concern would be to misunderstand the depth of his ethical investigation. Williams Carlos Williams knew this when in his 1934 *Poetry* magazine review of Oppen's *Discrete Series* he locates this ethical importance of Oppen's poetry not in what it says but in what it "*is*," its form ("New Poetical Economy" 267). Like the figures of the women above, Oppen's poetry is not simply vulnerable to its obligation to the Other because the poet desires it—that would imply the poet possesses a power to "let be" that would thereby void passivity.[6] Instead, I am claiming Oppen writes in such a way not merely to "respect" the Other but literally to sub-ject his writing to an obligation already there (in the saying of language). As Levinas writes, "[s]peaking, rather than 'letting be,' solicits the Other" (*Totality* 195). In a sense, Oppen seems to agree, speaking paradoxically through his choice of form, that the poet does not have to *do* anything to invoke ethics except to use language. In other words, ethics happens, as Burton Hatlen has pointed out, "in between" the words ("Opening" 265–66). Because Objectivists like Oppen believed that poetry was *formed* language, this sub-jection happens on the level of form or, better yet, where form de-forms.

But the question then becomes, how can we read an ethics in the form of poetry? More precisely, how do we read an obligation for the Other in the saying of poetic language? For much of the twentieth century, many critics and thinkers, including Levinas, have precluded modern poetry, particularly in its most avant-garde formulation, from the category of the ethical. One reason being that formal experimentation nihilistically destroys the kinds of systematic thinking on which conventional moralities are built. But in the time period we are dealing with, the distance between the poetic and the philosophical domain of ethics is occluded.

For Oppen and Levinas, mere experiment in art does not signal ethics, as they understood those terms, but for different reasons. Many readers of Levinas, particularly Jill Robbins in her book, *Altered Reading: Levinas and Literature* (1999), have pointed to *Totality and Infinity* (originally published in 1961) and "Reality and Its Shadow" (originally published in 1948) to argue for a Levinas suspicious of art and poetry as unethical discourses.[7] In such early work, Levinas explicitly attacks art and poetry as akin to idolatry. Poetry seems to receive, in a very platonic way, Levinas's harshest critique because (1) it is written, as opposed to spoken language, and (2) it is self-centered. A few brief passages from *Totality and Infinity* can illustrate these critiques. "The alterity of the I that takes itself for another," Levinas writes, "may strike the imagination of the poet precisely because it is but the play of the same" (*Totality* 37). This mere "play" is made possible by writing, which does not require the author to answer for his language. "Speech," on the other hand for Levinas, "better than a simple sign, is essentially magisterial" (69). Written rhetoric for Levinas in 1961, "would consist in suppressing the other . . . [b]ut in its expressive [spoken] function language precisely main-tains the other" (73). Considering these critiques from his major early works, the interpretation goes, art and writing cannot be ethical for Levinas be-cause they do not lead to a dialogue with the Other; art is outside society and arrests the face of the Other in a plastic image. Oppen is similarly skep-tical of art, especially the European avant-garde as witnessed by several of the poems in *Of Being Numerous*—one being section 10, which I excerpted above—so Levinas's caution toward art is germane to an understanding of Oppen's poetry (Hatlen, "Opening" 275–76). Both writers, despite com-ing from a generation that was skeptical of the morality of art, were working toward a more ethical discourse in the 1950s and 1960s. Even in light of Lev-inas's seeming rejection of art, I firmly maintain that his work is relevant and, indeed vital, to the study of poetry. Yet neither do I want to dismiss his caution because it offers valuable lessons to those who think poetry should become ethical either by battling philosophy on its own didactic ground (as Plato and Pound perhaps thought) or by completely separating itself from logic and rationality (as is perhaps the case in nineteenth century aesthetics or some Modernist verse). However, Levinas's skepticism of poetry is not total and begins to change after 1955. Through his relationship with Maurice Blanchot,[8] Levinas begins to explore the relationship of philosophy and poetry in such essays as "The Servant and Her Master" (originally published in 1966) and "Le regarde du poete" (1956) from *Monde Nouveau,* as well as books like *Otherwise than Being or Beyond Essence,* (originally published in 1974) and *Noms Propres* (1975). Levinas comes to regard poetry as providing the perfect conditions for witnessing *le dire* (the saying) and the obligation it invokes.

Despite his disparagement of writing in favor of speech in *Totality and Infinity,* Levinas's later notion of the saying places ethics within every mode of language, including poetry.[9] "The Servant and Her Master," Levinas's essay on Blanchot's novel *L'attente l'oubli,* begins to redefine the poetic in ways that resonate with Oppen's practice. In response to Blanchot's writing, Levinas submits the rejoinder that language is not a closed entity but, rather, the site where philosophy, defined as logical propositions aimed at possess-ing truth, is opened by what he will call *the poetic.* However, this poetic is not translatable into a poetics or a genre for the simple, yet philosophically important, reason that Levinas (along with Oppen) will provide no firm definition of poetry.[10] Instead of providing an essential structure by which to identify or judge poetry, Levinas opens language and poetry to his notion of ethics, while Oppen opens ethical philosophy to his notion of poetry.

Poetry, for Levinas and Oppen, becomes like ethics because it is not purely reducible to a set of rules or propositions: "The mode of revelation of what remains other, despite its revelation, is not the thought, but the language, of the poem" (Levinas, *Proper* 130). Indeed poetry reinscribes alterity into the text, which is opened to what remains other and shocks language. It is vulnerable.

In Levinas's essay, the endorsement of poetry hinges on the distinction he makes between *le dire* and *le dit*.[11] As defined in the introduction of this book, *le dit* (the said) is the supposed totality of language that includes the langue and parole of any system of signs—it is the how and what of language. *Le dire* (the saying) is the poetic underside of that system—that of language's very expression—and haunts the said with an ethical obligation to the Other. According to Levinas, the saying has no proper content but says only that "I am obligated," an asymmetry or curvature in relationship rather than a message. Unlike form, theme, or political stance, the saying cannot be "identified" at all and only leaves a *trace*. This trace traces and retreats within the said of language comprised of its content, form, and figures. The poetic for Levinas approaches a meaning similar to the saying, as what allows for meaning to arise, congeal, and collapse. However, the poetic cannot exist outside such static structures as form, grammar, signifier, logic, but, as such, those structures bear poetic responsibility as the saying. Therefore, the poetic interrupts, but does not eliminate, the philosophical language that "speaks without a stop." But by tying poetry to the saying, Levinas suggests a way out of this (Hegelian/Heideggerian) circle: "Is it possible to get out of the circle otherwise than by expressing the impossibility of getting out of it, by speaking the inexpressible? Is not poetry, of itself, the Exit?" ("Servant" 152). Poetry embodies ethics for Levinas, and for Oppen this embodiment becomes his poethics.

Oppen's poetry, even in (and especially in) its oft-touted silences, resists the drone of rational discourse, much like the saying resists the linearity of the said and provides us with an exit from proscriptive notions of ethics and poetics. This is the importance of a deconstructive approach to Oppen: the call of the Other can only be "read" as a trace in the said—as disruptions, contradictions, anxieties, spaces, and silences—created by certain poetic techniques (actively enacted by the poet) and their effects (beyond intentional authorial control, enacted in reading).[12] So the key, as Steve McCaffery points out with David Antin's poetry, would be to find the traces left by "foregrounding the saying" within the said ("Scandal" 180–82). One may trace responsibility via Oppen's poetry in a number of ways not limited to the following: nonjudgmental diction, deixis, ambiguous reference, question marks, parataxis, quotations, ellipses, gaps, internal contradictions, multiple connotations, line breaks, page space, lack of subject-object agreement, unconventional syntax, and other poetic innovations that avoid judgment while remaining vulnerable to responsibility.[13] Many such techniques can be located in the work of other Modernist poets, as Krzysztof Ziarek does with Celan or Tim Woods with Zukofsky; but they occur in conjunction with the theme of obligation and with such frequency in Oppen's poetry (as well as in the work of many poets in the experimental strain after Oppen) that they cannot be overlooked as integral to the way ethical obligation inflects its language.

A qualification: I want to make it clear that this poetic enterprise is bound to fail in its attempt to not judge or totalize the Other. Poetry can never completely "let the other be," "respect" the other, or even fully invite obligation into the poem. Despite his admonitions against language as communication, Oppen still relies somewhat on unity, grammar, action, and rationality in his poetry. On that score, Oppen is not so different from many Modernists. Neither are these techniques successful in fully capturing the obligation to otherness in the text, but it is through that failure, ironically, that we can find the traces of ethical saying.[14] According to this middle ground between dialectical oppositions, herein lies Oppen's sense of obligation: to keep seeking the Other in language even if such a search is doomed. However, ethics happens in poetry even before the seeking properly begins, and Oppen's verse seems fully susceptible to that fact. Beyond the power to seek, his poetic elements open the poetry to the Other *always already there* and at the same time allow for the questioning of how we, in language, make moral decisions at all.

Deforming Ethics

Because "Of Being Numerous" is Oppen's first poem to consciously deal with the issue of "humanity" (Schiffer, "Interview" 14–16; Dembo 162–64), it allows us to "see" how this poetic deferral of action and intention turns toward obligation to other people in this text and in the succeeding works as well. But this deferral reveals itself, if you will, only in between the lines, where the poem does not (or cannot) "make sense." The most obvious instance of this tracing is that many of the sections of "Of Being Numerous," in fact all 40 sections, do not seem complete. This is also another clear rejection of totality, only on the formal level. Many of the poems begin or end with ellipses (sections 16, 35, 37, 40), in the middle of a sentence (1, 11, 13, 20), or contain a quotation from another person or text (1, 9, 12, 16, 17, 23, 25, 34, 37, 39, 40). These simple gestures make poems that are not coherent wholes or "rested totalities" but witnesses, open to the fact that they are indebted to other texts, other words, other people for their existence. As Hatlen puts it, "Oppen, indeed, has allowed the voice of the Other to inhabit his own discourse, for a perilous moment" ("Opening" 270). Perilous because the obligation petitioned by the Other does not decide on the proper moral action for the subject, a topic that will be explored in more depth in the next chapter in the context of Reznikoff's work.

Even the poems that contain quotations, in addition to the fact that Oppen has included them in the poem itself, contain formal "quirks" (for lack of a better word) that signal ethical responsibility. A simple illustration would be the last section of the series, section 40, which contains only one word that "belongs to" Oppen—that word, oddly enough, is "Whitman." The only sign of choice or action on the part of Oppen, the word (and the line break that sets it off) is not simply an object, an end in itself, but an invocation (an inspiration, a response, and an obligation), and the rest of the words belong to Whitman's text. Ironically, however, this word of Oppen's is a proper name belonging to someone else and, thus, does not even really belong to Oppen in the sense that he crafted it with his own originality. This irony deepens our sense of the alterity-through-passivity that such a technique signals. Another curious part of this poem, besides its subject matter about the "new" capitol building at sunset, is the way in which Oppen sets off the final word on its own line, "curious . . ." (*New Collected* 188). Many may read this dislocation of the quotation as an ironic political statement that juxtaposes Whitman's optimistic adoration of the building with the current crises at the time in the United States, such as the war in Vietnam, that Oppen is commenting on throughout the entire poem. Some may read it in other ways because it is ambiguous. Yet, in spite of the interpretation one might place on this section of the poem, it is impossible to deny that a response to Whitman has been made without saying a word. In fact, the words of the Other speak through Oppen's poetry (in a way over which he has no control), while the very form sounds its obligation to the quotation/borrowing. As Oppen says himself of this passage, "I suppose it's nearly a sense of awe, simply to feel that the thing is there and that it's quite something to see. It's an awareness of the world, a lyric reaction to the world" (Dembo 164). The form is a lyricization—which is not the same as thematization—of the wonder inspired not just by the capitol dome but by Whitman's text and by the Other and a responsibility to that Other. In Whitman's text, we see his awe at the Capitol; in Oppen's, we see awe at the traces of Whitman in the text. Oppen's Objectivist lyric then is not just a particular form embodying the subject's voice, but an ethical way of responding to the Other. Oppen's poetry finds a way to invite and expose responses in the very formal gaps of the poem. In other words, the Other's words remain unsaid yet motivate the saying in the poem.

Yet how can this type of reading that focuses on unidentifiable aporiae be important in a poetry that often seems to "make sense," rather than in a more abstract poetry, such as zaum poetry, Gertrude Stein's cubist poetry, or more recent, Language poetry? In an Objectivist poetics, one expects the poem to name or visualize objects, persons, or states of mind as they are encountered in the world. Especially in Oppen's poetry, the philosophical diction and subject matter along with "plain" English in American dialect seem to suggest explanation and "clarity," a favorite word of Oppen's and one that guides much Oppen criticism down the path of ontology or representation. This type of reading prevails especially when one looks at his negative attitude toward obscurity as a poetic technique, which seems to place him squarely against the type of reading I am proposing.[15]

Yet, there is a certain *opacity* to Oppen's language that has an ethical effect because it draws attention to how language works in the rendering of moral decision. Rather than resorting to manipulation or trickery, this vagueness, or opaqueness, refers back to Oppen's lack of assertion and judgment. In a sense, Oppen attempts a *clarity of uncertainty* that I read as an ethical event. In fact, much of Oppen's poetry leaves things open, as in not explained, but also the sense of meditation:

17
The roots of words
Dim in the subways

There is madness in the number
Of the living
'A state of matter'

There is nobody here but us chickens

Anti-ontology—

He wants to say
His life is real,
No one can say why

It is not easy to speak

A ferocious mumbling, in public
Of rootless speech (*New Collected* 172–73)

The paratactic juxtaposition of the elements in this poem prevents a systematic way of drawing meaning from it. Yet a certain sense (which is really a non-sense because it posits no foundational reading of the text itself) can be made by looking at the aporiae of the poem, that is, at the moments when sense or identification is frustrated. First, in the overall thematics of this section, each stanza initiates a new and unrelated twist in the poem's subject matter, but, again, the poem remains silent on their relation—there are no connectives. This parataxis leaves interpretation open, that is, vulnerable to the Other, to the indeterminate. Meaning becomes a possibility rather than a prescription. On the other hand, lack of punctuation, with the exception of two commas, seems to run the different stanzas together, as if they formed one sentence. There seems to be the makings of four complete sentences here, but where do they begin and end? Take for example the stanzas after the dash: "He wants to say his life is real, no one can say why it is not easy to speak a ferocious mumbling, in public of rootless speech." Is this one sentence? Before these stanzas in "Of Being Numerous" were written, a line break in Oppen's work usually coincides with a syntactical or grammatical unit.[16] However, does a line break keep "a ferocious mumbling" from being the object of the infinitive, "to speak"? And what about this "ferocious mumbling"? Is this a denigration of a public that cannot communicate except in a mumbling "of rootless speech"? This may be a judgment on Oppen's part, but at the onset of the poem the words *do* have roots that show dimly in the subways. So is this condemnation complete, or is the mumbling a metonymy for the poet's perception of the public that is separate and other from him? Such a metonymy, rather than a metaphor, reveals an obligation to that otherness by not equating it and replacing it with another figure.[17] Although the correct meaning of the poem lies beyond me, I think the poem cannot answer the question of clarity with what it has provided.

In this poem, the difficulty of speaking is enacted; in other words, this opaque and confusing (and some might say "arcane") way that Oppen uses to explain that "it is not easy to speak" in the "dim subways" is itself a way of speaking, a way of mumbling a rootless speech. This rootlessness—as the absence of center, ground, or origin—is not a loss of meaning but the very possibility of conversation with an Other. In his reading of Blanchot's novel *L'attente l'oubli*, Levinas characterizes this impossible possibility as the ethical saying of language ("Servant" 156). Emblematic of such rootlessness, the disruptions of "correct" grammar and punctuation are a way to respond to "the madness in the number of the living," which in its double entendre serves both as metonymic figure of sympathy for collective humanity and an expression of antipathy at the sheer numbers. Furthermore, this contradiction seems to qualify his outright judgment of such a "public," as seen, for instance, in "Of Being Numerous" section 13 as it indicts the "shoppers and choosers." Such vagueness in Oppen's poetry is more than just a reluctance to totalize; it opens the poem to a responsibility because it cannot reduce, reject, or refuse the realities the poet sees around him. The point of these poems is not to make a point, to make a particular "sense," or to project a certain message; instead, they foreground the very attempt of responding to the call of the Other through language, the saying, whether that response be a failure of charity or a refusal to judge. As Cid Corman states, Oppen's poetry "is heroism that refuses heroics, confronting only the terrible history, past and present and destined to come into more terribleness, in the name of man as a principle of nature. And in the possibility of speech, of addressing one to another, granted the most painful limits, but refusing not to try to work them through" (118). All speech is rooted in that it must exist and be expressed, yet language too is rootless because it does not connect me with anything or anyone but with what is other and beyond reach. In spite of this paradox, Oppen's poems say, we must and do respond to the Other in spite of "the most painful limits" that all but make such speaking impossible.

This lack of explanation bordering on vagueness—which I read as *the saying*, an ethical "clarity," a clearing of a place from which to respond to the Other—appears in the role of silence in Oppen's poetry, which has garnered much critical attention because of his own biographical silence from 1934 to 1958. Adding to readings of silence as witness, as politics, and as aesthetic care, I interpret Oppen's silence as an ethical event because it invites indeterminacy to inhabit the poem:

Clarity
In the sense of *transparence,*
I don't mean that much can be explained.

Clarity in the sense of silence. (*New Collected* 175)

This silence is certainly a political statement, but it is also more than that.[18] It is also an ethical silence, as opposed to an excluding silence. An ethical silence not only lets a situation be, but passively witnesses the very difficulty of relating, thinking, and communicating. Silence is vulnerable to the Other because it does not explain, and, most of all, silence admits that explanation would be impossible because such "things" are beyond control and cognition. Yet this foregrounding of the difficulty of speaking of things, without actually speaking of the things themselves, responds to that very difficult and elusive otherness. This ethical silence affects both things and people, as Woods points out (217), but I want to emphasize the primacy of the neighbor, the other person, in Oppen's work (a priority he shares with Levinas). This becomes a tricky distinction to trace in a poetry that does not make such definitive judgments; section 9 in "Of Being Numerous," for example, invites obligation and otherness by not naming what is:

The absolute singular

The unearthly bonds
Of the singular

Which is the bright light of shipwreck (*New Collected* 167)

Rather than confidently reporting on events in the world, this lyric singles out the unearthly quality of existence. But the ethical question remains: If Being is singular, shipwrecked, then to whom am I bound? On this paradox the poem is silent, except perhaps in the suggestive title of the entire series in which the "Numerous" is not an object but a manner of being *beyond* Being that rejects the neutrality of Being by peopling it. There is another person to whom I am bound. Rather than exclude by answering, Oppen leaves the question of responsibility in silence. Unlike Levinas, however, Oppen creates in his work a tension, between singular subject and numerous others, a relationship with "the unearthly," the Other, who is also "singular." The way the phrase "The unearthly bonds" is set off as the second line here positions it as a qualification of "the absolute singular." This qualification signals an inarticulate responsibility because those bonds are not codified or understandable, as they are in a religious morality or a social contract. In a sense, these bonds "shipwreck" the language of the poem in terms of reference or grammar. As Levinas says in "The Servant and Her Master," poetry disrupts or hinders the logic of what is said by reminding us of the saying that obligates (150–51). Oppen's version of Herman Melville's famous saying from *Pierre* that "Silence is the only voice of our God" might be something like, "Silence is the very sound of my obligation to the Other."

Similar to the role of silence in Oppen's poetry is the function of gaps, which seem to occur in two varieties: "internal," within the lines as well as between lines and stanzas, and "external," around the entire poem itself. In a useful elucidation, Randolph Chilton explains this space in terms of Heidegger's clearing of the "Nothing," the place where "what is" can emerge. Contrary to the weblike totality of relations that marks the autonomous work of art, Chilton argues, Oppen "evokes the space between those particulars that allows them to exist as discrete entities" and from which we can "contemplate both the limits and the depths of language, thought, and our own being" (112). And, I would add, this contemplation of Being in Oppen is disturbed by a responsibility to the Other that characterizes not just interpersonal relations but all relationships. In other words, the spaces in Oppen's poetry do not seem to contain simply "nothing" or even "Being"; they are spaces left open for the Other where the saying can obligate us, as a space at the table is left for Elijah at the Seder. Here is an example of such "external" use of space in "Of Being Numerous":

A Theological Definition

A small room, the varnished floor
Making an L around the bed,

What is or is true as
Happiness

Windows opening on the sea,
The green painted railings of the balcony
Against the rock, the bushes and the sea running (*New Collected* 203)

The rushing of the poem out the window over the sea far away from the room mimics the transcendence of the saying: the "theological" is in the everyday, the bed, "happiness," yet it opens out onto the open sea and runs on to the indefinite, if not the infinite.[19] The "running" happens despite the poet's intent or control. This tripartite structure—the object, the state of being, and the inescapable opening onto the Other—characterizes several of the poems of this book (see also sections 17 and 23) and functions as an analog to an Objectivist ethics perhaps as a whole. What is left out, through the imposition of internal "space," in the figure of the letter *L* is the connection between the three parts (as is left out of much of the juxtapositions in the book). The juxtaposition is a call to respond, but it does not dictate the response. This silence is a trace of an interpretation that is always to come.

In his later work, such as *Seascape: Needle's Eye* (1972), Oppen comes to emphasize gaps in his poetry by putting them in th very middle of lines. In an interview with Reinhold Schiffer, Oppen claims that "[w]hat happens is that the poem is more open . . . my interest in that was precisely the application always of all which is beyond and all that is within" (23). In other words, Oppen uses internal gaps consciously to open up a line to otherness (as well as to the poem and subject within), but the gaps open the poem to what the poet can never foresee. For instance, "From a Phrase of Simone Weil's and Some Words of Hegel's" (Oppen, *New Collected* 211) and "Exodus" (234) the gaps and disrupted syntax add to the exposure of the saying and the vulnerability of the poem to responsibility:

Exodus

Miracle of the children   the brilliant
Children   the word
Liquid as woodlands   Children?
When she was a child I read Exodus
To my daughter   'The children of Israel . . .'

Pillar of fire
Pillar of cloud

We stared at the end
Into each other's eyes   Where
She said hushed

Were the adults   We dreamed to each other
Miracle of the children
The brilliant children   Miracle

Of their brilliance   Miracle
of

There are eight internal gaps within lines in this poem and each serves a different function that is not specified by the text and whose meaning can only be speculated. However, each seems to enact a space that at once signals a bond of relationship and at the same time points to the otherness that pervades relationship. The first internal gap, between "Children   the word" in line 2, seems to put some self-reflexive distance in the poem, to show that the narrative of the biblical story (as well as of the poem) is constructed of language. "Liquid as woodlands   Children?" also inserts distance—to describe the sound of the word as well as the geographical distance between the present state and the desired Promised Land—but also questions the very semantics of the term selected to describe the Israelites. On the other hand, the gaps heighten a sense of desire for relationship, a relationship of language that is ethics itself: "We stared at the end / Into each other's eyes   Where / She said hushed" (ll. 9–11). The lines not only describe a dialogue between Oppen and his daughter who asked "Where were the adults?" but calls attention to the language again. The gap between "eyes" and "Where" sets up a tension in which the face-to-face relation of the father and daughter becomes itself the site of language, its saying. The gap (in poem and in presence) opens the possibility of conversation (or, one might say, conversation opens the gap) in language where the "eyes," the face itself, do the talking (Levinas, *Totality* 66). In addition to conversation, this is the space of the Other (and) the unsaid, and it is in these types of gaps and silences that the obligations in Oppen's later poetry trace themselves out. These spaces are traces of the saying itself.

All of this discussion of silence, vagueness, and things left unsaid is crucial to understanding the ethics of Oppen's work, but there is a problem. What keeps this silence from becoming a violent exclusion, a complicity, or an omission? Oppen seems to silence the Other, and at the same time he constantly invokes the Other. This is why, paradoxically, he at once must keep the Other as a theme and why otherness uncontrollably disrupts that theme. In fact, he even figures this disruption in a dangerous attempt to invoke the Other in his last book of poetry, *Primitive* (1978):

> in events the myriad
>
> lights have entered
> us it is a music more powerful
>
> than music
>
> till other voices wake
> us or we drown (*New Collected* 286)

Only through hyperbole does Oppen try to name the voice of the Other as "a music more powerful / than music," so the voice remains elusive and unsaid. In a reversal of T. S. Eliot's "Love Song of J. Alfred Prufrock," Oppen simply invokes the saying of the Other without which we all are doomed to drown. It's not *what* the Other says, but *that* the Other speaks that gives us life. While I do think that Oppen's obscurity here leaves the Other other, the forms of deixis continually invokes what is other, beyond the control of the poet, whose attempt at control runs the risk of complicity, in Simon

Critchley's meaning of the term, in destroying otherness by making a said of it (48). In this risk, though, is an obligation that cannot be codified or understood because it faces the Other in the full light of its culpability.

As with representing atrocity, Oppen runs the risk of complicity in destroying otherness by making a said of it. In this risk is an obligation that cannot be codified or understood. In "Some San Francisco Poems" from *Seascape: Needle's Eye,* Oppen simply "points" to the otherness that obligates in poetry:

These little dumps
The poem is about them

Our hearts are twisted
In dead men's pride

Dead men crowd us
Lean over us

In the emplacements

The skull spins
Empty of subject

The hollow ego

Flinching from the war's huge air

Tho we are delivery boys and bartenders

We will choke on each other

Minds may crack

But not for what is discovered

Unless that everyone knew
And kept silent

Our minds are split
To seek the danger out
From among the miserable soldiers (*New Collected* 224–25)

First, Oppen literally points out the others by figuring them: From among the miserable, dead soldiers, these "delivery boys and bartenders," and "these little dumps," these marginalized, destitute figures are what have been excluded by society and a Modernist poetry that is more intent on building a bridge to the lost greatness of our Western culture. In addition to the figures of otherness, lack of punctuation disturbs the flow of this passage to create deixis that merely points to the Other. To what does "that" refer to in "Unless that everyone knew"? This silence points to something that is indeterminate, other. Perhaps what is discovered is the very existence, the very being of the earth, the war, the atrocity, the self. But if they had discovered it, Oppen points out, they had not told him. The otherness of the Other prevents complete totalization or objectification of beings by cracking or splitting the objectifying subject. This otherness obligates us even though "we choke on each other." The form enacts the splitting of the mind that Oppen refers to thematically. Although that split cannot be brought into the poem itself, only the two halves (one that flinches from danger and one that seeks it out). Yet the poem, as it says, concerns "these little dumps," these holes (not wholes) in the ground, these gaps in our mind. In the gaps between these single lines rumbles the unsaid atrocity of war and silence. This type of reference—vectors that go nowhere and do not grasp their object—is what Levinas calls in "The Trace of the Other" a work of pure loss (349–50). In other words, there is no return or payoff on a pronoun that does not refer to any-thing. Instead, that "anything" remains open to, vulnerable to, uncertain of "that" while still tracing that otherness.

Even to a greater extent than deixis, which only points to otherness by not grasping it, Oppen's poetry proffers many kinds of multiplicity that mag-nify the sense of otherness by proliferating it:[20]

4
For the people of that flow
Are new, the old

New to age as the young
To youth

And to their dwelling
For which the tarred roofs

And the stoops and doors—
A world of stoops—
Are petty alibi and satirical wit
Will not serve. (*New Collected* 164–65)

First, Oppen's diction, especially in "Of Being Numerous," is marked by multiplicity. The choice of the word "flow" is interesting in that it serves as substantive noun or as a possible metonymic figure for the vast numerousness of young people flooding into New York City. Such possible interpretations realize the notion of relativity in the context of a poem and present the possibility of an ethics not based on universal representations but on the specific point of view of the Other. Meaning, because of the slipperiness of language, depends on the reader and is not determined by the poet. Also, the old/new dichotomy that characterizes the difference between generations is reduced to relativity because the "old" are also "new" to old age. Such relativity does not allows us to "know" the Other but allows us to substitute ourselves for the Other. The one-for-the-other of inescapable responsibility implied in substitution, in fact, is not understandable without the decentering effect of relativity. Here we may at last see the realization of what Williams sought in his notion of the "relative foot": Write in such a way that by encouraging as many meanings as possible, we welcome the Other into our language. Finally, both the syntax and parataxis of the last stanza splay univocity in the poem.[21] What, especially, is the alibi? Stoops, doors, roofs, or all the above? And earlier: does the "And" of the third stanza connect two parallel elements in "youth" and "dwelling"? If so, then youth and dwelling are the petty alibi. But an alibi for what? More important than an answer is the question itself, for, in encouraging such multiple readings, Oppen is encouraging otherness within his poem.

The parataxis, or unexplained juxtaposition of elements, in "Of Being Numerous" and many of Oppen's other later works also multiplies otherness. By not explaining the relationships between parts of a poem, which would be the function provided by logical syntax, the poet leaves interpretation more to chance and the whim of the reader. In a way, the four divergent stanzas of this poem invite the unknown and unknowable into the poem through the unanticipatable, from the view of the poet, reaction of the reader:

39
Occurring 'neither for self
Nor for truth'

The sad marvels

In the least credible circumstance,
Storm or bombardment

Or the room of a very old man (*New Collected* 187–58)

Thematically, as Hatlen suggests, this poem works well with section 4 above because it takes up again the motif of aging and returns us to the "sad marvels" of section 1, of which the "stoops" and the stooping old man seem to be examples. Formally, though, this poem works against such thematic continuity. The simple fact that it is not even a complete sentence causes it to resist predication and consumption. The "sad marvels" do not do anything, nor do they need any response other than what the poet has given it, that is, to marvel at their very occurrence and to deal with the circumstances that they have created. The poem may tie up several of the themes and motifs of the poem, but it simultaneously defers them indefinitely. Without a judgment that gives a moral to this fractured story, this poem inscribes otherness simply by wondering at the coexistence of such things, which occur "'neither for self nor for truth.'" Instead, their occurrence is due to the Other and saying them is for-the-Other.

This tendency toward multiplicity, a type of entropy, does not provide the opposite effect of silence, that is, speaking therefore totalizing the name of the Other. Instead, it enacts the uncertainty inherent in a responsibility that questions language's very ability to name by giving the Other many possible names; neither name is more correct than any other. Likewise, it puts into question the very self-identity of the subject. Hatlen reads Oppen, I think rightly, "as if we were hearing, not a seamless discourse spoken by a single voice (presumably the voice of the author) but rather a brief dispute between two voices" ("Not Altogether" 269–70). The supposedly stable, unified voice of the poetic speaker is opened and exposed to disruption and uncertainty that signals an Other that demands, supplicates, a response. After all, the book is titled *Of Being **Numerous*** (my emphasis), an admission that there are *many* "others" (and many "selves") without trying to make those others part of a common humanity, a sameness. This multiplicity leaves these others and responds to these others *in their radical difference* from the poet and from each other.

As seen in this detailed anatomy of Oppen's use of language, his work can hardly be considered a simple example of Levinasian ethics. His interrogation of multiplicity, or *numerousness* to use Oppen's term, is only the beginning of what Oppen can teach Levinas, whose philosophy is more interested in the phenomenon of a one-on-one relationship. Such Levinasian singularity is inadequate for an urban, American poet of the nuclear age, so Oppen has augmented his ethics with appropriate attributes, in this case, an engagement with the numerousness of modern life. Oppen gives us, with this linguistic ethics, a different way of "dwelling poetically," to use Heidegger's terms, in a world that is full of people and all that goes with them: exile, isolation, war, atrocity, duties, death, joy, and, most of all, obligation. Such realism and specificity distinguish his poetry further from Levinas's more abstract ethics, especially because Oppen's poetry seems to more radically enact the very ethics about which Levinas only philosophizes.

Composing a Levinasian reading of a text does not involve proving that your partisan poetics loves otherness and is more ethical than other poets. This is a mistake many readers make with Levinas's work because—from the perspective of a philosophy that insists ethics is beyond the intent or will of the subject—even the most totalitarian, formal, closed, and thematically inhumane poetry can be revealed as ethical because obligation to the other (the saying) inhabits/inhibits all language (the said). Some writing, however, clearly capitulates to this dilemma, and it is the job of criticism to uncover that special subjection. Oppen's delicate and vulnerable poetry, by falling subject continually to otherness, encouraging uncertainty, relying on disruption and multiplicity (as well as didacticism and thematics), gives us, in Krzysztof Ziarek's words, a "nearer trajectory" to the ethical saying that inhabits language than most other poetry before it (Inflected 10–19). For Oppen, ethics is that sense of nearness, "Not truth, but each other" (*New Collected* 183); thus, without the pretense of "reality" or "truth," Oppen's poetry is free, open, vulnerable to welcome and respond to the Other in a way that, although risking exclusion, violence, or totalization, does not go gently with such rational seductions. Not trying to shirk the hold that responsibility has on it, Oppen's poetry shows us that one can work—not to settle one's account with the Other but—to respond to that inescapable and irredeemable call that is obligation without denial or self-congratulation. And even if Oppen's poethics does succumb to violence (which it must do because Oppen himself is aware of the failure of any ethical system), his poetry is there to face the risk of violating the Other—to respond, to accept, and to carry forth that responsibility-without-end.

A Phenomenology of Judgment
Charles Reznikoff's *Holocaust*

PORTIA: Therefore, Jew,
  Though justice be thy plea, none of us
  Should see salvation. We do pray for mercy,
  And that same prayer doth teach us all to render
  The deeds of mercy. (*Merchant of Venice* IV.i)

Since the women's movement of the late 1960s and early 1970s, the word *objectification* has come to assume a more negative cultural valence than it had in 1931 when Louis Zukofsky was writing his manifesto, "Sincerity and Objectification: With Special Reference to the Work of Charles Reznikoff" for *Poetry*. In 1967, Zukofsky revises the article but keeps the definition of *objectification* as a "desire for what is objectively perfect" in order to achieve what he calls a "rested totality" in a poem (*Prepositions* 12). As I have pointed out, many poems by the Objectivists develop themes involving other people, and from the feminist or postcolonial perspectives that began to develop after the 1960s, to objectify people is to strip them of human agency, not to mention human dignity, by reducing them to an object or an "Other." In this contemporary context, the ethical consequences of the failure of totality and objectification are clear: if the (lyric poet) subject is incapable of fully objectifying, then those who typically suffer from being objectified will be free from such domination, at least in terms of representation. In fact, Zukofsky seems to be intuitively aware of the violent potential of objectification when, in the February 1931 *Poetry* version of his essay, he defends Charles Reznikoff's poetry: "There is to be noted in Reznikoff's lines the isolation of each noun so that in itself it is an image, the grouping of nouns so that they partake of the quality of things being together without violence to their individual intact natures" (278). In Zukofsky's mind, the kind of objectification that juxtaposes nouns clearly, even if totalizing, respects the integrity of the thing at hand and is the "desired" objective of poetry.

In his 1969 poem "By the Well of Living and Seeing," Reznikoff has fully honed this awareness of the violence of language that allows him to enact a desire that does not try to totalize its object. This nontotalizing desire manifests in the poem, for example, in the figure of two lovers:

They hold their arms about each other
and no sooner do they stop kissing
than they fall to kissing again,
as if they could never have enough. (*Poems* II: 95)

The remarkable thing for Reznikoff about the desire of these lovers (as well as Reznikoff's desire for them as aesthetic figures) is that it is insatiable; however, the lovers do not desire each other because they are ostensibly lacking something. Instead, getting "enough" is not even a possibility because the Other, it seems, is beyond a total grasp that would sate desire. Levinas, during this time, understood desire for the Other in the same way. The alterity of the Other is so radical, according to Levinas, that it creates in the self a "metaphysical Desire" that is unfulfillable (*Totality* 33–35; *Ethics* 35). This never being able to get enough that Reznikoff captures in his poetry arises not because the subject lacks something and tries to fill that lack; instead, the subject lacks nothing, and the desire grows on its own feeding because the Other is not consumable. This notion of radical alterity is further illustrated when the couple that the poet at first thinks to be heterosexual turns out to be two men:

As I pass them,
the figure in slacks turns and smiles—
a fixed smile
not unlike that of an archaic Apollo—
the grey eyes shining and glazed—
not a girl at all
but a young man
badly in need of a shave (*Poems* II: 95)

In the current climate of relative tolerance toward homosexuality and other sexual orientations fostered by the gay and lesbian movement and queer theory, Reznikoff's poem seems ahead of its time in its progressive politics and compassion. Reznikoff's sympathetic portrayal of an act that would have been defined at the time in the state of New York as sodomy not only directly challenges legal injustice but also the social prejudices that give life to them.[1] More important than his politics, however, this poem exhibits his nonjudgmental ethics that privileges the victims of ontological, as well as physical, violence. Unlike some critics of Reznikoff, such as Peter Quartermain and Robert Franciosi, I argue that Reznikoff can be called an ethical poet because of this accepting, nonjudgmental posture toward the Other, not because he is didactic or moralizing (Quartermain 150). Reznikoff's dispassionate relation of a passionate homosexual kiss refrains from moralizing even as it qualifies the kiss "as if they could never have enough." To put it in Levinas's terms, desire from and for the Other overcomes the judgment of what the Other *should* be. The bulk of the poem is devoted to the unfolding realization that the couple is not a man and a woman, as the poet surmised, but two men. Rather than repulsion, all Reznikoff gives us in terms of judgment is that this young man is "badly in need of a shave." The comparison of a slighter figure in slacks to an "archaic Apollo" gives a heroic slant to the poem that makes its lack of moral condemnation of sodomy even more conspicuous. If one reserves judgment, the poem implies, one might find the beauty and passion in any human situation.

But it is comparatively easy, one might say from the standpoint of applied ethics, to accept those who are outcast, as are homosexuals, because of who they are and whose actions are consensual and hurt no one. It's much more difficult to accept those who are criminalized because what they do hurts others against their will, as in the case of, say, rapists. When that distinction is made, Reznikoff's challenge to antisodomy laws and antigay attitudes seems less of a risk. Through a poetic process of objectification, the desire for the Other can be related in an almost romantic way because no one gets hurt. But what if we are talking about something egregiously evil—like genocide or murder—that *should* be identified, objectified, and labeled as "bad" for the safety of the Other? What if our objectifying powers fail then, allowing atrocity to occur because we took a position of "nonjudgment" toward the crime? Surely our ability as humans to identify and contain dangers that threaten us as individuals and as a species—that is, our reason and ability to judge and measure—constitutes one of our most important evolutionary attributes.

Unlike the penchant for totality and coherence that we see in the modern epics of Zukofsky, William Carlos Williams, and Ezra Pound, the long poems of Charles Reznikoff stand as veritable monuments to the failure of objectification, judgment, and measure.[2] Like George Oppen, Reznikoff engages, instead of totality, the theme of responsibility to the Other (as the other of the subject) but in the context of unimaginable violence. In the crucible of the Holocaust, Reznikoff's poethics puts the typical rational mechanism of morality, that is, judgment, to the test. The result raises the questions of what obligations do we have to both the victims *and* perpetrators of violence.

Toward the end of his obscure career, Reznikoff began writing long, documentary poems with material culled from legal documents addressing not the triumphs of civilization, as does Pound in *The Cantos*, but the *failures* of humanity: from the mundane to catastrophic atrocities in history. Reznikoff's two-volume poem, *Testimony: the United States: 1885–1915: Recitative* (begun in 1965), brings together legal testimony about crimes and industrial accidents at the turn of the century from every part of the United States, divided by regions (North, South, West). Similarly, *Holocaust* (1975) recounts events, in roughly chronological order, from the Nazi attempts to eliminate Jews from Europe as told by witness at the Nuremberg and Adolf Eichmann trials after World War II.[3] Both poems relate accounts of crimes and injustice in the sparse Objectivist style of reportage and fit nicely within the ethical turn as a response to the failures of modernity. Because of their stylistic handling of such subject matter, these long poems present formidable challenges to articulating an Objectivist poethics, particularly if we think of it in terms of Zukofsky's emphasis in his prose writings and long poems on knowledge, vision, and reason. Rather than encompassing the totality or truth of these events, Reznikoff's poems, through their rhythm and numbingly relentless detail, gesture toward the ineffable and uncontainable quality of disaster within history. "Unless it be the case," Maurice Blanchot writes in a fragment from *The Writing of the Disaster*, "that knowledge—because it is not knowledge of the disaster, but knowledge as disaster and knowledge disastrously—carries us, carries us off, deports us (whom it smites and nonetheless leaves untouched), straight to ignorance, and puts us face to face with ignorance of the unknown so that we forget, endlessly" (3). This ineffability, as well as perhaps Reznikoff's own fear of the dangers of knowledge and objectification and forgetting (Franciosi 241–43), is underscored by the thirty-year lapse between the end of World War II and Reznikoff's response to it. Considering Reznikoff's nonjudgmental stance in his other poetry, a major question arises: What keeps Reznikoff's *Holocaust* from being a mere objectification and, thus, a reduction or even endorsement (in that it "deports us straight to ignorance"), of an unspeakable atrocity perpetrated on the Other?

To begin with the assumption that Reznikoff completely refrains from commentary in his poetry would not be fair because debate exists as to whether or not Reznikoff does actually withhold judgment in *Holocaust*. Sidra DeKoven Ezrahi, in *By Words Alone: The Holocaust in Literature*, claims that Reznikoff's long poem exhibits "the absence of any visible editorial hand" that allows for the testimony of Nazi and Jew to be seen on an equal plane, thus blurring the moral line between them (37). Ezrahi sees this equation in the poem as a threat to a moral order that would ensure genocide never happens again. But is this assessment, which Reznikoff shows *no* editorial intervention, a fair critique? First, Reznikoff's editorial hand certainly appears in the way that he selects, edits, and rewords the testimony culled from the Nuremberg and Eichmann trials. As Franciosi remarks, ". . . his selection and presentation of the documents are comments, are rhetorically determined acts. He sought the kinds of narratives that *moved* him" (249). Reznikoff did add words, such as the ones evident in Franciosi's analysis, such as "hardly" and "little" and "nothing to be wasted!" that add emphasis, judgment, or sympathy (Franciosi 255–56). But for the most part, the consistency in tone comes from the nature of the documents themselves; they are all told in the dispassionate and rational language of a court of law. In fact, *Holocaust* does not read as an amalgamation of quotations taken from various sources and told in various voices. It has a very steady and consistent tone. Franciosi argues that "Reznikoff does indeed embellish his material by deliberately attempting to instill the 'bare facts' of the transcribed testimonies with a rhetorical, an emotional power" (243). However, I am not convinced. In his rush to find an emotional force behind Reznikoff's words, Franciosi overemphasizes the role of emotion in Reznikoff's poetics. As evidence, Franciosi quotes Reznikoff from L. S. Dembo's "The 'Objectivists' Poet: Four Interviews" where Reznikoff says, "I see something and it moves me and I put it down as I see it. In the treatment of it, I abstain from comment" (249). There is a twofold error here. First, Franciosi mistakes the "movement" that initially draws Reznikoff to a document with "emotion" within the long poem. Second, he does not see the separation Reznikoff makes between what "moves" him and the "treatment" of that document. Reznikoff instead says that his process of abstention actually relieves the poetic production of the influence of any initial emotion, if it exists at all. In other words, emotion may affect the selection of the materials, but not the poetic treatment of those materials. This aversion to sentimentality is a well-known tenet of Modernism, and Reznikoff strove for abstinence even while acknowledging that the total excision of emotions is impossible. Although I am sympathetic to Franciosi's analysis of that failure to totalize all emotion, I do not think Reznikoff's ethics is primarily an affective one; instead it is one less of self-centered will and more of vulnerability to the Other. Am I saying that Reznikoff felt no emotions about the Holocaust? No. But Reznikoff is less interested in expressing his own emotions through his poetry than he is in pricking the conscience of himself and his readers.

There are more convincing arguments that Reznikoff withholds moral comment in *Holocaust*. Since Reznikoff worked for years as a writer of legal definitions for the American Law Book Company in New York, such a move to a serial documentary style with minimal editorial comment seems natural, particularly considering his attitude toward poetics (Fredman, *Menorah* 146). In *A Menorah for Athena*, the fullest treatment to date of the life and work of Charles Reznikoff, Stephen Fredman makes a startling claim about judgment in Reznikoff's documentary poetics in his later, long works:

> In *Testimony* and *Holocaust*, Reznikoff does not give himself a narrative voice, so that his witnessing the sufferings of others produces a shock in his readers: there is a sense of confronting the raw voice or materiality of the Other, without the filter of an actual or implied narrative voice. (47)

Mimicking the "full sounds and tight sentences" of Hebrew, Reznikoff, according to Fredman, "pare[s] away every inessential detail and rationalization from the legal testimony he gathered" and presents it "without interpretation" (*Menorah* 32, 47–48). In other words, Reznikoff does not pass judgment on the encyclopedic list of atrocities catalogued in these texts but instead "perform[s] the remarkable feat of allowing the Other access to the page" (*Menorah* 46). Rather than claiming that Reznikoff's discerning narrative position justly allows him to condemn the history of violence recorded in these texts, as does Franciosi, Fredman assigns to Reznikoff's work a kind of Jewish negative capability in which the author witnesses the suffering of others as unobtrusively as possible. Essentially, only the words of the witnesses themselves remain, telling the graphic details of personal tragedy in the "driest" dispassionate testimony of the modern judicial system. Perhaps this is why, according to Fredman, some people have said that these texts are "almost unbearably difficult to read" (*Menorah* 47).

This example from *Holocaust* gives a sense of Reznikoff's distance and detachment from represented violence:

> The Germans were gone.
> She was naked,
> covered with blood and dirty with the excrement of those in the
> dugout,
> and found that she had been shot in the back of the head.
> Blood was spurting from the dugout
> in many places;
> and she heard the cries and screams of those in it still alive. (37)

In this passage, as in the rest of the poem, no lyric voice of the poet or speaker provides a moral perspective on this numbing violence. Mere ownership of the language of the poem is problematic, since most of the words come from legal documents. Although some shaping by Reznikoff occurs, the question becomes does that shaping yield a clear moral judgment. Representative of the rest of the poem, Reznikoff's tone in this passage remains detached and consistent, even though the words throw us in among the bleeding, mangled bodies. There, the girl merely "found" that she had been shot in the back of the head, a wound that in most cases would be fatal. We see the blood and hear the screams, but they are objectified in a very plain style that eschews hyperbole, and this might be one case where no hyperbole is possible or necessary. What can be identified as editorial intrusions do not, therefore, provide a coordinate moral response. Although Reznikoff allows, as Fredman asserts, "the Other access to the page" in the form of quotation, how can we call ethical a poem that allows such bald atrocity to pass before our eyes without comment? Many historians and Jewish scholars have pointed out how silence often aided and abetted the Nazi rise to power and implementation of the Final Solution.[4] So why would Reznikoff refuse moral pronouncement? Surely Reznikoff, himself a Jew, is not promoting the violence depicted in *Holocaust,* but does his silence unconsciously endorse it?

Many commentators have addressed this issue of violence in poetry by the original Objectivists, but most critics stick to the dichotomy of either defending the poetry as subverting violence, which is the usual conclusion, or dismissing the poetry for being complicitous in the violence and atrocity it represents (Hooker; Perloff, "Shipwreck"). I believe that by examining the poetry closely without the urge to either defend or dismiss, we can see emerge in Objectivist poetry at large a different sort of response to violence and atrocity. This response does not reduce or objectify the facts of a horrific historical event but witnesses and welcomes the Other. Ultimately, Objectivist poetics assumes responsibility for the suffering of the Other *and* one's complicity in that suffering.

Responsibility for the Devil

Levinas's phenomenological analysis of ethics is preoccupied, like Reznikoff's long poetry, not just with the victims of the Holocaust but also the perpetrators of the violence. In his last major work, *Otherwise Than Being or Beyond Essence,* published the year before Reznikoff's *Holocaust,* Levinas expands his notion of the face-to-face ethics of *Totality and Infinity* to include what he calls "the Third" or "the third person," grammatical pun notwithstanding. In the proximity of the Third, Levinas argues, the self and the Other become coequals, as would defendant and plaintiff in a court of law, before the justice and judgment of the third person (*Otherwise* 157–58). At the same time, this triangular structure, which serves as a microcosm for all sociality, does not absolve the self of responsibility. In fact, the subject not only retains his originary obligation to the Other (the kind we see in Oppen's poetry) but also inherits the Other's responsibility for *his* Other, or the Third (84). In this understanding of responsibility, which Levinas and Reznikoff share, the subject's responsibility is geometrically increased ad infinitum.

As with Oppen's section 34 of "Of Being Numerous" on "the courage of women," Reznikoff's poetry seems to be part of a trend during the ethical turn of using maternity as an analogy for infinite suffering *and* responsibility. Levinas particularly uses the figure of the mother-child relationship to drive home his idea of infinite responsibility (*Otherwise* 75, 76, 88, 91). This dyad resonates with the many scenes of mothers and children that Reznikoff selects for *Holocaust* (28–29, 35–39, 43–46, 55–56, 59, 68, 70, 80), not to mention the section titled "Children" that might especially impact readers who are parents (65–70). As an illuminating context, I offer the most representative and important passage where Levinas employs this maternal analogy, eerily reminiscent of experiences related by witnesses of the Holocaust:

> Is not the restlessness of someone persecuted but a modification of maternity, the groaning of the wounded entrails by those it will bear or has borne? In maternity what signifies is a responsibility for others, to the point of substitution for others and suffering both from the effect of persecution and from the persecuting itself in which the persecutor sinks. Maternity, which is bearing par excellence, bears even responsibility for the persecuting by the persecutor. (75)

The strange aspect of this analogy is that the terms of the analogy are reversible. On the one hand, the self is the mother, responsible for the child and its care. A bit later, Levinas reiterates this structure: "In proximity the absolutely other, the stranger whom I have 'neither conceived nor given birth to,' I already have in my arms, already bear, according to the Biblical formula, 'in my breast as the nurse bears the nurseling [*sic*]'" (91). In other words, even if I am not a mother, I bear responsibility *like* a mother. On the other hand, the child is responsible for the burden it places on the parent, namely the struggle the mother went through in giving birth. Levinas describes in this phenomenological analysis an experience that all children have with their parents and then, in turn, with their own children. In the context of this all-too-familiar sense of guilt, Levinas points out that I, as a self, am always mother *and* child, two reversible yet inescapable subject-positions that share the common experience of responsibility for the Other. But the analogy's meaning does not stop there. In its universal, triadic ethical structure, the relationship between mother and child oddly resembles murder and genocide, which Levinas alludes when he asks, "Is not the restlessness of someone persecuted but a modification of maternity . . . ?" (75). In other words, a mother suffers for her children like a hostage does for his captor.

The connection between murder and maternity is made by these writers often through the notion of "survivor guilt." At the time Levinas and Reznikoff were writing their books, research was being done about this phenomenon, mostly as a result of the West finally facing the aftermath of the Holocaust after two decades of relative silence.[5] As a matter of fact, both Levinas and Reznikoff were Jews who survived the Holocaust, which could account in part for their interest in the idea. But for my analysis, the important thing is the way survivor guilt works rhetorically in tandem with the figure of maternity. Although Reznikoff devoted an entire volume to the disaster of the Nazi genocide, Levinas rarely mentions it explicitly in his work.[6] By drawing on this emerging concept of survivor guilt, Levinas, without naming it, brings the Shoah into his text. In a rather transparent allusion to the death camps, Levinas writes, "A face is a trace of itself, given over to my responsibility, but to which I am wanting and faulty. It is as though I were responsible for his morality, and guilty of surviving" (*Otherwise* 91). On that same page, as quoted above, Levinas uses the "Biblical formula" of the maternal analogy to characterize responsibility. The unstated connection being that, as subject, I am guilty of surviving my own birth. As the mother, I bear the guilt of surviving the trauma of childbirth. In *The Writing of the Disaster*, Blanchot explains Levinas's connection of survivor guilt and ethical responsibility in the context of disaster: "Responsibility is innocent guilt, the blow always long since received which makes me all the more sensitive to all blows." Then Blanchot makes the same connection to maternity that Levinas does: "[Responsibility] is the trauma of creation or birth. If the creature is 'he whose situation is ceded to him by the other,' then I am created responsible" (22). For all of these writers, maternity and survivor guilt share one thing that makes them attractive tropes for what these writers are trying to express: They both represent an ethical burden that is inescapable and always already passed. This burden Reznikoff bears himself in *Holocaust*.

Through his poetry, Reznikoff dramatizes the responsibility of survivor guilt and maternity even more than do Levinas and Blanchot, and thus the reversibility of the terms becomes even more shocking. To continue the previous quote from *Holocaust:*

> She began to search among the dead for her little girl
> and kept calling her name;
> trying to join the dead,
> and crying out to her dead mother and father,
> "Why didn't they kill me, too?" (37)

Reznikoff is sensitive, as are Levinas and Blanchot, to the sensation of responsibility that arises from surviving a trauma that others do not. In this scene, the daughter, who herself lost a daughter, wants to "join the dead" out of an overbearing confusion as to why she was not shot and the others were. The guilt follows from an overwhelming yet irrational belief that one could have done something to prevent the tragedy. Reznikoff orders the text chronologically, and thus the representation of mothers (or parents) and children ceases a little more than halfway through the book because, as Reznikoff documents in the "Work Camps" and "Children" sections, families were split up on arrival at the camps. In later sections, such as "Marches," we can see that the concentration camp experience from torture and hard labor has rendered basic human functioning, let alone childbirth, physiologically impossible. Mothers, in a sense, cease to exist, much like the other identities these people brought with them into the camps. But what does persist is the inescapable responsibility of the one for the Other that maternity represents.

More striking than the reversibility of mother and self or even the guilt of survival, however, are the implications of Levinas's maternal analogy for understanding the dynamic of victimhood. In a rhetorical move that seems almost unthinkable, Levinas implies that the victim, the Jew, could be responsible for the Nazi morality of the Final Solution. In the passage I quoted above, Levinas introduces this incredible concept via the trope of maternity: "Maternity, which is bearing par excellence, bears even responsibility for the persecuting by the persecutor" (*Otherwise* 75). In the last analysis, the mother becomes responsible for "the persecuting by the persecutor," in other words, the child's responsibility for the mother. So not only does the mother bear responsibility for the child but also doubly the child's responsibility for the mother. When taken to its extreme conclusion, this logic dictates that the victim becomes responsible for the victor, which means that the Jew (mother) becomes responsible for any persecution done by the Nazi (child). What is more, in the phrase, "suffering from . . . the persecuting itself in which the persecutor sinks," Levinas suggests that any mere *dis-*

comfort that the persecuting SS soldier might suffer inflicting suffering on the Jew becomes the responsibility of the Jew. Drawing on Levinas's structure, Blanchot describes this reversal by transforming the figure of the mother into the figure of the camp overseer: "And then, the other becomes rather the Overlord, indeed the Persecutor, he who overwhelms me, encumbers, undoes me, he who puts me in his debt no less than he who attacks me by making me answer for his crimes, by charging me with measureless responsibility which cannot be mine since it extends all the way to 'substitution'" (*Writing* 19). In his poem "Kaddish" (meaning prayer for the dead) from *Separate Way* (1936), Reznikoff employs liturgy to encourage responsibility for the devil:

> upon Israel and upon all who meet with unfriendly glances,
>> sticks and stones and names—
> on posters, in newspapers, or in books to last,
> chalked on asphalt or in acid on glass,
> shouted from a thousand thousand windows by radio;
> who are pushed out of class-rooms and rushing trains,
> whom the hundred hands of a mob strike,
> and whom jailers strike with bunches of keys, with revolver
>> butts;
> to them and to you
> in this place and in every place
> safety; (*Poems* I: 185–86)

The details of this poem unmistakably invoke the various injustices inflicted on Jews in Germany and Eastern Europe during the rise of Nazi power before the war began. But its most striking feature is that it wishes safety not just for Israel, but for "all who meet with unfriendly glances." Not only does this phrase refer to Jews—with whom Reznikoff is certainly sympathizing the most—but to anyone who is persecuted, including ostensibly Nazis. The syntax of the line even makes possible the reading that those who are making the "unfriendly glances" are included in the blessing: "upon Israel and upon all who meet [Israel] with unfriendly glances." As prelude to the escalated atrocities detailed in *Holocaust* almost thirty years later, this poem more explicitly comments and therefore demonstrates Reznikoff's ethical posture of forgiving and even blessing one's enemies. To wish them safety, furthermore, implies that it is the Jews' responsibility to wish *and* ensure that safety for those who hate them. If such a reading seems implausible, consider this stanza from *Inscriptions: 1944–1956* (1959):

I have no word of blame, no stick or stone,
because I died. The fault, the weakness,
was mine, of course. Mine alone. (*Poems* II: 74)

Echoing the "stick or stone" trope from "Kaddish," this passage underscores the assumption of responsibility for the persecution inflicted on one by the persecutor. Rather than indignantly rejecting responsibility in the victim, this kind of thinking deepens and even embraces the vulnerability of the victim. In the victim we see the most radical form of ethical responsibility.

From this view, we can understand Reznikoff's amoral authorial posture (or negative capability) toward the Nazis as a taking responsibility for everyone—family, friend, and foe. In one way, Levinas's unusual analysis of the victim's responsibility for the persecutor can explain Reznikoff's attention to the mundane scene of the Nazi soldier smoking a cigarette as he dangles his feet in the mass grave full of murdered Jews:

The soldier doing the shooting was sitting at the narrow end of
    the pit,
his feet dangling into it;
smoking a cigarette,
the machine-gun on his knees. (*Holocaust* 39)

In this passage we can see what Hannah Arendt meant, in reference to Adolf Eichmann, by the phrase "the banality of evil" (252). The scene impassively depicts a soldier on his break, and, though Reznikoff again refrains from comment, we can almost feel his fatigue from having to exert himself to the point where he would have to sit down. Most of us who have ever done physical labor of any kind know this unpleasant fatigue. There are other hints of normal, everyday life amid this horror. Like any other worker on a break, he is idly smoking a cigarette. Why, in the middle of the mass executions full of images that would more aptly occupy the poetic eye, does Reznikoff choose to include this little vignette? As a kind of clue to this question, the line breaks in this stanza serve to highlight the incongruity between the banal and extreme elements being here described. The first and last lines of the stanza end with the themes of shooting and the potential for death and violence. Yet the middle two lines isolate two seemingly innocuous and commonplace images, of the soldier's legs dangling down the side and his smoking a cigarette. The setting off of such disparate elements is furthered by the length of the lines, as the commonplace images are shorter than their counterparts. These elements—line breaks, length of line, juxtaposition, identification, and silence—all undercut any firm basis for moral judgment with the effect of letting the atrocity speak for itself not just out of an extreme situation but also out of the everyday.

What is left out of this particular vignette—the piles of bodies beneath the soldier's dangling feet, the lines of Jews being marched into position for the next execution, and the attitude of the soldier toward his duties—would allow us to morally condemn this scene. As it is, Reznikoff's silence can expose that process of judgment by not delivering the truly damning details. He gives us nothing concrete with which to vilify this soldier. Apart from the fact that we surmise that under the soldier's dangling feet are piles of freshly shot corpses, details that we must transpose from the surrounding context, Reznikoff does not give us any commentary, no moral judgment against the soldier. The only given connection between the soldier and the executions is the machine gun on his knee. By not depicting this soldier in the act of shooting innocent victims, Reznikoff forces us to draw the conclusion that indeed the soldier has been busy executing people. Through the paratactic form indicative of Objectivist poetry, this text foregrounds the very leap of faith that subtends the act of judgment. Without conclusive proof, we must make an assumption based on circumstantial evidence in the poem, and this formation of judgment is what Reznikoff wants us to be aware of as much as the representation of the banality of evil.

On the one hand, the juxtaposition of this vignette with the others of similar executions in this section of *Holocaust* damns the soldier in a horrific irony. On the other hand, Reznikoff does not explicitly make that connection, so an ambiguity haunts the seeming irony. The fact that we have to use the conditional to speculate on the posture of the poet and the context surrounding the soldier attests to Reznikoff's silence. The reason why is because Reznikoff's ethics does not involve indictment but rather *bearing*, bearing even the fatigue and discomfort caused to the Nazi soldier who pulls the trigger to kill what must have been hundreds of Jews. Ultimately, Reznikoff's poem takes responsibility for those murders as well—this is the ethical import of testimony. By presenting the banality of this solider, who could be any worker we know, even Reznikoff himself, Reznikoff takes responsibility for the soldier's murdering of those hundreds. Furthermore, although seeming detached and indifferent, Reznikoff shows us an everyday, human perspective on a Nazi soldier—the need for a break from work, the monotony of repetitive work, and so forth—details that any soldier or laborer might have difficulty not identifying with in spite of their urge to condemn. Unlike Arendt (294–98), Reznikoff does not use the banality of evil to reinforce the need for judgment in justice but as the very reason to forsake it. Reznikoff's poem seems to say: "Who can tell where evil will arise?" And answering its own question it holds, "One can't. That is why one must take responsibility for all."

Ethical Complicity

A potentially disastrous side effect of this taking responsibility for the morality of the Nazi is that the poet becomes complicit in the atrocity and may even be seen as condoning the violence. Charles Bernstein answers this issue of complicity by claiming that Reznikoff's poetry means to "acknowledge [America's] roots in violence" and as "giving witness to what is denied at the expense of the possibility of America" (30). Similarly, Franciosi writes that "Reznikoff commits himself to these testimonies as his source, but he does not surrender the emotional and moral authority with which they were delivered to austere factuality, does not sacrifice the witness' humanity . . . to a naïve gesture toward the 'neutral' documentation of historical or political events" (243). Fredman locates the "moral impact" of the poem in "the 'purity' of an extremely concise, vernacular style" that shows Reznikoff's deep respect for others (*Menorah* 11–12). Although I am more convinced that Reznikoff is not willing to extract himself morally from this violence, I am less convinced that mere witnessing—which *Holocaust,* considering its source material, almost purely is—provides enough force to create the moral position of "acknowledgment," "humility," and "expense" that Bernstein, Fredman, and Franciosi assign it, respectively. Even in a court of law, a witness's testimony only has its full meaning in the context of the argument of the prosecution or the defense. And despite his background in legal work, I don't think Reznikoff acts as judge and jury in his poetry.

Few critics have leveled this charge of complicity against Reznikoff. Perhaps the sacrosanct position in our culture of representations of the Holocaust, such as *Night* or *Schindler's List,* prevents outright political sniping.[7] But the charge of complicity has been raised against Reznikoff's friend and fellow Objectivist, George Oppen, whose poetry doesn't deal directly with the Holocaust but with related issues of war and violence.[8] Even so, these poets have plenty of arguments in their defense against such a negative charge. First of all, qualifications could be made by appealing to their biographies. While Oppen was wounded fighting against fascism in Europe, Reznikoff married a Zionist, composed several major poems, such as "In Memoriam: 1933," documenting the long history of anti-Semitism, wrote antifascist pieces for the *Menorah Journal,* and supported his wife's exposing of the atrocities of the death camps in 1942 as an editor of the *Jewish Frontier* (Franciosi 245; Fredman, *Menorah* 31).

Second, I am convinced that these Objectivist poets would willingly plead "guilty" and not deny their own involvement in the violence they render into verse. Their poetry makes no such distinctions of intent—they do not articulate their poetics as resisting or avoiding violence. Through their "objective" style, they instead flirt with complicity in the actual violence and the violence of representing violence, which for Oppen become intertwined. For instance, throughout the series "Of Being Numerous," Oppen includes himself in representations of atrocities by using the first person plural:

Now in the helicopters the casual will
Is atrocious

Insanity in high places,
If it is true we must do these things
We must cut our throats (*New Collected* 173)

Critic Jeremy Hooker casts the poem as Oppen's straightforward indictment of America's involvement in Vietnam and "not, at this point, an admission of complicity" (83).[9] But Oppen's use of the first-person plural in the line, "we must do these things," implies that he too is part of "the casual will." Although the indictment of the "casual will" is clear, Oppen is wary of judgment at the same time he makes one. First, the decision to burn people, an "event as ordinary as a President," is what Oppen is judging as bad, a sentiment reflected in the words "atrocious" and "insanity." In turn, the line "If it is true *we* must do these things" (my emphasis), tests the judgments just made in the poem because it implicates Oppen in those very atrocities. Although the conditional verb leaves the possibility open, the response is that a decision to cut others' throats is to cut our own, just as every judgment of others is a judgment of oneself. At its base, then, judgment deals with a relation between the subject and the Other, and Oppen's interrogation of judgment itself reveals this relation. Judgment does not determine an ethical relation but is determined by a relation that always already exists before judgment. This relation is the relation to the Other par excellence who demands my responsibility.

In fact, the very form of Oppen's poetry enacts this complicit and ethical relation to violence in a way that puts judgment itself on trial. Consider this quote from "Of Being Numerous" section 26:

> We stand on
>
> That denial
> Of death that paved the cities,
> Paved the cities
>
> Generation
> For generation and the pavement
>
> Is filthy as the corridors
> Of the police. (*New Collected* 178)

Denial of ethical responsibility is the worst kind of violence for Oppen because it perpetuates murder through history, just as Germans from top Nazi officers down to ordinary citizens denied that Hitler was capable of liquidating twelve million people. Seeming to distance the poet from the violence, the line breaks heighten that condemnation by setting off the violence (embodied in the line "That denial") as its own line. Yet, the form of this poem goes further than sheer indictment by undercutting interpretation and finally judgment itself. If this passage is considered as one sentence, then there is an ambiguity in the referent of "That." Is it death that paved the cities, or is it the denial of death that paved the cities? In true nonjudgmental fashion, the poem does not distinguish. Thus, the filth of corruption implicates the capitalist system that has exploited generation after generation in the name of progress (the other sense of *generation* meaning production). Yet this "filth" also implicates us, the poet included, for denying that such death is underneath progress. Not only does the sentence structure invite ambiguity, but the syntax seems to rupture, making the logic of judgment weak in this poem, which raises more questions than it answers: What function does the repetition of "paved the cities" serve in the sentence? Is it an adjectival phrase that modifies the "denial of death"? This confusion and ambiguity are heightened most of all by the fact that this "denial of death" is not really described or specified. We know only vaguely that it has something to do with generation and with the police. The point of this uncertainty is to foreground the very way we make moral judgments by making us fill in the details of the representation. The onus is on us to decide what the "denial of death" is and how much we identify with "we," and Oppen does not make such identifications and decisions easy for us.

In the poem, "Separate Way" from the volume of the same title, Reznikoff exhibits the kind of first-person complicity Oppen's poetry exudes:

We heard your jokes, your stories, and your songs,
know of your rights and all your wrongs,
but we are busy with our own affairs.
Sorry? O yes! But after all who cares?
You think that you have something still to say?
Perhaps. But you are growing old, are growing grey.
And we are too.
We'll spare another friendly word for you;
and go our separate ways to death. (*Poems* I: 171–72)

The ironic voice of "We," the editorial first-person plural, seems at first to be the target of Reznikoff's moral, though tacit, judgment. However, the last three lines cannot fail to include the poet himself, who because he too must die is not separate from those he might satire. With the short line, "And we are too," which is also set off by line breaks, the satiric tone attenuates and thus draws the speakers and the poet into the same pronoun. Even though he writes to warn us not to take life for granted, Reznikoff, too, is complicit with those who ignore the lessons of injustice and death because "we are busy with our own affairs." All in all, the enemy is We—you and I—and we are forced to face how we make ethical judgments at all, a phenomenology of judgment that is the primary preoccupation of *Holocaust.*

A Phenomenology of Judgment

Although nobody has linked Reznikoff with Nazi ideology as a young Oppen has been with Stalinism (Hooker 96–98, Naylor 102n), one could certainly do so, following Hooker's logic, because Reznikoff's poetry is even less didactic than Oppen's. Not surprisingly, though, Reznikoff's poetry acknowledges a similar complicity in atrocity that Oppen's does. Because his style is more lyrical, Oppen's poetry often makes direct, indicative statements that give some moral frame of reference, even if they are almost entirely nonjudgmental. From this position of complicit distance, Oppen interrogates judgment itself. Take, for example, the first three lines of section 29 in "Of Being Numerous" in which Oppen responds to a question in such a way as to perpetuate the very asking of the question: "My daughter, my daughter, what can I say / Of living? / I cannot judge it" (*New Collected* 181). As Oppen says of his treatment of the terrible events of war in *Of Being Numerous,* "I really had to tell it as quietly as I could" (Dembo 171), so this questioning of judgment is not always overt. By asking the question but withholding judgment, Oppen reveals a third response to violence and atrocity that lies beyond the condemning/condoning dyad. This response is characterized by a refusal to deny complicity in atrocity and, furthermore, by a commitment to be true and responsive to that violence. Oppen admits complicity at the same time he attempts to relate atrocity in an "objective" way. In this poetry the atrocity is not merely whisked away with the wave of a moral wand.

But the kind of proscriptive statement we find in Oppen, such as "we stand on that denial of death," is almost entirely absent from Reznikoff's work, particularly *Holocaust,* and this absence presents a problem when trying to interpret the purpose of the book. The problem is not merely that we *have* represented violence and are therefore implicated in it; Reznikoff is not trying to avoid complicity simply by refraining from moral comment lest he be judged by the same measure. Instead, the problem is how do we read and interpret this absence of moral judgment. My assertion is that in this formal choice of omission, this un-said, lies the Reznikoff's ethical response to the Holocaust. Seeing himself complicit as Oppen does in the violence around him, Reznikoff brings to our attention through form how we make sense of and judge the data of violence that language and the senses give us. I call this attention *the phenomenology of judgment,* and in terms of Reznikoff's poetry it has three main facets.

As I explained in the introduction, merely naming the Other, especially if one has defined that Other as beyond being, violates alterity. In his famous essay on Levinas, "Violence and Metaphysics," which was first published in French in two 1964 issues of *Revue de Métaphysique et de Morale,* Jacques Derrida criticizes Levinas for naming the "infinitely other" without allowing the other to be a self like me and thereby for denying the "very foundation and possibility of his own language" (*Writing* 125). To lend the Other to language, Derrida writes, "*to every possible language,* is perhaps to give oneself over to violence, or to make oneself its accomplice at least, and to *acquiesce* —in the critical sense—to the violence of the fact . . ." (125). Levinas, and by implication all Objectivist poets, are committing the ultimate violence, what Derrida calls a *preethical violence,* by invoking the Other (both the real victims of the Holocaust and the unspeakable terror the Shoah evoked) into language without recourse to the realm of ethical decision. Ironically, this embroilment in the very anathema of ethics—violence and atrocity —comprises the first acknowledgment of Reznikoff's phenomenology of judgment.

However, Oppen and Reznikoff, along with Levinas, never deny that they might be committing the gravest violence because that would mean that somehow they were above and beyond responsibility for atrocity. Foregoing redemption is the second element in this critique of judgment. In their ethics, the "debt" of obligation is far too great to ever pay off, so the subject is always being violent to the Other in one way or another; thus, they might plead guilty to the charges Derrida levels at Levinasian ethics without ever wanting to be innocent. In "The Trace of the Other," Levinas calls this obligation a "pure loss" and a movement "without return," in which no reckoning, salvation, or payoff can be made (347–49). It is important to notice that the subject, me, is left alone to face my responsibility, and this moment is always before I make an ethical/moral decision. Because he no longer desires exoneration, a poet like Reznikoff is "free" to face atrocity in which he is always already condemned. Such frankness (which is perhaps a version of Zukofsky's "sincerity") precedes moral judgment and thus provides a perspective from which to view the workings of decision. In other words, once free of the possibility of escaping being violent, redemption from violence no longer being a possibility, then a sincere, temporal responsibility can take place without the interference of ulterior motives, such as eternal life. One becomes more aware of the choices that lead to violence.

Thus, the acquiescence to violence, as Derrida calls it, is not only an admission of the poet's possible complicity in atrocity but also a challenge to the reader's morality, the third facet of Reznikoff's phenomenology. As Reznikoff says before delivering a reading of *Holocaust*, "So, in reading or listening to the facts themselves, *instead of merely [coming] to conclusions* of what happened in the life of a person or to a people, the reader or listener may *not only draw his own conclusions* but is more apt to feel actually what happened as if he or she where—fortunately—only a spectator" (Franciosi 248, emphasis mine). This type of questioning of firm moral judgment that allows the reader to "draw his own conclusions," although seeming to leave no direction in a violent world by undercutting codes by which we can make moral decisions, can have the opposite effect of creating a space for a responsibility not founded on the reciprocal notion of a debt or account. In fact, Reznikoff desires to make his audience "feel actually what happened" by inviting them to put themselves in the place of the Other (not through identification, it should be noted). This desire also suggests he wishes he were somehow something more than a mere "spectator" of the events. By substituting us for the victims of the Holocaust, Reznikoff is at once addressing his own survivor guilt and taking responsibility for suffering that cannot be denied or undone. Furthermore, as part of this group of spectators who were not there, Reznikoff admits his own complicity in this process of judgment, and undoing his own judgment is tantamount to taking responsibility.

One representative example of the phenomenology of judgment in *Holocaust* is the scene where a group of Hasidim are burned after they are told to pray to God for help:

> They gathered some twenty *Hasidic* Jews from their homes,
> in the robes these wear,
> wearing their prayer shawls, too,
> and holding prayer books in their hands.
> They were led up a hill.
> Here they were told to chant their prayers
> and raise their hands for help to God
> and, as they did so,
> the officers poured kerosene under them
> and set it on fire (40)

At first reading, Reznikoff seems to be showing what horrible monsters the SS officers are that they could burn people alive and taunt them at the same time. Certainly, Reznikoff has provided us with the opportunity to "feel actually what happened" to these innocent victims of senseless violence. The cinematic portrayal of the events invites us to substitute ourselves for the Hasidim and to curse their fate—and only through the empathy substitution effects can the full horror of this scene be felt—no one could wish to be humiliated by having one's faith mocked before being immolated. It's an unimaginable way to die. Such interpretations of this scene, along with the rest of the poem, rely implicitly on certain assumptions: that humans value life, that valuing life is good, that murder is wrong, that immolation would be a terrible way to die, and that one should treat others as one would want to be treated. More specifically, the limits on legal judgments enshrined in the Eighth Amendment of the Constitution of the United States would condition American readers (or any readers from a culture with such values) to react against this form of death as "cruel and unusual punishment." These warrants, and others I haven't mentioned, allow us to pass judgment on the scene and are uncovered by Reznikoff's poetics.

A tacit layer of irony, however, complicates this judgment and forces a self-conscious examination of this reading and its underlying assumptions. Because these Jews die horrible deaths at the hands of the Nazis while praying, we are posed with the nihilistic question of why the prayers of the Hasidim are not answered. From the poem, it is impossible to tell which prayers the victims recite—they may have simply been praying to be killed or for God to forgive the Nazis—but the most common prayer in Jewish tradition is the *amidah,* which consists of nineteen blessings that are recited in the morning, afternoon, and evening. Several of the blessings reinforce the supplication that Reznikoff inscribes in the line, "and raise their hands for help to God," and sharpen the irony of the situation by opening the possibility that the victims were praying for their own lives (as many of us would no doubt). For example, the second prayer of the amidah praises God for his powers, which include healing the sick and raising the dead, while the seventh and twelfth blessings ask God to save Israel and destroy its enemies. Clearly, none of these petitions are fulfilled in Reznikoff's scene. In closing, the prayer thanks God for life itself, something that the Nazis take away from them. Because they are killed by enemies, does that mean that the Hasidim's pleas were not answered? Because there is no authorial comment, we cannot know for sure how Reznikoff intends us to read this possibility. Is Reznikoff saying that God could not help them because, like the secular Nazis, Reznikoff does not believe that there is a God? A worse possibility is that Reznikoff believes that there is a God but He abandoned the victims of genocide in their direst time of need. Both readings reveal a heretical lack of faith lurking under the text of the poem. Reznikoff's stark arrangement of these details cuts both ways, aligning him (and us) at once with the Hasidim and the SS officers who, in their atheistic disdain, kill them. On a cursory reading, this vignette seems, through its obvious depiction of cruelty toward these Hasidic Jews, to condemn the flippant and irreverent violence of the SS officers. However, the bitter irony seems to justify, or at least support, the Nazis' viewpoint: When the people turn their hands to God for help, there is no response, at least not one of salvation; they are immolated despite their devout piety because there is no God but Hitler and the Nazi state. But where does *Holocaust* come out on these questions—did their deaths occur because God is dead and science and rationality rule our decisions, or is it because the ways of God are beyond our ken and those who were murdered may well be martyrs to a higher cause? On this, Reznikoff is silent and, instead, runs the risk of complicity with Nazi ideology in order to reveal something more fundamental, that the complexity of the situation presented above precedes or defers any judgment concerning the morality of the actions and asks us to examine our own assumptions that would allow a subsequent condemnation. Furthermore, the fact that God does not save the victims in *Holocaust* suggests responsibility for human acts of violence must be born by us humans, not transferred to a Redeemer.

Shielding Reznikoff from the charge of complicity, Franciosi is quick to point out that Reznikoff, with his adaptation of Polish Protestant Kurt Gerstein's testimony in the "Gas Chambers and Gas Trucks" section of *Holocaust,* is merciless in his indictment of the German people as they facilitated the Final Solution of the Nazis. What is more, Franciosi points out, Reznikoff implicitly convicts "the conduct of Gerstein himself" who, even though he joined the SS to thwart their crimes, "continued during that time to sign the purchasing orders to transport tons of Zyklon B to the death camps" (255). However, Franciosi does not take it a step further to implicate Reznikoff himself as a perpetrator; instead, Franciosi defends him as heroically memorializing, like Elie Wiesel, the voices of dead "to preserve their words from being lost in the dust of history" (248).

But I'm not sure Reznikoff's poem needs Franciosi's defense. That would too easily separate the poet from both perpetrator and, worse yet, victim. Separating poet/victim/reader from perpetrator would not allow for the phenomenological examination of judgment occurring in the poem. In this section of *Holocaust,* for example, Reznikoff strips away extraneous matter, such as specific Polish and Ukrainian person and place names that might prevent readers from readily putting themselves in the place of the subjects being inscribed. If the name of the town were left in the poem, then it might prevent a reader from seeing that this could be any town, which is part of Reznikoff's "point." Such distance would short-circuit complicity between reader and subject matter. The problem judgment presents us with is that we have represented violence and are therefore implicated in it, as a voyeur is implicated in what he watches. In addition, Reznikoff's poem brings to our attention through its form how we make sense of and judge the data of violence that language and our senses give us. As Quartermain says of some of the poems (not *Holocaust,* oddly enough), Reznikoff "invites" us to judge but does not judge himself (150). For instance, I had to make judgments above in my reading of the scene with the Nazi soldier smoking on his "break." By not commenting himself, Reznikoff forces me to form my own opinion, which confronts me with my own moral sensibility without the crutch of an authorial voice. Of course, *I* think what the soldier is doing is inconceivably horrible, but, if I am honest with myself, I also know what it is like to take a break in the middle of a hard job. By implicating the reader through a process of identification and substitution, an Objectivist poethics deemphasizes decision by invoking the inescapability of violence. Franciosi says Reznikoff's poetics is geared to "encourage our disgust toward the perpetrators" (255), then why earlier on does Franciosi say that Reznikoff humanizes "the faceless evil of the Nazi operation" (250)? Again, the "banality of evil" blurs the line between our everyday actions and what we might like to distance ourselves from by calling "evil" and therefore extraordinary. The logic is: We know our lives are banal, and we can see Eichmann's banality, so therefore we might also be capable of evil just like Eichmann. Likewise, Reznikoff could have easily excised the detail about the diesel trucks carrying the gas for the chambers breaking down:

> In the gas chambers
> the police wedged the people closely together
> until men and women were standing on the feet of each other—
> and the doors were closed.
> But the engine to furnish the gas
> could not start.
> An hour and two and almost three went by,
> and in the gas chambers cries were heard
> and many were praying (*Holocaust* 46)

Reznikoff leaves the mechanical failure in just to show that "the process is all the more horrible" by prolonging the agony (Franciosi 250). Certainly, the joke by the Professor of Public Health, who is overseeing the executions, that the prayers from inside the gas chamber sound "'[j]ust like a synagogue'" creates even more horror through irony. But the point of the passage is not just for us to pity the horror delivered upon the victims but to reveal to us our own process of judgment. The irony works because we bring to the poem the assumption that being forced into a small space with many others for hours in the back of a truck waiting to die would be horrible for us. When that assumption is exposed, the logic that allows us to judge the situation as terrible deconstructs itself. Instead of a concern for the actual victims of the Holocaust, such an identification evinces a self-involved horror at the idea that something like that could happen to me. Furthermore, the poem implies that praying with one's spiritual community, especially when dire circumstances call for it most, as it did for the Hasidim, is a futile and noxious experience. Beginning with this assumption thus unintentionally confirms the Professor's joke. Regardless of intent, Reznikoff's choices confront us with our own judgments, the assumptions that allow them, and the potentially contradictory consequences of them.

In addition to exposing assumptions, this passage uses the logic of identification not only for sympathy with the victims but to collapse any distance we would like to keep from the perpetrators, a distance that is key to the process of judgment. The historical details also allow us, ostensibly as working-class people who also drive trucks for a living and who also know what it is like to have equipment break down, to identify with the perpetrators —people like us or people like the ones we know could and did do this. One reason Reznikoff reminds himself in his notes to "change all Latin or French terms to words of Anglo-Saxon origin" is not only, as Franciosi points out, to "remind us of the complicity of the German populace" (258), but also to facilitate easier identification with another set of Anglo-Saxons, the American reader. Reznikoff himself is included in this latter category, even if Jewish, and he certainly preferred words of Anglo-Saxon etymology to those of Latin in his own writing.[10] Such humanizing tends to blur the lines of distinction that allow for easy moral judgments (they are evil because they are *not* like me) and make the possibility of complicity even more real (I may have driven a truck just like that, had I lived in Poland at the time). What Reznikoff puts in relief in his poem is not just the horror of the Holocaust. He also exposes the mechanisms that Western minds have used to make moral decisions, namely identification and detachment. The phenomenology of morality, an "ethics of ethics," is one of the main themes of *Holocaust.*

Even if I question the effects of Reznikoff's poetic tone, the one thing I will not question is his willingness to take responsibility for the consequences of his poetics and the potential complicity they entail. This willingness keeps us in the here and now from which we must face reality, but in facing the reality of atrocity, even in the face of another person, we open up the possibility of ethics. As David McAleavey so succinctly puts it, Objectivist poetry, "besides affirming the reality of the existent world [and its horror and atrocity] . . . confronts that world" (404).[11] There is no shying away from atrocity; before we can judge it or fix it, we must first face up to it. I ultimately believe, my reasoning based as much on faith or will as on logic, that Reznikoff's intention with *Holocaust* was to strip any mediating and buffering moral perspective from the documents of the Nazi genocide in order to allow the unspeakable acts, spoken by witnesses who were there and experienced it, to speak for themselves. The sheer amount and dulling repetition of the horrors related in Reznikoff's matter-of-fact yet almost absent poetic tone and voice leaves me (and perhaps many other readers, though I cannot prove *all*) with a sick feeling of repulsion and abjection. Reading the poem renews my vehement rejection of the Nazi state and its racist and genocidal vision, but it also places before me my own judgmental procedure. Will Reznikoff's style eventually dull me to atrocity to the point where I am used to it and can coolly analyze its content? Perhaps, in a sense, these words before you are a testimony to another unfortunate secondary side-effect of Reznikoff's poetic experiment and attempt to take responsibility. As Bernstein says of Reznikoff's poetry, it is not "reports of things seen (narrow definition of the 'objectivist' as ocular or transparent Imagism) but bearing witness to things not seen, overlooked." In witnessing, the witness is not simply the one who "beholds" the world but the one who is "beholden" to the Other (21). A witnessing that is a linguistic response, a poetic response to what is "overlooked," that is, the Other but also the uncritically held assumptions behind moral judgment. Reznikoff's vulnerability to moral judgment for his own choices testifies to his willingness to be complicit and to his willingness to suspend judgment in order to welcome the Other, who is undecidable and unknowable. Beginning with the words of the Other, his editorial changes blend self with Other and reinforce not only the complicity in the violence but also show how self (author) is bound to Other (human beings caught up in both sides of genocide). In Reznikoff's poetics, moral judgment, which divides self from Other and claims a higher moral ground for the self in exclusion of responsibility for the Other (even if a Nazi), is actually not ethical at all. It is an evasion of one's infinite and inescapable responsibility to the Other, a denial that one is responsible even for the responsibility of the Other for the Third, of the Jew for the Nazi. In this way, Reznikoff's phenomenological reduction of genocide to its most basic terms becomes more ethical, as responsibility to the Other, than would a flat-out moral rejection of the atrocity. Furthermore, as Franciosi points out, Reznikoff avoids the "cliché, propaganda, and editorialism" that has infected and diminished many other engagements with the twentieth century's most profound ethical crisis. Reznikoff, with his objective poetics, has perhaps found the narrow and barely imaginable ethics behind the Holocaust itself.

part 2

EXCESS AND EROS

DUKE. If music be the food of love, play on,
   Give me excess of it, that, surfeiting,
   The appetite may sicken and so die. (*Twelfth Night* I.i)

In "Projective Verse" (1950), an essay that had a major impact on the aesthetic and ethical posture of innovative American poetry at the time, Charles Olson states that he wants to do two things: first, to explain open or "projective" verse and, second, to explore "what stance toward reality brings such verse into being" (147). Much in keeping with the poets and philosophers after World War II, Olson conflates poetry and worldview and brings to fruition a philosophical revision of the relation of aesthetics to truth. He calls this stance toward reality *objectism*, which he traces back to Ezra Pound and William Carlos Williams's involvement in "Objectivism" as a "necessary quarrel" with "subjectivism." While he dismisses the subjective view of poetry (which means personal, academic, syllabic, or lyrical forms), Olson renames Objectivism by focusing on the object. The word *objectism*, he says, is

a word to be taken to stand for the kind of relation of man to experience which a poet might state as the necessity of a line or a work to be as wood is, to be as clean as wood is as it issues from the hand of nature, to be as shaped as wood can be when a man has had his hand in it. Objectism is getting rid of the lyrical interference of the individual as ego, of the "subject" and his soul, that peculiar presumption by which western man has interposed himself between what he is as a creature of nature (with certain instructions to carry out) and those other creatures of nature which we may, with not derogation, call objects. For man is himself an object, whatever he may take to be his advantages, the more likely to recognize himself as such the greater his advantages, particularly at that moment that he achieves an humilitas sufficient to make him of use. (155–56)

In this passage that lays out Olson's ethical "stance toward reality," we can see similarities with Louis Zukofsky's and George Oppen's urge to treat the poem as an object—Olson uses the metaphor of wood—and to get rid of the "lyrical interference of the individual as ego" in order to arrive, as does Charles Reznikoff, at a deeper *humilitas*. Both statements prompt an existential shift in the place of man in the universe and move him from godlike dominion over the creatures of the world to a humble object himself among other objects. This ethical stance of being an object and embracing "small existence" will allow the poet, as the rest of the essay explains, to draw on internal nature, specifically the objectlike "breath," and then project outside of him "dimensions larger than the man." *Projective verse*, as Olson calls it, is not exactly Zukofsky's rested totality or Oppen's invocation of Otherness because Olson mutates Objectivism in key ways, but Projective verse does raise similar ethical issues of how the (notably male) subject relates to the world.

This brief analysis demonstrates not only the connections of poets in Olson's Projectivist circles—Robert Duncan, Edward Dorn, Denise Levertov, and Robert Creeley—with Zukofsky and the Objectivists, but it also begins to hint at the way poets writing after World War II mutated Zukofsky's original Objectivist tenets. For example, we can see how *sight*, which was so crucial for Zukofsky, is less important than *sound* for Olson. By emphasizing the breath, for example, Olson can say "not the eye but the ear was to be [writing's] measurer" ("Projective" 155) and, thus elevate the nonvisual and nonrational. Olson's argument is indicative of the issues in many of his contemporaries: the relation of subject to social, inner to outer, sight to sound, law (syllabics) to freedom (open verse), containment[1] within the body (lyrical insight) to excess beyond the body (projections into realms "larger than the man"). Such issues certainly occupy the poetry and poetics of Robert Duncan and Edward Dorn, who nevertheless deviate from their comrade-in-verse in several key ethical ways.

Most striking, Dorn and Duncan differ from Olson and their Objectivist forerunners in their deemphasis on the object, or more precisely, the *what is* of "reality." As I portray the Objectivists, the ethics of Oppen, for example, comes from a proximity of poetry with what is—otherness traces itself in the images that are mostly of objects or given objectlike status. Olson, it seems clear, emphasizes the ontological relation of man to the world, and, at the same time, he assumes in this essay the didactic tone (how a poet *should* be writing) of Zukofsky and Pound. On the contrary, Dorn rejects the *what is/should be* problematic of Olson and provides a third ethical possibility, that is, the *could be*. Duncan, likewise, infuses what he calls the *What Is* with polysemous contradiction that returns us to the alterity in and before Being. Dorn and Duncan push beyond the dichotomy of *is/should* into a realm of transformation and possibility free of the judgment of *should* and unbound by sincerity to some objective "Being." This excess shows in their thematics and in their formal experimentations. By experimenting with what has been and what should be, both poets invoke the obligation of otherness via modes of excess and eros. During their careers, Duncan and Dorn wrote a poetry of fantasy, futurity, and fiction and saw themselves as visionaries of a completely new reality. Furthermore, unlike Reznikoff and Oppen who deal heavily with the other of the subject in the theme of responsibility, Dorn and Duncan primarily deal with the other of language and are therefore participating more in the linguistic turn of the period.

But Dorn and Duncan's poems are not untouched by problems related to reading them within a poethical context that favors nonjudgment and alterity. Their poetry is still troubled by the issue of didacticism—not in the way of Olson, who admits that his poetics is "dogma" and employs his pounding dictum, "ONE PERCEPTION MUST IMMEDIATELY AND DIRECTLY LEAD TO A FURTHER PERCEPTION" ("Projective" 149)—but in the way of moral *passion*. Dorn and Duncan both have strong moral and political views that pervade their poems in the form of accusative statement. Enikó Bollobás, the first critic to yoke Dorn and Duncan together in terms of their specific Black Mountain ethos, takes their declarative style as the essence of their morality. Borrowing heavily from Donald Wesling's "morality of attention," Bollobás sees a specific difference of these two poets from their Black Mountain colleagues because they deal with more "moral" issues. Although Bollobás defines Dorn's ethical responsibility as political commitment and moral didacticism and Duncan's as a historical revisionism as well as a "humility, tolerance, and openness to the other," her formulation stands as the inverse of my project that attempts to show a new kind of ethics in their poetry (43–46, 48–49). Although she claims that attention in Duncan and Dorn's poetry is an "ethic of failure," Bollobás does present them as politicians self-appointed to carry out their moral vision of the "whole earth" (47). I do not disagree that Bollobás's notion of morality is at play in the work of these poets; I simply think there is more to being a prophetic voice than saying "I told you so." Instead, I examine what in Duncan and Dorn's poethics allows them to assume these kinds of duties as poets. For Dorn, it is the deconstruction of the ethical relationship between subject and community, and for Duncan it is the eros of the body that opens the self to the Other. The question I wish to address in the following two chapters is, What are the conditions for such ethical possibilities?

3

The Ethics of Excess Edward Dorn's *Gunslinger*

KING. Presume not that I am the thing I was,
    For God doth know, so shall the world perceive,
    That I have turn'd away my former self;
    So will I those that kept me company.
    (*King Henry the Fourth, Part II* V.v)

In a 1995 debate on the Internet, Edward Dorn and his *Gunslinger*—a postmodern epic wherein a motley band of hippies undertake a quest to seek out their perceived enemy, Howard Hughes—are accused of everything from not being funny any more to being outright pompous, while some critics even resorted to echoing Eliot Weinberger's famous 1984 indictment that Dorn is a fascist AIDS-basher ("Case" 170–72). Only one lone voice rose in the din of cyberspace to defend Dorn against "unforgiving moralistic judgments" and to charge Dorn's critics with "masquerading plain old bad blood behind a facade of aesthetic and political theory" (Boughn). Although the polemic eventually simmers down into a tame discussion of the lineage of satire in *Gunslinger,* the confluence of the two topics, morals and satire, in Dorn's poetry is a productive and problematic one. The question is, why, after twenty years since the poem was published and after several important critical works have emerged about Dorn's writing, such as Donald Wesling's *Internal Resistances,* do debates about Dorn continue to return either to the poet's personal morals or to his mode of satiric humor? A better way to frame this question from the perspective of conventional morality might be, how can a poet whose work is constantly contradictory and overstepping bounds (even ones that it lays down via satire and polemics) be considered moral?[1]

My response is that neither Dorn's moral framework nor his brand of satire have found a context in which they can be constructively read without the taste of "bad blood." True, satire is Dorn's primary mode of ethical observation and intervention, but this satirical, moral posture is far more complex than has been recognized. To address this complex relation of Dorn to morality, I place him within the context of postmodern analyses of the relation between self and society or, more precisely, *subject* and *community.*

Because Dorn's poetics is bound up in a rethinking of these terms through what I will call an *ethics of excess,* a mode of the "could be," his poem ultimately calls for an entirely new mode of satire *and* morality. If thought of in these terms, Dorn's excess (in form, language, content, and figure) takes aim at the very foundation of morals, so the ethical implications of *Gunslinger* might be viewed from a different perspective, a perspective that gouges the eyes of vision altogether and leaves only a visionary realm of the beyond.

Dorn's Re-vision of Satire

Satire is, in *Gunslinger,* a form of excess itself, and I begin my chapter with the contention that Dorn's satire has been cast in unbefitting robes. Published as a whole in 1975 under the title *Slinger* by Wingbow Press, the poem was originally written and released in parts between 1968 and 1972 and then reprinted in 1989 and 1995 by Duke University Press as *Gunslinger.* This extended period gives Dorn ample opportunity to amend his poem and respond to many of the events of the day, including political and philosophical developments. But primarily this book is a satire of the "sicksties" and the reactionary backlash to its massive social changes. Because of this focus, most of his critics want to make of Dorn a typical Augustan satirist who hordes an elite knowledge and harbors, underneath the wit and contradictions, a proscriptive set of political and moral values.[2] But Dorn's satire is not that simple. Traditionally, satire is thought to be ethical because it uncovers the evils of society and the corruption of its individuals through a clear vision for representing what is.[3] Because ethics are often conceived as conventions, as laws or rules that instruct us on how to live a good life, a moral poet would usually affirm such values by adopting normative modes, even in satire.[4] But not Dorn. Or, at least, the ethics at play in *Gunslinger* does not merely rely on didactic language but, rather, continually attempts to exceed it. Entering the topography of southwestern Colorado, for instance, the character called "The Poet" diminishes measure and judgment as a way of getting at the splendor: "its scale is revelatory / not comparative" (178). Such is the scale of *Gunslinger* itself.

The linear reason of causality, which founds the logic of consequences in a moral system that rewards good and punishes evil, is satirized in several figures in the poem that show both Dorn's debt to satiric tradition and his move beyond it.[5] In *Gunslinger,* The figure of Howard Hughes, famed aviator and filmmaker of the 1930s and aeronautics tycoon of the 1950s, exemplifies the necessity of law and order (even if he makes all the laws) in his capitalist system: "We're gonna have Order / Even if we have to inject it" (152).

This line epitomizes the totalizing nature of systems founded on reason, which ultimately provides the order necessary to the free trade of capitalism, Hughes's ultimate goal being "to hold the property lines" (151). Reason is also symbolized by Hughes's train that "has no front it's All rear" (98). Like logic that functions on similarities and noncontradictions, the train tracks are great "equal signs," in Michael Davidson's phrase, homogenizing the countryside: "Parallels are just two things / going to the same place that's a bore" ("To Eliminate" 97, 137). The (at least) temporary derailment of the linear train of logic by "The Cycle" provides an ethical perspective from which to uncover the violence inherent in any rational system. Dorn's satire, echoing Henry David Thoreau, is incisive:

> The scream of the Accomplished Present
> A conglomerate of Ends, The scream of Parallels
> All tied down with spikes These are the spines
> Of the cold citizens made to run wheels upon (97)[6]

Although Dorn's invective is severe, it does not imply that there is a "better" way to live than through capitalism and reason; he simply is questioning their status in our culture as the infallible Good.

With reason no longer left unchallenged as the basis of moral or political judgments, the focus in *Gunslinger* is on ethical uncertainty. For Dorn, political commitment is questionable at best because, as Robert von Hallberg points out, Dorn hates choosing sides (58–61). Dorn's lack of political moorings and refusal to believe in the power of reason means that he possesses no ideal to replace what he is satirizing. The real difference, according to Wesling, between Dorn and other satirists is that Dorn is the "self-mocking solitary" voice (3). But this voice is more that of an ecstatic prophet than of an intelligentsia. Dorn's poem, therefore, does nothing to shape the people into a new order, as Wesling argues (15), but rather to open the community through language to an otherness that will allow for a transformation that has yet to be determined. The suspension of political decision, which begins with the dismantling of the decision maker, the rational subject, is the opening of ethics in *Gunslinger*.

The Subject's Split, Man

An ethics of excess appears first in the poem through the new forms of subjectivity that arise out of the satire of linear reason.[7] In short, Dorn is participating in the deconstruction of the subject and "author function" reminiscent of the linguistic turn of poststructuralism where, as Jacques

Derrida writes, the proper name is not a person but a problem, a question (*Of Grammatology* 107–18). This critique is one of the first steps to rethinking ethics because the rational, unified subject, not to mention the very authority of the idea of authorship, is at the heart of most conventional moralities, especially the ones Dorn satirizes. The "I" of Book I (the Book of "I") is a pun in that the entire first section of the poem relates the crumbling and transformation of what has formerly been called the "first person." "The curtain might rise anywhere on a single speaker" (1), and it might fall on one as well. As Davidson points out, I is "'the last vestige of the self-conscious, rationalizing ego' of Cartesianism, the unitary self whose trust in linear logic and rationality leads him into an endless series of questions that the Slinger and his friends find inappropriate if not ludicrous" (Perloff, "Introduction" x). As a dinosaur of Western Civ and, as Slinger calls him, "a past reference," I insists on defining meaning as the one-to-one correspondence of signifier to signified, word to idea. But his collapse, along with the poem's corresponding shift to language of subjectivity, causes confusion in I who seeks an answer: "And you want some *reason*," Slinger points out (Dorn, *Gunslinger* 29). The Appropriately Named Horse, Claude Lévi-Strauss,[8] tells I,

> I study the savage mind.
> And what is that I asked.
> *That*, intoned Claude leaning on my shoulder
> is what you *have*
> in other words, you provide
> an instance
> you are purely animal
> sometimes purely plant
> but mostly you're just a
> classification, (35)

The dependence of I's mind on viewing the world purely as an object for his knowledge and meaning—the very processes of reason—betrays him and reduces him to a "classification." But if the rationality needed to underwrite the unity of a subject is severely compromised, the poem seems to say, then how can we talk of the subject as singular or even as a subject?

Traditionally conceived, the subject, through reason, grasps and synthesizes the world in a complete, total gaze. This totality is conceptualized dialectically as the self's constitutive relationship with an object, but Dorn is quick to jab at this philosophical beast with two backs. When Slinger questions the seriousness of Dr. Flamboyant's dissertation, titled *The Tensile Strength of Last Winters Icicles,* the doctor replies:

> Not at all, it was
> that conjectural—
> it's whats called a
> post-ephemeral subject
> always a day late, their error lay of course
> in looking for an object (82)

Flamboyant's dissertation seems ridiculous at first glance on account of the title, but Dorn is dead serious in his critique. This new idea of the subject, the "post-ephemeral subject," is not constituted in its totality or totalizing relation to an object as in Hegelian phenomenology. Instead, this subject, "always a day late" for such completeness, is conjectural and, as such, exists only by being true to what is possible. Existence is at best a conjecture.[9]

However, despite its conjectural "strength," Flamboyant's subject can never really be exactly what it is,[10] for it "exists" only as a supplement or excess of an absent original, essential subject. Slinger adds to the doctor's description above:

> When it gets to you
> them in their case, me
> in mine,
> it doesn't exist
> Like the star whose ray
> announces the disappearance
> of its master by the presence of itself. (82)

Like a ray from a dying star or like water from a melted icicle, this "new" subject "announces" itself only by being a trace of what no longer exists, that is, the total subject. The subject is not just "what it is" but is the remainder, the excess of what is, what was, and what never could have been. In these tenses lies the tension of excess, and though Dorn does not replace the subject, he does muse on what it *could be.*

The poem exhibits an excess of subjectivity as a splitting of the subject, or as Dorn says elsewhere, "the relaxation of the ego" (Dorn, *Interviews* 100). As the Slinger explains:

> The Ego
> is costumed as the road manager

of the soul, every time
the soul plays a date in another town
I goes ahead to set up
the bleechers, or book the hall
as they now have it,
the phenomenon is reported by the phrase
I got there ahead of myself (57–58)

If I must be preserved, as the Slinger says, then it must take a demotion from the discerning cogito to "the road manager of the soul" who simply prepares the way for another self yet to come. For the subject is/has now split, as "reported by the phrase I got there ahead of myself," and is no longer unified. But this split does not mean that the self is lost because, as Dorn points out, in order for the ego to relax "the person has to be assured that destruction isn't around the corner" (*Interviews* 100). The poem suggests here that the I simply becomes other to itself. This split is literalized in the transition of the titles from "Book I" to "Book II," where the I is doubled.

Such splitting and fracturing of the subject can be seen in the simple way the character's names change throughout the poem. In Book II of *Gunslinger* and thereafter, enacting the very satire of naming that occurs didactically throughout Book I (19, 25–29, 32–33), Dorn breaks a great, unwritten rule of narrative: consistent character names. The character, the Gunslinger, for instance, begins in Book I as the epitome of the epic Western hero who depends on his name as the badge of his reputation "of impeccable personal smoothness" (3); however, through Books II and III, he is referred to almost exclusively as "Slinger," and by section two of Book IIII he is called "Zlinger."[11] The Horse's name changes the most, beginning as the "mare lather[ed] with tedium" (7) and picking up a new epic epithet, such as "the Stoned Horse" or "the Turned On Horse," almost every time he is mentioned. He is also called "Heidegger" and "Claude Lévi-Strauss" interchangeably by his friends—both "homonyms" (36), itself a possible pun on Jonathan Swift's humanlike horses in *Gulliver's Travels,* the "Huoyhnhynms." As Robert von Hallberg points out, in the Horse's name "actually two homonyms are crossed with a pun: Clawed Lévi-Strauss → clawed jeans → clawed genes" (67). So the names not only change but become multi-referential, which further dilutes the authority of a subject that relies on its name as a metonym of wholeness.[12] Such morphing of names in the poem splinters the fantasy of the unified subject, spoofed by Flamboyant's "Turning Machine," which teleports only parts of his body from Beenville.

The punch line? He is left "quite without / the authority of the Whole Body" (137).

Free of the fetters of unity, reason, and consistency, the poem is able to experiment with new (and ethical) modes of subjectivity. After being pickled in five gallons of LSD, for instance, I is a new man. He does not say a word after he steps off the coach in Universe City, and we don't hear from him again until the end of Book III in the "Nightletta," which he writes as the secretary to Parmenides. As others have pointed out, this letter means little beyond non-sense and yields at best only "FLAPTRAP INFORMA-TION TEETOTTER" (140), when read cursorily; but the lack of sense signals that I has moved beyond his dependence on reason into a new type of consciousness. Also, by Book IIII (the use of "IIII" instead of "IV" again underscoring the proliferation of versions of "I"), he has become much more laid back and accepting, for he no longer wants "to know / what something *means* after you've / seen it, after you've *been* there" (29).[13] This new kind of wisdom avoids the unified subject altogether:

> I had one eye out
> for the prosecutors of Individuality
> and the other eye out for the advocates
> catching in that spectrum
> all the known species of Cant (162)

This paranoid, critical stance fits well with the "I" named Dorn who hates taking sides. The pun on "eye," too, suggest that the subject is split, since there are two eyes. Because the split subject cannot be pinned down to one side or another, it is freer to explore the paradoxes and contradictions that comprise life in a postmodern world. In this more Nietzschean mode of existence, I exists above the law and has "an ability / to hear Evil praised" (159).

This kind of being-outside-oneself that Dorn describes in the phrase "I got ahead of my I" (57–58) is reminiscent of Heidegger's notion of *ekstasis*, which Heidegger elucidates in 1947 in "Letter on Humanism," his famous response to the rise of the ethical turn in French thought.[14] In this context, the split subjectivity of the poem gains its full ethical significance. This term *ekstasis*, as the etymology implies, describes a state in which one exists outside of one's body. For Heidegger this is not simply one state among others, but man's mode of being and thinking. In standing outside oneself, Heidegger claims, one remains no longer isolated from the world by the boundaries of skin, senses, and perception. Just as a writer like Dorn must become someone else in order to write in another voice, so the Poet/singer at the end of

"The Cycle" ecstatically takes on the identity of Al and Rupert as his narrative switches (as does the poem as a whole) from a first-person, omniscient reflection on "Robarts Wallet" to that of a third-person, limited dialogue. In this ecstatic state, the Poet virtually becomes Rupert, the subject of his cycle. Such a mode is ethical for Heidegger because we are being-with or being-there with things, and Everything (an unavoidable pun) is part of who we are, so in letting others be, we let ourselves be.

In addition to Heidegger's use of the word, Dorn may have understood what I am calling *ekstasis* in terms of what Charles Olson called *proprioception*. As Olson words it, proprioception relates to an experience of the body—"SENSIBILITY WITHIN THE ORGANISM/ BY MOVEMENT OF ITS OWN TISSUES"—which implies that a perception of the inside is a perception of the outside, "or participation: active social life" ("Proprioception" 182).[15] Perhaps Dorn invokes this idea in his phrase, "the inside real and the outsidereal" (*Gunslinger* 110), where both in and out are not total, but fluid and connected: "connection is not by contact . . . nothing touches, connection meant is / Instant in extent a proposal of limit" (115). Like Gloucester and Maximus in Olson's *The Maximus Poems*, man cannot be distinguished from his locale, which for Dorn exceeds simple geography.[16] Slinger, with his connections to the movement of the sun and stars, as well as his ability to eliminate the draw,[17] epitomizes proprioception. I also draws on the language of proprioception when he writes in his nightletta, "ALL PRESENT SCHEMA KNOWN CONFORM LOCAL STRANDS : SET BIOLINES AT GROSS BODY MOTIONS" (141). Considering that the context of this passage borders on non-sense, Dorn seems to be gently mocking his teacher's revered concept, but at the same time Dorn affirms, through the excess of his language, the effacement of the inside and outside.

The ecstatic alternative to the unified subject lies in the excess of the "collective" subject that proprioception enables as "active social life." If boundaries cease to exist between the subject and the world of objects, the logic of the concept goes, then boundaries cease between subjects, so all subjects are somehow bound. But this erasure does not mean that people become the same and lose all sense of self. As Olson says in "Proprioception," "it [the object of perception] is inside us / & at the same time does not feel literally *identical* with our own physical or mortal self" (183). But Olson is not the only person to discuss the collective aspect of subjectivity. In *The Inoperative Community* (1991, *Communauté désoeuvrée* 1986), Jean-Luc Nancy takes Heidegger's idea of *ekstasis* to mean that through the exposure of the body we, as singular beings, share singular Being (25–31). Although Being, according to Heidegger, continually withdraws from us and is therefore not an essence that we share, this sharing for Dorn ultimately makes us collective in our identity.[18] The ganglike movement of the characters in *Gunslinger* suggests they are a collective subject, which Dorn refers to in the poem as "the constellation" or the "pliead" (which denotes either to one of the cluster of six stars in the constellation Taurus, the seven daughters of Atlas who were turned into stars, or the name of a group of seven sixteenth-century poets who took their name from a group of ancient Greek tragic poets). We may consider them as a collective subject because being-together, in which they share only nonessential Being, makes them who they are. No genetic, individual identity (personified in Hughes and his "genetic duels with other men") gives them commonality. Therefore, in *Gunslinger* the phrase "Our company moves collectively" (46) means slightly more than merely they departed together.[19] In fact, just as the sharing-Being of this group forever mutates the singular being in the poem, so I's transformation, oddly enough, becomes evident only upon his return from the "cultural collective" (148), which seems to provide a macrocosm to the *Gunslinger* microcosm. Dorn states that the problem with the first-person pronoun is that the ego has lost its use; in turn, the egocentrism of our stories makes them and us interchangeable (*Interviews* 49). Although I remains a part of our cultural heritage, he acquires transformative potential because he converts from a unified, individual to a collective subject who shares with others the singularity of his being.

Wandering/Wondering Community

By implying in his figure of the ecstatic subject a type of community that itself crosses boundaries, Dorn moves us toward an ethics of excess. As Nancy points out, Heidegger's notion of *ekstasis* ultimately provides a figure of community (6–7). Thus, their work gives us a model on which to begin considering the ethical implications of the notion of community at work in the text of *Gunslinger.*

The collective subject of the *Gunslinger* opposes what Nancy calls the *immanent community.* Within the immanent community, which has dominated most discussion of community in the West for centuries, individuals are bound together by means of some presumed essence that depends usually on the exclusion of difference and the communion of sameness (Nancy 1–12). Such a community is exemplified in the poem not only by Hughes but by the citizen in Book I who seeks to remove the Horse from the saloon because of his difference, especially because he's "even a *negra* horse"

(*Gunslinger* 26). The Slinger silences this "fabrikoid coat" and his bigotry by calling him "a plain unassorted white citizen" (28), the very essence that the citizen is trying to preserve by excluding the black horse. The tables of discriminating judgment have been turned. Similarly, when I de-coaches in Universe City after being preserved in LSD,

> A band of citizens gathered.
> They blocked the way. They too
> were meshed with the appearance of I
> Tho their interest was inessentially
> soldered to the surface, and tho
> they had nought invested, an old appetite
> for the Destruction of the Strange
> governed the massed impulse of their tongues (68)

The "citizens" preserve their essence and identity only by focusing on appearance and "the Destruction of the Strange." Such a focus characterizes an immanent community that must exclude the Other, both the other of the subject and the other of language, and thus precludes ethics in favor of the law. The Slinger defends I and confronts the crowd by admonishing that "your identification is the *same* / as your word for fear" (70). The Slinger points here to the paradox that immanent community must deny: Identity, in seeking to protect the unity of the subject and community, actually prevents any immanent community from taking place at all. It is a fiction. Conversely, Dorn creates an alternative community in a utopian but nonidealistic way in order to open a space of social and political transformation, what William Lockwood calls a *renewed society* (196).

As one of the characters in *Gunslinger* points out, "if you have a name you can be sold" as part of the immanent community (32), so the very resistance to naming and the continually changing names of the troupe make them perfect ambassadors for a new type of community—to use Nancy's term, an *inoperative community*. In such a formation, according to Nancy, community is constantly being "unworked" (*désoeuvrée*) because there is no immanent myth that would unite everyone in communion (31–70). Such an unworking of any stultified, tyrannical institution, is what keeps the possibility of change open. This model of revolution allows us to see the Horse's resistance of "the Owner" in Book II of *Gunslinger* as a good example of how community always exceeds any attempt to totalize it via property or any other means of control.[20] "Bringing news / beyond the heads of most of them," the Horse convinces the other horses in the plaza that their "reins are not fixed to the ground." In other words, the horses are not essentially bound to their subservient status in community, and this news prompts them to run off. The Owner, troubled by "some deep somatic conflict," gets irate and fires both of his pistols, which the Slinger quickly "jammonings." He can jam the guns because, as he points out, "this can only be / *materialism*, the result / of merely *real* speed" (74). Slinger's community consists of hipster coolness in which everyone gathers, not for profit or reassurance of unity, but to hear the Poet's "Cycle." Bound only by poetry and not a unifying myth, this ragtag assortment of "curious refugees" grows continually throughout the poem. Eventually, the group must and does disband, because, as both Nancy and Blanchot show, community must unwork itself in order not to reify the very exclusion perpetrated by immanence.[21] Slinger's community wanders around the desert Southwest without a purpose and wonders at the myriad miracles.

A community without purpose would be at odds with one that seeks order, profit, and dominion.[22] Therefore, Dorn's critique of authority enacts that conflict and seeks to resolve it through excessive satire and humor. This critique of the authority of immanent community takes several different self-reflexive forms in the poem. One, the Blakean song, "*Cool Liquid Comes,*" resembles Thoreau's description of the morning from *Walden* and envisions a communal world of *ekstasis* in which the singular, the worldly, and the cosmic are aligned and resonant. The cool liquid of the sun's light

> branding morning
> on the worlds side
> the great plaining zodiacus
> The great brand of our crossing
> the fabulous accounting
> of our coursing
> the country of our consciousness (50)

The Slinger responds with an allusion to Blake's *Marriage of Heaven and Hell*, "all things of the imagination must be."[23] Although the Slinger says that he has "lyrcd somewhat predestinarian," the song has rendered "the Panorama" as a place so present ("morning sensing congealing") that it actually lies Beyond the future and beyond a single destiny: "Oh Narrowness of protestation!"(52).

On a less cosmic and more cultural scale than "*Cool Liquid Comes,*" "The Cycle," a vision within a vision, enacts a mode of excess in its satire of authority. In a seeming reification of authority, "The Cycle" opens with an invocation by the Slinger who suggests that the Poet totalize and thus normalize the ethics of the citizens of Universe City:

> make
> their azured senses warm *Make* your norm
> their own   deliver them
> from their *Vicious Isolation* (89)

Yet, Slinger urges the Poet to "Make your norm / their own" not by making them comply with a set of rules but through warming their "azured senses" by making them feel "the Cycle of Acquisition" that "Robart the Valfather of this race" is perpetrating on them. In other words, the Poet must transform their sensibilities through language. Likewise, to "deliver them from their Vicious Isolation" would open them to the Other by exposing them to the proprioceptory subjectivity and ecstatic community that the Poet represents. Here we see a resemblance to Bruce Andrews's second model of language, the libidinal: Authority arises when language and attitudes are imposed on a people, and liberation comes from turning the cycle of language to open it to possibility, uncertainty, and otherness. Such a proprioceptory consciousness will be crucial if the citizens in the audience are to acknowledge and then face the threat represented by Hughes.

Although not a civic power, Hughes is associated in "The Cycle" with the larger military-industrial complex that uses jargon and propaganda ("Save the Cheeze [*sic*] Programs") to propagate the proverbial hustle on the "lewdness of the multitude" (*Gunslinger* 91). Hughes surrounds himself with clones who think like he does, embodying the idea that immanent community relies on identity not difference, and he imposes an order on the world that no one can escape:

> This Grand Car with the Superior Interior
> Moves with a basal shift So Large
> It would be a dream to feel time curve
> For no masses so locked serve straight time
>
> Thus rhythm has a duty to de-tour the Vast
> Contra Naturum? Baby you ain't heard nothing yet (100)

Like a black hole, Hughes's presence curves space so that the masses are imprisoned, serving "time." The "shades are drawn against / The organ of the Imagination," which might serve as challenges to Hughes's authority. The Poet also insinuates that it will be impossible to escape "the vast Contra

Naturum."[24] Although set up as the symbol of capitalism, the figures in "The Cycle" are hardly model Junior Achievers, but they reveal the dark side of their business of giving people "choices." For example, the Atlantes, Rupert's Atlas-like entourage of cronies who are motivated only by "Fear and Surrender," can "pick the pockets / Of the passing guard," produce almanacs, or take "tintypes of Brigham Young in drag . . . [b]ut they cannot count" (102). They also cannot speak very well, "Their conversational English is limited / Yet they mimick its rehearsal very cleverly" (103). Simply put, the Atlantes are a whining bunch of yes-men, who are also ruthless:

> They fear one thing and one thing only
> And that is the avaricious Vice-Versas
>
> An obscene and gluttonous order of rat
> The Supreme Janitor unleases on the floor
> After Lunch where they destroy themselves
> With madness
>
> When they find nothing
> But their Raving Expectations
> And upon this Nought
> They bloat and bloat and bloat
>
> And Rupert cackles and grabs for Breath
> And hollers This!
> Is what we keep the slums awake with (103)

In other words, these henchmen fear the paradox and uncertainty ("Vice-Versas") unleashed by the Janitor of *Naked Lunch* fame ("After Lunch"), which they resist by replacing certainty with "their Raving Expectations." Ultimately, the whole show of the Atlantes going mad is Hughes's to control, and he plays for an exploitative end, to "keep the slums awake." Only formally can such a system be exceeded, so the poem's form itself—as the cycle of the acquisition of power and wealth that must be repeated and repeatedly satirized—works against the linear, narrative authority of the poem.

Although "The Cycle" satirizes authority, it does not suggest that the complete destruction of authority is possible or even desired, and this simply shows that Dorn's "thirst" for contradiction is part of his ethics. Alarmingly, though, the power of Hughes/Robart/Rupert/Al and his cronies seems to continue to grow and coalesce despite certain setbacks, as well as the Poet's mockery ("And human hands first mimicked and then mocked" 90–91).[25]

Eventually, the same cackling figure—who, disguised as a cheeseburger, was shuffled in a stretcher through the train station in Boston narrowly escaping an angry mob—peers haughtily by the end of "The Cycle" over Las Vegas and the world:

> Rupert snapped on
> And moved his amber shades
> Like a sweep from the conning tower
> And His finger poised over the button
>
> Which could activate the Vice-Versas
> And either way it's far out   how
> He cons the present to hustle the futchah
> By a simple elimination of the datadata (108–9)

By eliminating the evidence of the "datadata" through the monological effect of his "language cleaner" (an apocalyptic figure made real in the cultural understanding in the atomic age of the 1960s of "The Button"), Rupert reseals and reinforces "the system" to support his "Used War for Sale" campaign and to pick off telegrams from pesky pre-Socratic philosophers. The presentation of these actions of capitalist exploitation is satirical: substantial evidence is only "datadata" and Hughes's muse is the one singing "Used War for Sale." But Dorn provides no overt condemnation and thus no ideal solution. Rupert here is not exactly a weak figure who has been divested of power by the Poet's cyclical satire; in a certain sense, Dorn suggests that figures like Hughes are here to stay as part of the present historical landscape. Instead of willing the elimination of authority to be replaced by a more idealistic world, the satire of "The Cycle," a satire without idealism, becomes a revolutionary act in simply opening the given, present world (of capitalist entrepreneurs) to the *possibility* of change as opposed to the necessity of a new replacement system. This kind of satire emphasizes that authority itself is vulnerable to the transforming effects of language even if that system of authority can't be completely erased. To William J. Lockwood, "The Cycle" is "simply a vision of Blankness whose sinister implications, if viewed in a comic perspective, may be appropriately neutralized" (182). But I see this intermediary book of *Gunslinger* as doubled, at once a foreboding of an impending evil that lurks in the void of postmodernity and an objective revelation of the mind-set of the moment. Either way, Lockwood's ultimate conclusion is that Dorn is trying, like the Poet, "to create a cognizance in the society of itself and to furnish the means for a self-appraisal and self-evaluation" (182–83). The control implied in self-reflexive evaluation surely exhibits a moral position and signals a deeper ethical resistance.

The Ethics of Excess

Once we understand how Dorn recasts both the subject and the community as excessive, the question becomes what is the ethical implication of such re-definitions that oppose "the Destruction of the Strange." One possibility is that by questioning ego subjectivity and by unveiling the lie of immanent community, *Gunslinger* invites into its erratic lines the trace of the Other—or as Jacques Derrida calls it, *différance*—that summons change and difference.[26] In other words, *Gunslinger* envisions an ethical relation between the ecstatic subject and the community through an excess—in figure, form, and content, as well as in discontinuity—which creates not vision but, to use a phrase of Emmanuel Levinas, "goes further than vision" (*Totality* 290) to a visionary ethics of how things could be. Because vision, both in terms of the senses and also as a measuring, relies on "seeing things as they are," Dorn resorts to a more shamanistic, visionary poetic to impress excess upon his reader.

Book I does begin with an emphasis on sight, but because sight obsti-nately claims a monopoly on truth and mimesis, the poem insists, vision has no room for change and must be exceeded. This exceeding happens when the poem is the most formally and thematically challenging, that is, when it is open to strangeness. The opening of Book II shows the movement in the poem from the critique of vision-centered description (as in Slinger's query to I during the saloon fight, "Tell me what you see") to a visionary mode that attempts to look beyond being:

> born on the breathing
> of a distant harmonium, To See
> is their desire
> as they wander estranged
> through the lanes of the Tenders
> of Objects
> who implore this existence
> for a plan and dance wildeyed
> provided with a schedule
> of separated events
> along the selvedge of time. (45)

"They," the collective subject, begin their quest in the realm of vision, "To See," yet this is not a vision of stasis and rested totality.[27] The desire, the estrangement, along with the allusion to Wallace Stevens's distant "roman-tic," visionary voice breathing in the background, unsettle our heroes "as they wander estranged / through the lanes of the Tenders / of Objects." Al-though these "Tenders of Objects" might be motivated by a sheer awe of mere existence inspired by Olson's Projectivist poetics, the phrase also sug-gests the exploitation of objects by capitalism (the objects, after all, are cap-italized in the line). These lanes of poetry eerily resemble those of Wild West souvenir vendors at a roadside curio shop, such as Stuckey's, which was a chain popular in the 1960s and 1970s. Regardless of the function of objects in the field of vision, the last four lines of the passage move us into a differ-ent realm entirely. The first of the lines opens with an ambiguous pronoun: "who" may refer to "Objects," in which case they are asking for liberation; it may refer to "Tenders" who act as tour guides of Being; or it could refer to "they," our heroes. The latter is the reading I prefer because it makes their strangeness "heroic." Any way you read it, though, the word "who" ushers in an excess of meaning not controlled by the poet. No matter what the refer-ence of "who" is, "existence" is implored to provide "a plan," or vision, of how to move beyond the merely given or capitalized. This plan is to "dance wildeyed," a Dionysian dance of excess in the wilderness of the Wild West, where "a schedule / of separated events" comprises the "selvedge of time."[28] "Have you ever noticed," the Slinger asks, "how everboring / the following day is, / If there be nothing new but that which is?" (47). In Slinger time, or "apache time," the discrete present moments never remain to congeal into a discernible what is but rather open the universe up to a vision of a plan of what could be.

But how are we to understand this "estrangement" that opens the collec-tive subjects and time to "wildeyed" possibility as ethical? According to Lev-inas in *Totality and Infinity,* the Other cannot be known by a set of attributes or substantives. Instead, the Other only manifests in the form of *excess,* through which he or she overflows reason, "exceeding the idea of the other in me" (48–52). Levinas refers to this excess as *infinity* or *trace.* What qualifies each of these terms is the sense that the Other is beyond description, much like the phenomenological world of *Gunslinger.* More importantly, through this beyondness, the Other obligates me before any law, reason, or duty. Dorn himself describes a similar structure in his phrase "Obligations of the Divine," which he glosses in *Interviews* as meaning "to be alert to the Spirit, and not so much to write poetry as to compose the poetry that's constantly written on air . . . to be as varied as possible since the instrumentation is lan-guage" (66). As Dorn explains the individual terms, *Divine* takes on the verbal form, "divining," in the scientific sense of an "imaginative leap" that can stay attuned to others and envision a "world mind." And *Obligation* has to do with language as pure expression, language "as varied as possible," which Levinas might describe as *le dire* (the saying), a structure that mirrors the obligation before any law. If language is reduced to a "function," Dorn continues, or "a qualification of Expression," then there is no need for obligation to others because it would become self-centered: "All of that attitude and result would be irresponsible. Expression is not responsible to anything" (67). Instead, Dorn maintains, the poet is responsible to the reader (66), and this responsibility, if I may infer, is visionary expression itself. As Levinas might understand Dorn's statements, the poet is responsible to the Other by writing out of the saying, a condition before rationality and judgment have established "meaning." However, Dorn's statements do not fit completely within a Levinasian framework. Not only would sober Levinas not endorse the Dionysian Dorn (cp. John Caputo, *Against Ethics*), he would not agree that "expression is not responsible to anything," unless "expression" means "self-expression." Where their ideas coincide is in the poet's responsibility to the reader, which for Dorn opens communal possibility through strangeness and excess. Ethics, for Dorn, would then be based on the excess of language over form and content.

My point here is that Dorn's poem is a communal "space" in which and over which the Other may manifest as excess. There are, then, certain formal "signatures" of excess as an ethical relation to the Other in both the movement of figures in the poem and the failure of figure and narrative in their discontinuity and gaps. Robert Creeley's pronouncement, which Olson uses to anchor his Projective poetics, that "form is never more than an extension of content,"[29] is altered in Dorn's work. For him, *form always exceeds content*.

Puns are one of the tools Dorn employs to open words to other meanings and thereby otherness in an ethical way. A brief example of this type of pun is the phrase, "Turned On Horse." At one point, he is "turned on," meaning sexually or narcotically aroused, as he flirts with Lil and her girls and smokes huge, "Tampico Bomber" marijuana joints (*Gunslinger* 15). But later, he is "turned on," meaning confronted or double-crossed (in addition to wearing a "XX Stetson"), by the irate, bigoted "Owner" (29). On top of that, the pun also alludes to the Trojan horse, a gift that eventually "turned on," or betrayed, the Trojans.[30] Von Hallberg insightfully recounts in detail the "literalizing" of puns in *Gunslinger* (73), which seems to be a way of taking a joke too far; in other words—and please pardon the pun—it's like beating a

Turned On Horse. In their multifarious, ambiguous, and contradictory function in the text, puns relinquish control over meaning, by both the author and reader, and open a field of strange and compelling possibility.

One of the most obvious forms of excess in *Gunslinger*, hyperbole, by its very definition continually outstrips content. One example of the poem's hyperbole, which incidentally invokes the idea of totality, operates as excessively in its idiom as in its typographical presentation. The Slinger is warning his crew about what can happen when one tries to project the future. In his words, the mind gets

> to thinking so wide
> Eats head
> went out the side of the room
>   of the room
> and moved the stadium
> to declare its connections
> and the flashy scoreboard read
> THE OUT*OF*TOWN TEAM IS VERY MODAL
>   THEREFORE THIS SHIT COULD BE
>
>   **TOTAL** (125)

The difficulty in reading this passage comes from its hyperbole, among other things. The exaggerated scenario of a mind becoming bigger than a stadium reads as absurd and obvious, overdramatized in the enlarged, bold font of "**TOTAL**." Yet the implied totality of the content is undone by the exaggeration in the form not only because of the hyperbolic figure of the exponentially growing head, which mimics the growing font size, but because the referents of "TEAM" and "SHIT" are extratextual. The content of the text does, however, seem to acknowledge in some odd way the alterity presented in this form. On the next page, the idea of a totality is satirized as it becomes part of an Abbott and Costello "Who's on First?" routine:

> VAroom ! he said
> Whats that?
> The room he said
> whats that
> a bloom he said
> oh whats that
> the Bloom he said
> Oh what is that

Kartoum he said
oh what is THAT
it is the Imperial bloom he said
what is it?
Outside the room they said
What, Whats outside?
Everything says it must have come
from under his hat!

*   *   *   *

What, whats outside?
The outside, the OUTside the chorus chorused (126)

The joke here revolves around trying to describe (again) what exists "out-side" of the *what is* of ontology, with the pun on "everything." Just as the Slinger uses "the draw" of his absolute .44 that "registers what my enemies / can never quite recall" (37), slapstick comedy, play, and pun become the only appropriate modes that Dorn can find to talk about something beyond being and reason. This carnivalesque feel of what can never be "recalled" epitomizes the ethics of excess in the sense that one is obligated to "divine" the burgeoning and infinite meanings. To continue the questioning that has no single answer, as embodied in the chorus, is to belong to the inoperable community of the poem.

Personification is another figure of speech taken to extremes in *Gun-slinger*. Such figures as the Horse, the Cracker Barrel, and Sllab serve for Dorn as ways to invoke certain voices while retaining a trace of otherness to them so that they are not so easily assimilated into the old stories of the ego. Likewise, the use of onomatopoeia inflects the language of the poem with otherness by literally personifying sound itself. There are myriad examples of this in the poem: the "**STRUM** / **strum**" of a guitar throughout Book I; Everything's mimicry of the impotence of the Owner's bullets against the Slinger, "Plunk Plunk" (74); Lil's "Honk HONK, Honk HONK Honk" horn (7); and the touristy "'Click'" to the recording of Sllab's message on the in-tercom on the hill of beans (165). The power chord beginning of "Cocaine Lil": "CO-KÁNG!" (172) and the guitar solo at the end of "Cocaine Lil"— "thwang! thwang thwang thwang thwang! twang!" (177)—refer to popular songs like "Cocaine Blues," which was first recorded by T. J. Arnall in 1958 and subsequently rerecorded by the likes of Johnny Cash and Bob Dylan. It is also a prescient anticipation of Eric Clapton's guitar in his 1977 rock clas-sic, "Cocaine" written in 1976 by J. J. Cale. Of course, these excessive figures do not serve the function of representing the thing as signified, as does, say, a proper onomatopoeia such as "bzzz" for a "bee." Instead, the signs are unfettered, which means they both retain a sense of otherness (that it is beyond meaning) and refer to many *other* contexts. The "**Strum, strum**" not only stands in for the Absolute of the Poet ("which," as the Gunslinger points out, "this company took to be a guitar / in their inattention" [39]) but also invokes the sound tracks of old Westerns, which usually provide a guitar strum or Spanish-style riff to punctuate important tension points in the plot. Such an excessive use of the word *strum* (there are eighteen instances in Book I) not only implies sarcasm aimed at Hollywood but also draws attention to their own oddity within the poem:

STRUM

strum
      And by that sound
we had come there, false fronts
my Gunslinger said make
the people mortal
and give their business
an inward cast. They cause culture.
Honk HONK, Honk HONK Honk
that sound comes
at the end of the dusty street,
where we meet the gaudy Madam (7)

Self-reflexively, the sounds literally transport the characters to the typical Western film set, the "false fronts" that now comprise popular culture. Much more effective than the fake buildings of Hollywood, the bits of onomatopoeia work beyond their role as referents to becoming actual agents and forces of movement and satire that create an inoperable community. Such sounds are, like Cocaine Lil's nose:

      intense
to the switching of the Inner Trail
which leads by hidden passage
to the Absolute Outside (173)

Through a proprioceptory subjectivity, the senses are the passage from what is "inside," the singular being, to what is "the Absolute Outside" (for Levinas, the Other) and thus community. Sounds (and smells) enact this opening.

Otherness, however, infiltrates the poem not only in Dorn's use of figurative language but also through the gaps and discontinuities (intended or not) in the poem which serve, to use one of Dorn's favorite figures, as black holes leading to a realm beyond. The implication is that ethics in *Gunslinger* does not necessarily result of Dorn's poetic craft; rather, the ethics marks the way he uses language.

In part, the excess of multiplicity in the poem contributes to its discontinuity and therefore its vigilance for the Other. Aside from the multiple meanings of words and concepts or even the multiple and changing names of the characters that I have mentioned elsewhere in this paper, multiplicity in *Gunslinger* leads to ethical relations. Paul Dresman describes the "dialectic of otherness" in Dorn's work on the American Indians as remembering and reinscribing the victim of imperialism back into American history and letters (105–7). So too, multiplicity in *Gunslinger* makes room for excluded figures. "Creeps!" Lil complains to Slinger about I's incessant jabber, "you always did / hang out with some curious refugees" (8). In fact, Lil's statement is representative of the poem itself in that every character, including herself (as the Poet's song, "Cocaine Lil" shows) is a "curious refugee." This is the feel of a community of excess: when subjects once bound by rules of unity that enforce codes of sameness are allowed to be different through a language that makes compellingly apparent the trace of otherness, everyone can "be themselves" (and more) without fear or threat of exclusion. Thus, community and ethics can take place almost organically without being forced into any artificial order. Moreover, because Slinger's constellation accepts the riffraff of society, like Taco Desoxin, for instance, community can make room for the Other.

Much like the multiplicity of the character relations in the poem, the multiple tracks of this discontinuous narrative enact an ethics. Such discontinuities reflect, as others have pointed out, a rejection of the linear reason and time on which narrative is founded.[31] But the suspension of reason is not simply an act of nihilistic glee but an ethical act because it calls into question an airtight structure that might not leave room for the trace of an Other. One of the largest gaps in the narrative of the poem is the reasoning and motivation for Robart-Rupert-Hughes's departure from the scene:

Here, I've got it
I'm almost inside, the doctor cried
but that car has got so much lead
around it

May I present
sputtered thru the monitor
His Holinas the 19th Hodunkas
of Hot Springs

Krackle Krackle Krackle

Incarnation is bunk, Al
Get that Punk outa here
And send for the Hydralicx
we're in a fracture
surprise is no longer the mode
We gotta get as big as we can
as fast as we can, that's the game plan

Can't do that Patrón
He don't pray for rain no more
he was a happy man
but they kicked him upstairs
and moved him to Chicago

He travels fastest who travels alone
¡Adiós! (195)

The gap, or "fracture," comes structurally between Al's excuse for failure and Hughes's enunciation of a line so clichéd that any spaghetti western star could have utter it before riding into the sunset, "He travels fastest who travels alone." The gap in the narrative is not complete, just ambiguous, because there are implied explanations for Hughes's departure. At any rate, Hughes (now the "naked singularity" detached from community) hightails it out of there on his "Chester White Special" and heads for either Chile or Siberia (196) *on his own accord*, without having to be forcefully removed by the hero—a gesture that would simply repeat the violence of the immanent community. Even though he leaves, Hughes's space in this inoperative community remains open. And although the doctor says that "it looks like the Magma Source was saved" (196) while Lil declares "that Robart's redshifted again . . . we've effected the saneamento!" (197), there is no typical Wild West showdown. Sanity is ostensibly restored through nonviolence. In fact, this anticlimax is heightened when we learn that the hero, Zlinger, has slept through it all. But such dislocation and disappointment serve only to prevent the poem in its allegorical function from becoming a totalizing metanarrative. This finale presents at root an ethical situation, even if it does not prescribe the moral action, for no one, even Robart, is outside the text of the poem or can view or control culture as a totality—such a totality is the delusion of the ego who has interest in controlling a monological view of reality.

Such formal disruptions move beyond the tyranny of totality by inscribing a trace of otherness into the text. Note how the following passage, although thematically in keeping with the relation of finite being to otherness, is still twisted with excess. In this scene, Everything is posing a question to Slinger but is interrupted:

> Well, uh, the world is absolutely finite
> and the cosmos is indefinitely finite
> whats that?
>
> a cross between a billiard table
> ana sponge cake the Horse whispered
> in Lil's piercèd ear (134)

This, as Davidson has pointed out, is Olber's paradox, which theoretically describes the relation of the finite to the infinite ("To Eliminate" 139). On the "selvedge" of the two incompatible sides of the paradox, the finite totality and the infinite possibilities touch, as George Oppen might say. In Levinasian terms, this *edge* is where the Other manifests as the excess of the trace. Yet this paradox cannot be left by Dorn in an academic nonchalance that threatens to be another totalizing gesture of knowledge; instead, Dorn must exceed it by making an absurd joke of it. The "cross between a billiard table / ana sponge cake" makes only metaphoric "sense" and returns to the paradox a sense of strangeness.

Further, the impossible cohabitation of the linear with the multiplicity of uncertainty, another way of saying Olber's paradox (and another way of describing the form of the poem), is the site of the ethical relation. Davidson suggests that Dorn is liberating language from totalizing, exploitative systems ("To Eliminate" 148–49). And I would add that this liberation is part of the ethical enterprise of excess because freeing language from control and transcendental meaning also frees the self, community, and the Other. But this freeing is not merely an action that a man might play, for it is only a possibility opened in the pure expression of language, the "Obligation of the Divine."

Coda: A Hitch in the Ethics of Excess

In order to stay true to many of the claims I have made about uncertainty being ethical and to the spirit of a poet and a poem that refuses to take sides,

I cannot end this chapter without qualifying or unsaying some of my statements about the ethics in *Gunslinger*. Dorn's ethics and morality have been questioned elsewhere, and I too think there are problems with the poem that do not fit neatly into the kind of ethics of excess I am describing here.[32] At points, the poem explicitly disavows excess as a mechanism of ethics. For example, Sllab's final words via his messenger (made by Hughes, no less) make the connection between excess and *commercialization,* the very thing *Gunslinger* supposedly satires and resists: "altho there is much that I find sickening= / the excessive opulence & waste / the blatant commercialization" (165). Apparently not all excess is desirable, even if this passage is only a stab at Hughes because excessive consumption sustains his life of exploitative capitalism. And Sllab's disclaimer of all textual uncertainty seems to contradict my entire argument:

> Don't look for ambiguities
> or textual tickets
> as the vocabulary blended
> in this resumé
> prohibits the use of them
> "CLICK" (165)

Is this serious or tongue in cheek or both? In interviews, Dorn is often wary of "textual tickets," in other words, answers readily given to his poems. But how can one avoid ambiguities in *this* poem? The answers to these questions are impossible to divine, but one thing is sure: Even in denying excess, Dorn is excessive in turning satire on his own poetic and thereby ensuring undecidability.

Aside from its disclaimers, a major challenge to my ethical paradigm for *Gunslinger* is its negotiation of violence. For one, Robart/Rupert/Hughes himself serves as a caution to any ethical system, even one like mine that purports to reject systematicity itself. As Marjorie Perloff points out, the group cannot, ironically, help admiring Hughes, for they see the charm and "centerlessness" that make him a pop icon (Introduction ix). This, however, is a terrifying complicity. In terms of morality, Hughes reflects back to us the types of rationalizations that scientific knowledge and linear logic lead us to: "We're Scientists Al, Sometimes / we have to do things we hate" (*Gunslinger* 152). And in the interest of "science," Robart convinces Al to drop napalmlike hot oil on the "Single-Spacers" (who are, by the way, a "Low-Violence Army" a satire in itself in the context of Vietnam) and "to soakem / in all this draino" (152). The murderous intent is clear: "[T]his is no time for technological sentiment," screams Robart, "weve got to put those dusty feet / on the path to oblivion" (152). The problem is, through money and power, exploiters like Hughes can damage-control reality through misinformation campaigns without the public ever knowing about the destruction or even the wool over their eyes: "they'll think its all experimental," says a flippant Hughes (150). Such a statement, taken right out of the revolutionary tenets of the postmodern avant-garde, shows the shallowness of change done for its own sake and enamored with its own hipness. The complexity of the satire in Dorn's ethical vision teaches us never to trust any moral framework, and the implication is that even an ethics of excess based on "otherness" can be put to reactionary ends as Hughes's anonymous, centerless postmodernism demonstrates.

Very similar to Hughes's rationalized acts of terror, I's "act of oblivion" (153) in Book IIII is also problematic to an ethics of excess. How open to the Other is I being when

A 50 Caliber Derringer
sprung out of I's right sleeve
and drilled two test holes
in the managers skull (156)

Although murder, which I states that he "will enjoy" (153), is excessive in its own right, even more excessive is the joke I makes after he kills him: "Um, zymosis of the brain, I observed, peering thru the managers head" and mocking the trite seriousness of TV doctors. But it gets worse: "Those two flies mating on the opposite wall / were clean on line, still sitting there" (157). Additionally, none of the characters seem concerned, except Everything who only wants the manager's finger out of his ear. In fact, the Slinger ignores the whole thing and changes the subject, "Where's our poet the Slinger asked." This question is a moral one, where is our poet (i.e., Dorn) and his moral judgment that would make sense of this incident? Does an "ethics of excess" mean killing is OK as an act of political rebellion? As almost every other critic has pointed out by quoting I's line, "Entrapment is this society's / Sole activity . . . / and Only laughter / can blow it to rags" (155), there is a sense of political resistance in *Gunslinger*, especially considering the context of the Vietnam War. Also, Dorn's admiration for Dr. Samuel Johnson is clear in his interviews (*Interviews* 70–103). So, is he condoning I by quoting "as Dr. Johnson said: / if Public war be allowed / to be consistent with morality / Private war must be equally so" (156)? Or is this statement satirizing the entire idea of war by pushing it to its logical extreme: Of course we don't want legal private wars, so why should we have public ones? Yet this logic does not take into account that I does get away with murder, albeit one that seems to be understandable because it puts an end to the jerk manager who "kicked the table with a smirk / and presented the check" (156).

In spite of *Gunslinger*'s silence on these questions, Dorn does not leave us in a nihilistic void just because he does not provide a "correction" to society's ills (as does, say, Jonathan Swift's "Modest Proposal"). Such normative/normalizing judgment does not exist in Dorn's poem because, rather than working within the realm of politics or culture to change ethics, Dorn's satire questions what comprises the ethical itself. This questioning does not limit itself to asking what has gone wrong with society; rather, it posits a new take on the relation of the subject to the group (politics in the usual sense) and the normative relation of subjects to each other (morality in the traditional sense). For example, instead of gaining the key to a code of proper behavior from Parmenides, I achieves, through his "tour of the cumulus," an altogether new ethical mode. When Lil asks I about that "sicksties" stuff, I replies that living such an ethics is "[l]ike trying to read a newspaper / from nothing but the ink poured into your ear." In other words, although it is humorous and absurd, language is pure expression, like ink without content or form.[33] This pure expression is the saying of Dorn's "Obligation of the Divine" that requires a "poetry that's constantly written on air" (Interviews 66). As Levinas points out, *that* the Other speaks to me, not what is said, summons the singular being to responsibility for the collective (*Otherwise* 75–91, 157–58). I continues,

> First off,
> the lights go out on Thought
> and an increase in the thought of thought,
> plausibly flooded w/ darkness,
> in the shape of an ability
> to hear Evil praised (159)

This Nietzschean ability to stare into the abyss of uncertainty and lack of moral law ("Evil praised") is not to condone evil, but to face it, to admit one's complicity in "the assorted disasters / guaranteed to secure one's comfort" (159).[34] Ethics comes not from knowing the Right, but from self-questioning ("the thought of thought") and responding to the Other with the pure expression of an "Obligation of the Divine." In this spirit, I eventually qualifies his own violence. To the above line about blowing society's entrapment of us to rags, I tags the qualification, "*But* there is no negative pure enough / to entrap our Expectation" (155). I read this line not as the reestablishment of some *ideal* course for community to follow but as the persistence of a visionary *vision* that allows us continually to make a space for an Other who has not yet arrived and whom we can never know. Ex-spectation. To look out and take responsibility for the Other. This is the ethics of excess.

But such an ethics is not without risks. *Gunslinger* ultimately cannot defend itself from the ethical problems or the charges of immorality that I and others have raised, just as Dorn does not defend himself from charges of sexism, homophobia, or "counterrevolutionary" tendencies, because he is not dealing with ethics on the level of simply providing a "better louse trap." Perhaps Dorn does not want anyone to defend him here—as Wesling points out, he hungers for contradiction (60–1). This defenselessness, like Charles Reznikoff's lack of moral comment on the Holocaust, is the risk of an ethics of excess. Unlike Reznikoff, however, Dorn's ethics always wants too much, is too opinionated (von Hallberg 64–66), includes too many different kinds of people at its parties, stays too late, and is far too trusting. Yet its ethical power lies in its possibilities, in its (respons)ability to welcome the Other, no matter how atrocious, contradictory, or seemingly immoral (even if that welcome involves a fight). In fact, this type of ethics is an ethics only in the fact that it awaits an Other who may or may not come, who may kill and exploit, or who may join the community and be free in singularity. For without such an ethics that awaits the Other—that hopes for what is beyond hope, that inhabits what could be rather than just what is—transformation and change would never be possible, and things would remain as they are. If there is such a thing as a "better," more "ethical" political/moral world, as Jonathan Swift and Alexander Pope wagered there was, then we will never get there if we don't wander in the desert with the *Gunslinger* and wonder what *could be*.

The Body Ethical Robert Duncan's *Passages*

KING. But that I know love is begun by time,
And that I see, in passages of proof,
Time qualifies the spark and fire of it.
There lives within the very flame of love
A kind of wick or snuff that will abate it;
And nothing is at a like goodness still;
For goodness, growing to a plurisy,
Dies in his own too-much. (*Hamlet* IV.vii)

In the introduction to his 1968 volume of poetry titled *Bending the Bow*, Robert Duncan directly addresses perhaps the most important issue of the twentieth century: war. Although he was born the year after World War I and discharged from the U.S. Army during World War II due to his homosexuality, the impact of the Vietnam War is the primary ethical dilemma that preoccupies Duncan for most of his career after 1960. At various points in the book, he alludes to the far-reaching effects of the war via the images of mutilated bodies and destruction that were for the first time being beamed via uncensored TV signals into American living rooms (i). Unexpectedly, it is the figure of "the body," so vulnerable to the destruction wreaked by modern war and its mechanical, atomic, and chemical weapons, that Duncan takes up as his antidote/anti-strophe/antipode/antAres against the seemingly hopeless cycle of violence.

Formally, the introduction to *Bending the Bow* is incompatibly narrative and poetic, which makes it rather difficult to follow, but its structure provides a correlate of the paradoxes and tensions that pervade all of Duncan's work and demark his particular poethics. The narrative part of the introduction obliquely recounts a protest against the war at which Duncan is supposed to speak. Just before he is to go on stage, a line of soldiers confronts the unarmed protesters. In the midst of this "terrible wounded area," a confrontation converges between the bodies of soldiers and readers, which Duncan symbolizes respectively with the figures of the bow and the lyre.[1] Duncan asserts in the narrative that his poetry seeks a deep, visceral connection that might restore a "common humanity." It is necessary to do so,

Duncan believes, because such rigid, divisive boundaries are destroying us. Therein lies the ethical imperative of the poetic in Duncan's introduction:

> If the soul is the life-shape of the body, great stars, that are born and have their histories we read in the skies and will die, are souls. And this poetry, the ever forming of bodies in language in which breath moves, is a field of ensouling. Each line, intensely, a soul thing, a contribution; a locality of the living. (ii)

In this passage, Duncan explicitly conflates poetry and the body: the body/poem is the site of ethical responsibility in a time of war, a responsibility that goes beyond mere condemnation. But the interconnectedness does not stop with these two elements, as he magnifies them both astronomically to include the entire universe (similar to Charles Olson's proprioception but also a throwback to Louis Zukofsky's desire for totality, no doubt), which would connect all human beings regardless of political agenda. Contrary to most models, this universe, which he renames in the poem, "The Multiversity, *Passages* 21," is not total and closed, but collaged and open: "The part in its fitting does not lock but unlocks; what was closed is opend" (iv). Only through such exceeding of boundaries, Duncan testifies, can the poem heal a wounded people through love:

> But I have only the language of our commonness, alive with them as well as me, the speech of the audience in its refusal in which I would come into that confidence. The poem in which my heart beats speaks like to unlike, kind to unkind. The line of the poem itself confronts me where I must volunteer my love, and I saw, long before this war, wrath move in the music that troubles me. (iii)

Because the heart beating in the poem goes beyond mere metaphor for Duncan, the question that his work raises for us is how can exceeding the corporeal limits of the body through poetry lead us to a loving relationship with humanity. The poetic aspect of this introduction emerges not merely in the self-reflexive discussion of poetics, but also in its form. Duncan's syntax (e.g., "I saw, long before this war, wrath move in the music that troubles me"), his diction ("speaks like to unlike"), and his use of fragments and sound ("heart beats speaks") raise the introduction above mere narrative or pronouncement. Furthermore, the contradictory intertwining of narrative and poetry continually defers climax, interrupts predication, and disables argument. Such duality signals the deliberate tension that is the hallmark of Duncan's poetics.

These formal tensions raise the question of what the words "body" and "love" mean for Duncan, and how can they be ethical, especially when they are linked to sexuality. After all, many of Duncan's contemporary critics would not afford him, due to his perceived social "excesses," the title of ethical poet.[2] As a homosexual, as someone who more than just dabbled in the occult, as a man who led an unconventional social and political life, Duncan and his poetry are seen by many critics, then and even now, as brilliant but not necessarily a model of the Good Life. Coming out of a time in which "Free Love" was a bumper-sticker catchphrase, Duncan's notion of Eros can easily be obscured and not read for its full ethical significance. Because of its weighted, idealistic connotations, the word "love" was often rejected by the thinkers of the ethical turn.[3] Then, as it is today, "love" is also derided by conservative social forces as equivalent to a lawless and hedonistic promiscuity, so how can it defended as an ethical imperative? In this chapter, I will address these questions in the context of the long, open-ended series of *Passages* poems, the first thirty of which Duncan includes in *Bending the Bow*, that build on similar themes in many of his other writings in the 1950s and 1960s. Because he describes them retrospectively in the preface to *Ground Work: Before the War* as "a life/death tide back of the beat of the heart and the breath" as well as "passages of a poem beyond," the poems explicitly engage the issues of the body, language, form, subjectivity, and alterity that preoccupies the linguistic and ethical turns of postmodernity. More importantly, Duncan's poetic form—involving collage, paradox, unsaying, puns, gaps, and silences—engages these issues and enacts his embodied ethics.

Critics have tended to focus on the totalizing side of Duncan's poetics— his belief in a grand design, his interest in abstractness, totality, commonality, and wholeness. Here I am concerned, instead, with plucking, Ariadne-like, a thread in the other, complementary side of Duncan's poetics—that of particularity, openness, indeterminacy, and fragile embodiment—the side of the contradiction in Duncan's contradictory poetics that is obliged to alterity. This side has often been ignored to the detriment of Duncan studies in general. In asking the question, how does Duncan's poethics work, I kept returning to three recurrent ethical themes—alterity, sexuality, and love— and found that they all flow from the body for Duncan. The excess that Duncan's poetry enacts is to exceed the corporeal limits of the body through poetry and into otherness. For Duncan, the body opens us onto ethical relations through a process of poetic, disordering, and interpenetrating love. In my inquiry, I attempt to weave each of these threads together simultaneously rather than taking them one at a time, which Duncan's own fugal form would at any rate make impossible.

As I suggested in my discussion of the introduction to *Bending the Bow*, Duncan's paradoxical form keeps opposites interpenetrating, deconstructing, and reconstituting: narrative/poetry, self/Other, order/disorder, chord/discord, and so on, but not just on the level of thematic motifs. This poetics, which for Duncan amounts to an oscillating process as much as a typographical shape for his poem, pervades every level of his writing, from singular poems to long series to entire books and, ultimately, to his entire corpus. Duncan never stops contradicting himself or unsaying something he had previously said. But this contrapuntal form at each level pivots on the "threshold" (*Letters* ii) and seeks balance, what Duncan calls in *Bending the Bow*, "equilibrations" (61). This balance hangs on what Duncan will variably call the pivot, threshold, daimon, joint, trace, chord, inbinding—all akin to King Claudius's "wick." This threshold is the passage to the Other, whom Duncan calls "he does not know Whose Name" ("Parsifal," *Bending* 56). But this balance does not come for Duncan from parsing, minimalism, or discipline but through excess—excessive form, excessive themes, excessive emotion, and so forth. Rather than the excess leading us to the "could be" of possible futures, as it does in Edward Dorn's work, Duncan keeps us in the present moment, a moment that is not static but dynamic, always changing and open to the Other.

Amoral Life

Perhaps people interested in the moral issues of poetry pass over Duncan not only because of his lifestyle but also because of his own unease with the relation of morality to aesthetics. In a September 1957 letter to Robin Blaser, for example, Duncan confesses how the two issues "gnaw" at him, even though he clearly divorces them from poetry: "But it is the difficult equilibrium; the aesthetic and the moral are harpies for me as a poet. The poetic is neither, makes its truce or its war or its collaboration with those other modes as it can. I do find every conflict of allegiance in myself" ("Letters on Poetry" 114). In separating the "poetic" from the "moral" and the "aesthetic," Duncan presents us with a challenge for reading his poetry in an ethical mode. What does Duncan mean by "morality" or "ethics"? These two signifiers, like all the others Duncan employs, are susceptible to his paradoxical poetic process. Often, as in "Orders, *Passages* 24" or "The Torso, *Passages* 18," Duncan is concerned with "the good" and with order and obedience. Elsewhere, as in his

1961 essay "Ideas of the Meaning of Form," Duncan rails against enlightenment, rational ethics where "the goal is a system or reason, motive or morality, some set of rules and standards that will bring the troubling plentitude
of experience 'within our power'" (*Fictive* 102–3). Duncan seeks instead a
poetics and life "without bounds" that exceeds moral rules "where the counterpart of free verse may be free thought and free movement" (103). As an
antidote to rationality, Duncan writes that "love and knowledge are conditions that life imposes upon us if we would come into her melodies" (104).
Tellingly, in the last line of the letter to Blaser, Duncan defines morality in
terms of an Objectivist sincerity of being "true," so it is no wonder, as with
his Objectivist predecessors, he and his poetry simply do not fit most definitions of ethics as rules, codes, or moral laws.

There are some exceptions to the rejection of Duncan's life and poetry
as amoral, the most notable being Enikó Bollobás who sees Duncan's ethics
as founded on a liberal political ideology and a hippie, environmentally
friendly ecology. In this model, ethics is a search for an "inner law" based on
"humility," to which the poet should remain "true" (Bollobás 47, 50). Echoing Duncan's own definition of morality, Bollobás's claim provides insight-
ful readings for poems such as "The Multiversity, *Passages* 21," in which the
legislative Duncan denounces the Evil that silences that inner law (*Bending*
70–73), support Bollobás's claim.[4] Unfortunately, this remains a view of
Duncan as legislator, a stance that ignores the role of paradox and that Duncan himself has rejected. I feel that, contrary to some views, Duncan has a
far more postmodern understanding of ethics.[5] For example, Duncan rejects normative morality when he claims that evil is often called good by
institutions and cultures. "The moralist," Duncan writes in *Bending the Bow*,
echoing Dorn's "Obligations of the Divine," "must always be outraged by
what God finds Good" (vii). For in "In the Place of a Passage 22," Freedom is,
paradoxically, the Law, and Duncan turns legislation into permission. Under
this logic of contradiction, Law is not simply a limit but the excess of freedom, a following the contours of an open field, or better yet, poetry. As the
preceding "The Multiversity, *Passages* 21" tells us:

vowels sung in a field in mid-morning

      awakening the heart from its oppressions.

Evil "referrd to the root of *up, over*"
simulacra of law that wld over-rule
      the Law man's inner nature seeks, (*Bending* 72)

Here we see not only the "inner" law that Bollobás points to as the source of Duncan's nonviolent ethics but also the emphasis on ethics as something that is "true," as a vowel sung in a morning field. This law, which paradoxically for Duncan is freedom and permission, represents what Bruce Andrews calls, as I detailed in my introduction, the libidinal force of the Structuralist view of language that seeks to release energies and drives. But ethical "trueness" is the necessary counterweight to this libidinal free-for-all. In the preface to his 1958 volume of poetry, *Letters*, Duncan describes this delicate balance of opposites. In the context of asking what happens when sexual impulses are transformed into poetry (which he calls bodily "specializations" like the shells, fur, and combs of animals), Duncan writes that the goal is "to maintain ourselves at that threshold, as if satisfied, to work with a constant excitement at play" (ii). The lack of balance in the current historical climate, according to Duncan, has led to a privileging of science, which he equates with war, over art. When this happens, science is "irresponsible, in which diseases and explosions appear as inevitable pragma." As a counterweight to scientists, there are "the artists, whose delirium is responsible, appearing in the desire for a new order which radiates from their works" (ii–iii). In *Letters*, Duncan morphs "trueness" to a responsible "delirium," which is also a "tuning": "And here I declare a mood, a mode, in writing, conceived as a tuning of the language, as the ear, hand and eye, brain are tuned—towards a possible music" (iv). By the time *Bending of the Bow* is written, the lyre is tuned to an ontological reality that is *polysemous*, to use Duncan's term, and sometimes beyond the grasp of reason (*Fictive* 143). In "The Light, *Passages*, 28," Duncan invokes

> Pegasos / that great horse Poetry,   Rider
>   we ride, who make up
>   the truth of What Is (*Bending* 122)

Drawing on passages like this, some critics view Duncan's ethics in the mode of an ontological ethics in that the poetry stays true to *what is*, much in the Objectivist mode of "sincerity."[6] In the above passage from his letters to Blaser, Duncan clearly states that morality for poetry is "that it should be 'true,'" and the inference—based on the text of the above letter in which he next quotes a passage from William Carlos Williams—is that this is a being "true" to what is. Duncan then states that "I would keep the morality that asks that a poem not gratify, but testify. 'Only the passion endures' Pound wrote—and the passion is not (as the god damnd psychoanalysts at times suggest) a storm within but an energy defined in its participation in the real by its objective" ("Letters on Poetry" 114). Although he quotes Ezra Pound and alludes to Zukofsky ("objective") as his support for a new morality, the emphasis on "not gratify, but testify" also aligns Duncan with Charles Reznikoff's notion of testimony as nonviolently facing alterity in the poem. As Duncan implies in recounting his experience at an anti–Vietnam War protest, to be true to oneself is an ethics "to hold the ground of our testimony stubbornly, the individual volition of a non-violent action" (*Bending* iii).

Duncan's essay "Ideas of the Meaning of Form" (*Fictive* 1961) was published three years before he began writing the *Passages* poems, but the essay opens with many of the same motifs that inhabit the long poetic series:

> Phases of meaning in the soul may be like phases of the moon, and, though rationalists may contend against the imagination, all men may be one, for they have their source out of the same earth, mothered in one ocean and fathered in the light and heat of one sun that is not tranquil but rages between its energy that is a disorder seeking higher intensities and its fate or dream of perfection that is an order where all light, heat, being, movement, meaning and form, are consumed toward the cold. The which [*sic*] men have imagined in the laws of thermodynamics. (*Fictive* 89)

This prose gives us a little insight into why Duncan put into play in *Passages* figures of the sun and moon, mothers and fathers, science and myth, ocean and sky—each involves unity, origins, or a passage from one binary to another—but its form is even more instructive on that theme. The next paragraph, with its opening volta, predictably contradicts the previous:

> But if our life is mixed, as the suspicion comes from the Gnostics and from Blake, and rays of many stars that are suns of all kinds, Aie! if we are so many fathered, or if, as theosophists have feared, we were many mothered in the various chemistries of the planets . . . Thus, I say, "Let the light rays mix," and, against the Gnostics, who would free the sparks of spirit from what is the matter, and against the positivists and semanticists who would free the matter from its inspirational chaos, I am glad that there is night and day, Heaven and Hell, love and wrath, sanity and ecstasie [*sic*], together in a little place. Having taken thought upon death, I would be infected by what is." (*Fictive* 89)

Although it is logically impossible to have a cosmology of wholeness and a dualistic worldview at the same time, Duncan is trying to do just that. To be "infected by what is" is not merely to have a rational or even a phenomenological experience because "what is" is contradictory and paradoxical: "imagination appears as an intuition of the real" (92). It remains other to the systems of thought and interpretation that Duncan spends the majority of this essay critiquing. "Taste, reason, rationality rule, and rule must be absolute and enlightened," Duncan writes ironically, "because beyond lies the chiaroscuro in which forces co-operate and sympathies and aversions mingle" (91). But the ceasing of rational order and perfection is not only an aesthetic goal, it is ethical: "The end of masterpieces . . . the beginning of testimony." This testimony of what is not only stays true to reality, albeit a chaotic, dynamic reality in Duncan's view, but also desires "a free association of living things . . . for my longing moves beyond governments to a cooperation" (90). As the repetition of this word in the above passages attests, this "cooperation" is not a simple harmony but a harmony and discord comingled. Duncan seeks the movement toward "a universe of psychic correspondences, toward a life where men and things were beginning to mix and cross boundaries of knowledge" (91). The title to the essay collection, *Fictive Certainties*, which includes this text, suggests this paradoxical goal.

A Bodily Poethics

This will to testify provides a missing balance to the ontological view of Duncan's ethics because it restores Duncan's idea that poetry constitutes and is not merely constituted by reality, in a similar fashion that the linguistic turn defines language. "From the body of the poem, all that words create," Duncan writes in "Stage Directions, *Passages* 30" (*Bending* 128). In the introduction to *Bending the Bow*, Duncan puts it this way: "The poem is not a stream of consciousness, but an area of composition in which I work with whatever comes into it. . . . In which meanings and ideas, themes and things seen, arise. . . . The commune of Poetry becomes so real that he sounds each particle in relation to parts of a great story that he knows will never be completed. A word has the weight of an actual stone in his hand" (vi). "The Light, *Passages* 28" emblematizes this paradox:

and, as if Eros unbound, AntEros / bound
free to love, Chrysaor / of the golden sword—

> twins of that vision in which from the
> old law's   terrible sentence

wingd   the new law springs

> •

> darkling

lumen (*Bending* 122–23)

Not only do we see here the paradox of "bound" is "free," Duncan presents us with Pegasus's twin brother, Chrysaor, who along with Pegasus, was born of the blood from Medusa's severed head. Thus, poetry is twinned with AntEros—and anti-Eros who is also "bound / free to love"—the sword bearer who presumably destroys. In this pair, from the old law of pronouncement and morality, springs the new law of paradox, involving both dark and light, both equally bound. In fact, as the introduction of *Bending the Bow* implies, this law is actually "a multitude of laws" (v). Like Christ, this new law is "to be made or revealed anew as Love, the lasting reason and intent of What Is—this deepest myth of what is happening in poetry moves us as it moves words" (vii). But like poetry that "will never be completed," love initiates an open-ended process, much like the *Passages* themselves, which exceeds a single idea of "What Is" in order to attend on who or what is to come. In his contemporaneous essay on Dante's work, Duncan declares that Poetry, Love, and the Real are one, "they have their source in the same literal ground of the poem" (*Fictive* 143).

In this being true to "What Is" as loving testimony, Duncan is also being true to the larger ethical battle (which he cannot see but can feel in his body) being waged above the specific sides of the confrontation outlined in Duncan's narrative in the introduction of *Bending the Bow:* "The poet of the event senses the play of its moralities belongs to the configuration he cannot see but feels in terms of fittings that fix and fittings that release the design out of itself as he works to bring the necessary image to sight" (iv–v). To provide a moral counterweight to "fittings that fix," provided in abundance by America's military-industrial complex during the post–World War II period, Duncan's side of this argument involves "fittings that release," and these fittings are poetic—image, tuning, contradiction. Duncan, like Dorn, insists that providing an alternative is the poet's responsibility, and for Duncan fulfilling this responsibility requires a body with eyes that can see and/or ears that can hear and/or a mouth that can speak and/or a hand that can write.

We can see Duncan grappling with these same ethical terms as early as the mid-1950s. In a letter to Robin Blaser dated June 18, 1957, Duncan addresses the ethics of the poetic line:

> Re: responsibility=the ability to respond. To keep, that is, the touch green=necessary. In the poem this means shedding of effect. The right word is a tone (as in painting color) cluster, a felt stress in a recognized

movement defining the time of the poem, a reference (moving toward meaning that might be non-sense or theme or janus-faced) which in turn has another tone (mood, mode), a proposition of a possible syntax (ORDER) (DISORDER). Achievement here comes neither from talent nor from genius—but from conviction (gnosis/feeling) in awareness of the actual order and disorder of the universe. ("Letters on Poetry" 107)

What Duncan means exactly in this passage is not readily evident, but what is immediately evident is that Duncan does not define "responsibility" as adherence to a prescribed set of duties placed on the subject from an authority above. It is instead "the ability to respond," which leaves the actual response open to choice and interpretation as "conviction," which Duncan says elsewhere must be strife with oneself (*Fictive* 111). Contrarily, responsibility also is not a choice and involves disorder imposed on the poet. That Duncan chose to repeat the saying, "responsibility=the ability to respond," in his 1960 poem, "The Law I Love Is Major Mover," attests to its importance in Duncan's ethics during this period (*Opening* 10). This "janus-faced" focus on the moment between order/disorder and choice/imposition, which is "both here-and-now and eternity" (*Fictive* 87), distinguishes Duncan's ethics: "Becoming conscious, becoming aware of the order of what is happening is the full responsibility of the poet" (82). As he says of responsibility, it cannot determine how one understands that moment of threshold, but is only the "ability to respond" and, as indeterminate, leaves an opening for alterity. Indeed, "the order of what is happening" is for Duncan not a static or knowable structure or law, but a protean process or oscillation. This "ability to respond" that does not impose an order on what is to be said brings Duncan's notion of responsibility close to Levinas's notion of the saying, which is ethical expression before content.

Since Duncan's ethics is not predetermined by a universal law or indicative imperative but instead governed by responsibility, it is, in a sense, open to what cannot be conceived, what is other: "It is a boundary beyond our understanding" (*Bending* i). His ethics also is, in a sense, total—not that it totalizes in static order, but in that the responsibility is, as Levinas describes, inescapable. Stephen Fredman in *The Grounding of American Poetry* recognizes Duncan's paradoxical mode as an ethical stance in which he evidences "an awareness of one's complete responsibility for everything the I/eye perceives" (111). In discussing the ethical and political purpose of *Passages* in his 1968 essay "Man's Fulfillment in Order and Strife," Duncan equates this responsibility with raising "a conscience of order and disorder" that turns "moral outrage" over the war in Vietnam to complete responsibility for everything "so that the crimes of the Nation are properly my own, of having, in other words, a burden of original sin in the history of the Nation" (*Fictive* 130).

Next, this responsibility is again located for Duncan in the body, as "a felt stress," a "touch" or "gnosis/feeling," which is more capable than judgment ("talent" or "genius") in sensing the "rightness" of a particular tone or color. The point of this sensitivity to the body is that it allows the poet to be sincere, true to what is, what is given to the senses and to perception. In *Phenomenology of Perception*, which was first published in 1945 and translated into English in 1962, Maurice Merleau-Ponty similarly describes the body as the inescapable element of existence and perception, which he calls a "situation." As Toril Moi has shown, this body-as-situation is not the same as merely being in a situation (*What Is a Woman?* 62–72). In Merleau-Ponty's terms, the body is instead both the empirical "barest raw material" of flesh and also the "hidden *form* of being ourself [*sic*]" that must be interpreted (*Phenomenology* 165). In Duncan's terms, the body is the "What Is" of the subject. Moreover, the notion of the body-as-situation is crucial because it erases boundaries between the body and the mind as well as the body and the world. Duncan undertakes a similar phenomenological deconstruction of the mind/body split. As "The Earth, *Passages* 19" demonstrates, more is at stake in Duncan's employment of the body than the creation of mere matter necessary for an experience of subjectivity, defined as an individual person. In fact, the body is intricately implanted in the earth and universe. He quotes the Renaissance philosopher and mystic, Jacob Boehme:

> . . . for the stars have their kingdom in the veins of
> the body which are cunning passages (and the sun
> has designd the arteries)   where they drive forth
> the form, shape and condition of man (*Bending* 66)

Not only do the sun and stars "drive forth" the very veins of the body, as in the leaves of plants, but those veins are literally "passages," which the poem rhymes figuratively with "the words upon the page," the passages of writing. These passages, like blood, "flow away into" the page, and through this cosmic network, language is capillaried with the body. In a letter to Jack Spicer, Duncan proposes "a sensualitie of meaning" in which the "texture" of the language can literally impress the reader ("Letters on Poetry" 98). This texture is the embodiment of the sign in the figure of "the Angel Syntax" that pervades Duncan's work and serves as a mediator between the earthly and divine:[7]

```
        twisted out of shape, crippled
     by angelic Syntax
Look!    the Angel that made a man of Jacob
     made Israël in His embrace
```

was the Law,   was Syntax. (*Opening* 11)

Here, the angel, who also exists linguistically as the law of syntax, shapes the man and the nation in a bodily "embrace." Of course, the reverse is true in that the body of the man shapes the syntax. Duncan writes in an essay published the same year as *Bending the Bow* that great writers like Blake are "intensely incarnate" in their words and claims that "this idea of poetry is a very special one I've got, I *have* got it, it *has* me. In the intensity of the work, it, Poetry, gives me orders" (*Fictive* 124). Merleau-Ponty also describes during this time a paradoxical connection of the body to language. Continuing from the passage above, he writes:

> If we therefore say that the body expresses existence at every moment, this is in the sense in which a word expresses thought. Anterior to conventional means of expression, which reveal my thoughts to others only because already, for both myself and them, meanings are provided for each sign, and which in this sense do not give rise to genuine communication at all, we must, as we shall see, recognize a primary process of signification in which the thing expressed does not exist apart from the expression, and in which the signs themselves induce their significance externally. In this way the body expresses total existence, not because it is an external accompaniment to that existence, but because existence realizes itself in the body. This incarnate significance is the central phenomenon of which body and mind, sign and significance are abstract moments. (165–66, italics mine)

In this passage, which elaborates the linguistic aspect of the body-as-situation, Merleau-Ponty makes an analogy between the body and language. The thing expressed, the sign, does not exist apart from its expression just as the body is not an existent but the expression of existence itself. In this way, language and the body coincide. However, the analogy disappears when the body is a sign and doesn't just work *like* one. As Duncan writes in his 1983 essay "The Self in Postmodern Poetry," "[b]ut here (for poetry is, as Mallarmé long ago reminded us, written with words, not ideas) I mean how I hear or read the word 'self' to mean" (*Fictive*, 219). As with poetry, Duncan understands that subjectivity is mediated by language, as is the "body." This understanding allows Duncan to see his poetry as interpenetrating with the body through language.

The notion of the body-as-situation, glossed in terms of a relation to language, can clarify what the body means for Duncan's *Passages* poems. Not only are the mind, soul, and body fused and indistinguishable in the incarnate subject, but they are also infused into the poem.[8] Olson and Duncan's famous phrase, *composition by field*, does not simply denote a process accomplished by a detached artist separated from the work but is more a writing through the body and a writing the body into the poem. Composition by body, another way to describe Duncan's poetics, purports a unique relationship between the body and the poem, a relationship that includes the poet's body and the body of the poem. In regard to the latter, as Davidson points out in *Ghostlier Demarcations*, Duncan insisted that his publishers follow his exact layout instructions. Their failure to do so led Duncan to skip the middleman and to publish his straight typescripts as mimeograph packets or as *Ground Work: Before the War*. This attention to the material details of the text on the page shows that for Duncan the structure of the poem's body is integral to the poem's meaning (177–79). As we see in "The Collage, *Passages* 6," the body is inseparable from (or at least congruent with) the field of the poem:

> This way below is the way above,
>
> the mouth of the cave or temple growing moist
>
>   shining,   to allow   the neophyte
>   full entrance.
>
> The body of the poem, aroused,   having
>
>   what mouths? (*Bending* 19)

The passageway described here, possibly a vaginal or anal opening, evokes and arouses the body of the poem. Similarly, "As In the Old Days, *Passages* 8" equates in a long chain the passage of the birth canal with the passage of birth with the rites of passage of life/love with the passage of the poem—all are brought to bear in the poem. However, this does not mean that the body encompasses the entire universe, as it does in Williams's *Paterson* where the entire city-poem is figured, at the end of the first part, as a body. For Duncan, the body does not symbolize something larger or abstract. Quite the contrary. The body in Duncan's poetry always figures as the other of the subject—a material, human body—so when the body is thought of as a limited, existential situation, then it becomes entangled in the intersections of many different forces, experiences, objects, and matter. In fact, that node of specific relations in a situation (economics, sexuality, politics, history, morality, ethics, sex, genetics, environment, family, community) is the body. Drawing on Merleau-Ponty's notion of body-as-situation, Simone de Beauvoir writes in *The Second Sex* that the human being is "an historical idea" and is not limited to certain imposed notions of "natural" fact (34). Thus, when thought of as a body, Duncan's poetics of incarnation and "composition by field" become the inverse of the totalization with which he is often credited. Instead, the poem emerges as a historical gathering of infinite relations which, as Charles Altieri points out, is an event of destruction as well as creation (*Enlarging* 159). This poetic series of *Passages* also contains history, as Duncan says of Dante's and Pound's work, in a way that grounds the poem in the literal (body) of the day (*Fictive* 143–44). This ground serves as the most visceral aspect of the "What Is" because a body moves through it every day. In "The Fire, *Passages* 13," the most dominant strain in that daily ground is the war in Vietnam. Like many of the *Passages* to come, "Fire" is an adamant antiwar poem, and it doesn't shirk from pronouncement: "Satan looks forth from men's faces . . . the look of Stevenson lying in the U.N. that our Nation save face" (*Bending* 43). The thing to notice about this passage is its use of a body part central to the rhetoric of the ethical turn, namely the face, to expose "the glints of the evil that one sees in the power of this world" (44). For Duncan, the face opens the history of the body and the poem.

The Other Body

In keeping with the oscillating poetics I have been tracing in his work, Duncan's poetry exhibits a concomitant concern for otherness to compliment the immanent exploration of the "What Is." Several critics have explored the role of alterity in Duncan's texts, but few consider this working of otherness as an ethical event.[9] Yet we can tell Duncan, from the mid-1950s to the late 1960s, was concerned with traces of otherness that lie "beyond" the poem not only in terms of content but also of form. In another letter to Blaser from November 5, 1957, Duncan lists three goals for his poetry: "It's certainly that I want universal figures to move in the poems, for the art to evoke otherness, and to view the personal only as incident" ("Letters on Poetry" 115). "The first experience in poetry," Duncan writes later in 1968, "is to find in words not an argument or an explanation but a world, to see an other world or to be of an other world" (*Fictive* 122). The space Duncan places between "an" and "other" show his emphasis on the latter. The title poem of *Bending the*

Bow, which plays on the contrary figures of the bow and lyre set up in the introduction, also evokes an alterity in distinction to the "What Is," a tension that plays throughout the *Passages* poems also in the book. Flowing against the current of everyday life are the "Day's duties,"

> the litter
> of coffee cups and saucers,
> carnations painted growing upon whose surfaces. The whole
> composition of surfaces leads into the other
> current disturbing
> what I would take hold of. (7)

"The other current" enacts what Duncan calls in the introduction "the interruption of our composure," the "discords," and the "dissatisfaction in all orders" (ix). As the poem continues, however, Duncan associates this neutral "other current" with a correspondent, a woman to whom Duncan writes letters "reaching to touch / ghostly exhilarations in the thought of her" (7). His response-abilty, then, is not just to the opposition of alterity to what is, but to the Other who interrupts the writing of the letter. As with Oppen and Reznikoff, Duncan uses the words of others as a way to evoke otherness. Judging from both the title, "*Passages,*" and the "Notes" section that ends *Bending the Bow,* quotation constitutes a major formal element—as product and process—of Duncan's poetics in this series. As I argued in relation to Oppen, this method opens poetry to the Other by letting the Other speak through his or her own words.[10] At any rate, the three goals he sets for his poetry—universals, otherness, and the self-effacement—could only coexist in a poetics of paradox because, as Duncan says of his own poetic process, strife is the "breaking up the order I belong to in order to come into alien orders" (*Fictive* 112). Thus, an ulterior meaning of the title of "Orders, *Passages* 24" breaks up the idea of the current political regime waging war in Vietnam in order to reveal "another order" of the ethical good (*Bending* 80).

The following passage from "Variations on Two Dicta of William Blake," which was written in 1960 (Bertholf, *Bibliography* 239), published in *Poetry* magazine in 1961 and again in *Roots and Branches* (1964), constructs a relation between Being (what is) and the Other (alterity):

There was the event there was.

That is

recomposed in the witholding

The whole of time waits like a hand
    trembling upon the edge of another hand
    trembling upon the edge of not caring
    trembling upon the edge of its eternal answer

    That is

not ours in the witholding.

We wait, two Others, outside ever
    our eternal being

    That is

here, in this sad tableau too,
    (for us, unwilling actors)
    rapture. (*Roots* 52)

Reminiscent of Heidegger's description in "The Origin of the Work of Art,"
Being is not a static totality to Duncan, nor is it a process, total in itself, as
some critics might suggest (Johnson 22). Instead, this withholding, rather
than being solidly centered or self-possessed, is "trembling upon the edge"
of what could be called otherness in a handshake or caress, that is, "another
hand." And aside from this withholding of Being not being proper to "us,"
our relationship to it is that of a relationship to someone beyond Being,
"outside ever / our eternal being." This relationship for Duncan makes the
body not autonomous but obligated, a body-for-the-Other. Incidentally,
the capitalization in the phrase, "We . . . two Others," suggests that Duncan
is engaging the contemporary philosophical debate about alterity. In the last
stanza of "Variations" Duncan locates this relation to otherness beyond
being "here, in this sad tableau," which I read not only as the stage of the
actors but also their literal stage, their bodies, and the surface of the poem as
well. This tableau of the body is "sad" because it implies the loneliness of the
proscenial separation that implies unwillingness. Paradoxically, the body-
for-the-Other is also the possibility of rapture, dramatic and sexual. This
paradox of sadness and ecstasy is much like Dorn's *ekstasis* in that it implies
what Levinas calls *sociality*, but Duncan's relationship to the Other in his
poetry and poetics is always embodied. Likewise, this idea that the body
opens the subject to the Other was common during the ethical turn of mid-
century. For Merleau-Ponty, the hand is the part of the body that initially
opens us to the Other. For Luce Irigaray it is a woman's lips, and for Levinas
it is the face:

Hence one may in particular wonder whether such a "relation" (the ethical relation) does not impose itself through a radical separation between the two hands, which in point of fact do not belong to the same body, nor to a hypothetical or only metaphorical intercorporeity. It is that radical separation, and the entire ethical order of sociality, that appears to me to be signified in the nakedness of the face illuminating the human visage, but also in the expressivity of the other person's whole sensible being, even in the hand one shakes. (*Outside* 101–2)

As Levinas writes in 1961, "the whole body—a hand or a curve of the shoulder —can express as the face" (*Totality* 262). Because a person's "whole sensible being" faces the Other in nakedness, sensuality and sexuality are key phenomena in ethical relations. This notion, indebted to Freudian psychoanalysis, is widely held during this period, especially by Duncan.

Sexuality informs the figure of the body in Duncan's poetry and poetics as the site of an ethical relationship with alterity.[11] In "The Torso, *Passages* 18" (hereinafter "The Torso"), Duncan fully explores this notion of the situated, poetic body-for-the-Other. In the following passage, the poem emphasizes the uncertainty that the body as expressive sign implies:

> If he be Truth
> I would dwell in the illusion of him
>
> His hands unlocking from chambers of my male body
>
> such an idea in man's image
>
> rising tides that sweep me towards him
>
> . . . *homosexual?* (*Bending* 63)

The poem begins seemingly to idealize and universalize this body, a "torso," by objectifying it and calling attention to its beauty and abstract truth. But the universals ("Truth" and "Beauty") are as illusory as the naturalness of heterosexuality. They must be dwelled in and interrogated, as indicated in the question mark, to unlock the alterity and ambiguity within the body. This is why Duncan must emblazon the lover's body, to show the concrete, existential ground for the meanings that eventually exceed that specific site and open onto the body of the Other:

> At the root of the neck
>
> *the clavicle,* for the neck is the stem of the great artery
> upward into his head that is beautiful

At the rise of the pectoral muscles

the nipples, for the breasts are like sleeping fountains
    of feeling in man, waiting above the beat of his heart,
    shielding the rise and fall of his breath, to be
    awakened (*Bending* 63)

The crucial thing to note about this passage is that the meaning of the body starts in observation of the material without making that body just an objective correlative of the incisive poetic vision. The details stand on their own and do not refer to anything beyond themselves, nor do they, as in scientific discourse, simply serve as the positivist data from which to derive a hypothesis. The poem continues in the same balanced mode for two more stanzas, detailing the midriff and groin, respectively, and the body of the Other begins to take on ethical significance in a sexual context:

At the root of the groin

the pubic hair, for the torso is the stem in which the man
    flowers forth and leads to the stamen of flesh in which
    his seed rises (*Bending* 64)

The groin, which like the body is ambiguous and open to interpretation, forms the passage between torso and penis. In this passage, "the man / flowers forth" and is connected to all others through "his seed" (see fig. 1).

In a letter to Blaser in 1958, Duncan points out the pun "[t]hat *pubes* (the lovely hair of the private parts) and public are etymologically identical" and emphasizes the "contrapuntal" relationship between singular being and community ("Letters on Poetry" 117). What is more, this social relationship occurs in the situation that is the body, and this bodily relation is the opening of sexual desire, "to be awakened." Beyond the play of opposites, this embodied, and thus sexual, desire opens the body as a potential ethical agent in relation to the Other.

Sexuality as Ethics

Rather than being a hindrance to this embodied ethical response, as was conventionally thought in mid-twentieth-century American morality, sexuality becomes crucial to ethics both in terms of sexual desire and sexual orientation. With his 1944 article "The Homosexual in Society," Duncan became one of the first homosexual men (let alone artist-intellectuals) to openly avow his own gayness and also to argue for its acceptance in American society. What is more important to my argument, though, is that Duncan,

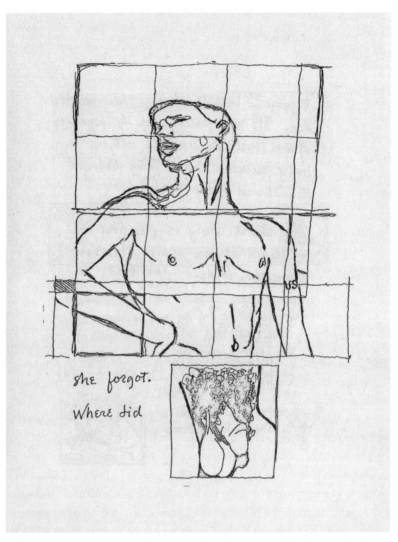

she forgot.

Where did

1. Illustration of torso from *Play Time: Pseudo Stein*, in a section titled "1942, A Story."
Dated "1/5/53," this book was not published until 1969, one year after *Bending of the
Bow*. Courtesy Literary Estate of Robert Duncan.

in his 1959 revisions, makes this not a plea for identity politics but a call to
"share in the creation of a human community good" (*Selected Prose* 38). His
argument is that, aside from being othered by mainstream society, a person's
sex and sexuality make a difference in the way she/he relates to the Other.
Yet, even with this difference, Duncan describes the original urgency to write
this essay, the desire to say, as a "public responsibility" (39). This responsi-

bility, the ability and necessity of responding to the Other, here in the form of an essay pleading for a common humanity, is the "agenda" of otherness in Duncan's poetry. This responsibility, born in the strife of sexualized love, is the beginning of ethics. Many writers during the ethical turn shared this characterization of the body as an intersection of the sexual and the ethical. Merleau-Ponty writes:

> Metaphysics—the coming to light of something beyond nature—is not localized at the level of knowledge: it begins with the opening out upon "another," and is to be found everywhere, and already, in the specific development of sexuality. . . . Sexuality is neither transcended in human life nor shown up at its centre by unconscious representations. It is at all times present there like an atmosphere. (167–68)

In other words, sexuality—both in terms of being a sexed being and in terms of sexual orientation—is an ethical relation because through it the subject opens to the Other. Pervading us like "an atmosphere," sexuality materially manifests ethical responsibility in interpersonal dynamics. With its pervasive nature not arising in knowledge, sexuality is ethical because it precedes judgment and exclusion. While it must be emphasized that sexuality does not determine every relationship nor is every relationship about having sex, sex and sexuality for Merleau-Ponty pervade the very situation of the situated body. Humans are situated sexually toward one another. And in Duncan's poetry, this sexuality is the most important expression of relation to an Other.

This ethical turn in the phenomenology of the body during this postmodern period does not take "sexuality" for granted but underscores that it too, like "the body," must be interpreted like a language. Hence, the linguistic turn accompanies the ethical one. For Merleau-Ponty, the body is (like) a language because it opens and closes the subject to others in spite of and because of its ambiguity: "Taken in this way, as an ambiguous atmosphere, sexuality is co-extensive with life. In other words, ambiguity is of the essence of human existence, and everything we live or think has always several meanings" (*Phenomenology* 169). It is important to note here that for Merleau-Ponty, as for Duncan, sexuality is at the heart of human existence. But if the sexuality of the body opens it to the Other both physically and linguistically, then Duncan's poetry should also be pervaded with ambiguity. "To be alive itself," Duncan writes in 1966, "is a form involving organization in time and space, continuity and body, that exceeds clearly our conscious design" (*Fictive* 82).

It is the exceeding of conscious design and embracing of bodily ambiguity that Duncan seeks in his use of collage form, which is the subject of "The Collage, *Passages* 6." In the opening of the poem, Duncan points out the morphological similarity of the body to the alphabet. He explicitly refers to Henry Miller's description of a woman's genitals as "the cunt," "the Delta," "his vehicle and / Her zone." Interestingly, after the word *cunt* appears, Duncan inserts an aside that interrupts the poem and clarifies his poetics: "I mean to force up emblems again into these passages of a poetry," as if he were anxious about the epithet. This bracketed aside not only thematically addresses sexuality, but it mimics the phallic thrust that forces the line into the passage, "the life-door" (*Bending* 19). In this context, Duncan's use of form captures the body's ambiguity in sexuality:

> no word, it's that clear,   is
> soft, shit, painty   •   Can consonants
>   so crawl or blur   to give . . .
> contrive to imitate juices, excretions, the body's
>   spit?
>   beyond how wet the air will
>   come and carry these vowels?
>   these dentals, labials, the tongue
> so adamantly insists upon? (19–20)

This passage abounds with puns that blur the distinction between "the language, the sea, the body," and most of them are sexual innuendos (e.g., "tongue," "labials," "spit," "wet"). Contradictory, Duncan says that no word is "soft," but later in the poem he writes, "this block with E for elefant is throne, is soft, and as far as I get in the play." In this play, sexuality is as much a part of language as it is our bodies. Moreover, the interrogative form of many of these lines increases their indeterminacy.

As "The Collage, *Passages* 6" indicates, Duncan was dedicated to that form. Through its paratactic placement of words that leaves exposed the seams of connection, collage reveals an ambiguous passage that signals an ethical relation with the Other. The body, like the poem, has a form. But that form includes a pivot, a navel, a bowel, a passage, that turns it back on itself, doubles it, and makes it Other to itself.[12] Duncan uses this figure in "The Torso":

> At the axis of his mid hriff [*sic*]
>
> *the navel,* for in the pit of his stomach the chord from
>   which first he was fed has its temple (*Bending* 64)

The navel indicates the middle of the body, the axis where it bends in half. Tellingly, this figure forms the axis and navel of the poem itself—it appears as the middle stanza—and is acknowledged thematically as "the chord" that first bound him to another, his mother. The musical spelling of the word *chord* emphasizes the centrality of musical form to ethical relationship, which I will discuss shortly. That the body is flexible, like language, makes it porous and available to the Other—first the mother and then the lover. Like the blood that fills the umbilical cord, the body's flexibility morphs into fluidity. Duncan invokes this fluidity earlier in the poem: "His hands unlocking from chambers of my male body . . . and at the treasure of his mouth / pour forth my soul" (*Bending* 63). This pouring forth of the soul connotes linguistic, familial, and sexual union. As Jack Rudman asks using the language of Martin Buber's *I/Thou,* "Why does so strenuous, though not strained, an act of mind remind me that I live in my body? It has to do with the act of thou/ing another being" (162). In addressing the Other, through sex or language, I am reminded of my body. But this address does not necessarily mean that I totalize, figure, or even name the Other.

The Navel of Passages
In "The Torso" we see this embodied "thou/ing" of the Other in the form of not naming. Not only does Duncan never name the lover, but the oscillating form continually unsays any positive statement the poet may venture to make about him, leaving both self and Other, "a trembling hieroglyph" (*Bending* 63). In "Orders, *Passages* 24," Duncan calls this oscillation *a contrapuntal communion of all things,* and this communion—a word that Duncan puns on throughout the *Passages*—is ethical:

> There is no
> good a man has in his own things except
> it be in the community of every thing (79)

This bodily double-bind places the poet's responsibility to the community first and deems "self-interest" a betrayal of "all good of self" (79). In deferring the self, the body remains an ethical element, a way to move beyond what Olson calls "the lyrical interference of the individual ego" ("Projective" 56). This deemphasis of the lyric self in poetry shifts the poetics to the world and the Other who is traced in the navel, or what Duncan elsewhere in 1966 calls *the borderline:* "Our engagement with knowing, with craft and lore, our demand for truth is not to read a conclusion but to keep our exposure to what we do not know, to confront our wish and our need beyond habit and capability, beyond what we can take for granted, at the borderline, the light finger-tip or thought-tip where impulse and novelty spring" (*Fictive* 87). Like Dorn, Duncan would rather we "keep our exposure to what we do not know." But unlike Dorn whose ethics lies in poetry's potential, Duncan's relation with alterity remains in the here and now. This paradox of otherness-in-presence seems to fit his focus on the borderline, the threshold, the hinge between opposites, the in-binding, as well as on the literal, the senses, the body ("light finger-tip"). This threshold is literally a passage to the Other who is "beyond."

As with "The Torso" specifically, the "navel" of the *Passages* poems as a whole is the silence Duncan builds into them, which occurs more often than just in the lengthwise "middle" of the poem. Even in what John Taggart calls Duncan's annoyingly excessive voice, the saying of language is empty of content and full only of the gravity of the ethical relation.[13] As Rudman explains: "Duncan's openness, his process of writing, also has to do with gaps —space, spaces that are left for the Other to fill" (162). I have in previous chapters cited silence as an opening for the trace of the Other in poetry, but in Duncan it is more difficult to locate such silence. In *Bending the Bow*, Duncan speaks of the situation in which the "sign appears— • — as if there were a stress in silence" (ix). This diacritical mark, or spot, a formal element that does not limit like a period, points to "a bounds out of bounds" and traces alterity in its unfamiliarity. This silence also connects to the body, as I will demonstrate.

"Moving the Moving Image, *Passages* 17" enacts its title and the form of the *Passages* poems. Both this poem and the series as a whole put into motion— Duncan uses the figure of the mobile (*Bending* ix)—the unconnected images and texts of the collage through the negative space of silence. Each section in this poem contains moving images that, to use Olson's words, "must MOVE INSTANTER" upon one another: The end of the pagan Kabiri and the rise of Christianity → the hanging of Christ upon the cross → the lifting of the "I" in an embrace → the setting/rising of the Sun → taking a breath → the changing of musical keys → the fall of the ancient, hermetic vision of the cosmos. The poem ends with four figures of balance, what Duncan calls the *equilibrations* lost in the fall of the dreamers of first things: Socrates's daimon, the Holy Spirit, Eros, and John Cage. Each figure is a mediator, a pivotal figure that connects "the divine and what perishes" (*Bending* 61). In this connection, this gap, we find silence—not just between the stanzas and lines but within them. In one particular passage, Duncan uses what I call, *the spot* for lack of a better term, to draw attention to the silence:

stream of bright water pouring over
      rocks gleaming amidst the cold
  current, s • words
Sept 5:   Sweet his mouth   bitter his mouth
Sept 7:   At dawn, your breath stirs   first light
     auras of the cool line of hill-horizons
ringing,   your eyes closed,   sweet smile
     bitter smile. The first ones are awakening. (*Bending* 58)

The silent spot is placed strategically to insinuate ambiguity into the line, which can be read in multiple ways. Not only does the spot interrupt the streaming current of words of the poem in the figure of a stream. But it divides and connects the "words" of love to the "swords" of war. Drawing attention to the "s • words," the spot also occurs directly above the phrase, "Sweet his mouth," and, continuing down in a column, "At dawn, your breath stirs." The mouth serves as the bodily source of language and also of silence, combined with the breath and eyes that indicate a body. But this spot is not merely a mental silence to be read to oneself. As Duncan writes in the preface to *Groundwork: Before the War,* which contains many of the *Passages* poems written after 1968, "The cadence of the verse, and, in turn, the interpenetration of cadences in sequence is, for me, related to the dance of my physical body." Directed by Duncan's "moving hand" and breath, these cadences include the "space-period-space," which means a "sounded silence" that stops the beat before it resumes. The spot, then, calls graphic and sonic attention to what cannot be said, and opens the space in the poem for love of another: "I loved all the early announcements of you, the first falling in love, / the first lovers" (*Bending* 59). But form, whether in excess of moving images and sounds or in silence, is not purely a curious spectacle but impresses on the poem and the reader the obligation weighing language with the burden of relation. Love, as the form obligation takes in *Bending the Bow,* is a "music that troubles me" (iii).

Like a troubling sonata, "The Fire, *Passages* 13" (hereinafter "The Fire") proves to be one of the most challenging poems in terms of form that Duncan ever wrote. Like many of the poems and the series itself, this poem operates in the paradoxical, oscillating structure that opens the passage via a "navel" or "borderline" or "binding" to ethical responsibility to the Other. The form is remarkable because the beginning and end of the poem are best described as a "matrix" of words, each with six evenly spaced columns and rows (see fig. 2). Duncan, in fact, uses the word *matrix* in "In the Place of a

jump	stone	hand	leaf	shadow	sun
day	plash	coin	light	downstream	fish
first	loosen	under	boat	harbor	circle
old	earth	bronze	dark	wall	waver
new	smell	purl	close	wet	green
now	rise	foot	warm	hold	cool

	blood	disk	
	horizon	flame	

The day at the window
the rain at the window
the night and the star at the window

    Do you know the old language?
    I do not know the old language.

40

2. First page of "The Fire, *Passages* 13" from *Bending the Bow*, showing the poem's first matrix.

Passage 22" as a pun to refer to the "mother of all images" (*Bending* 75). Notably, the matrix at the end of the poem differs from the one at the beginning, a change that we will discuss shortly as a key to understanding how the matrices fit with the rest of the poem. For now, though, I would like to explore the most pronounced feature of the matrices: their spacing. Although the matrix works as a whole to form a grand image, or pictogram, it spreads the words out and, in silence, almost irretrievably disturbs any syntactic order. This silent page space forces us to consider each word literally, as an object in itself, independent of syntactic context. "[E]ach word," Duncan writes in "The Concert, Passages 31" from *Groundwork: Before the War*, "a severd [*sic*] distinct thing" (12). The significance of this literal severing must be understood before we can read more of the poem.

Duncan discusses the moral importance of this emphasis on the literal in his 1965 essay "The Sweetness and Greatness of Dante's *Divine Comedy*," where he compares Dante to the Imagists and outlines a poetics of embodiment and love. Quoting a letter by Dante to his patron, Can Grande, Duncan points out that Dante saw his poetry as "polysemous," though Dante says in the second treatise of the *Convivio* that readers of his poetry must always start with its literal level. This statement prompts Duncan to compare Dante to Modernism and its emphasis "upon the image in its direct presentation." Duncan writes,

> This doctrine of the literal, the immediate and *embodied* sense, as the foundation of all others, is striking to the modern poet . . . something goes awry if in our adoration of the Logos we lose sense of or would cut loose from the living body and passion of Man in the actual Universe . . . but the universe and our experience in it is a text that we must learn to read if we are to come to the truth of it and ourselves (*Fictive* 143–44, emphasis mine).

Poetry literally incarnates the body, the world, and the truth, and our responsibility becomes to read that body. "We ourselves are literal, actual beings," Duncan writes, reminiscent of Merleau-Ponty and the existentialists: "This is the hardest ground for us to know, for we are *of* it—not outside, observing, but inside, experiencing. It is, finally, I believe, the only ground for us to know; for it is Creation, it is the Divine Presentation, it is the language of experience whose words are immediate to our senses; from which our own creative life takes fire, *within which* our own creative life takes fire." Herein lies an important meaning for the title of "The Fire," which serves as a representative example of how the literalness of language—in all its ambiguity—

can serve as the passage to ethical responsibility. From the literal, creativity ignites. But, Duncan argues, the moral and allegorical also arise from the literal; like flames from the Inferno. Drawing on Dante's discourse on virtue, Duncan theorizes how the moral virtue of poets arises from the literal. First, courage comprises one of the main parts of virtue for Dante, and Duncan implies that the poet's virtue is like Dante's courage that is a "consciousness of greatness." Duncan draws an analogy to the awe Dante felt for Virgil. The second side to the poet's moral virtue is what Duncan calls, drawing on the *Purgatorio*, a *sweetening* of the soul through the labor of making poetry. This aim must be ever present in a poet's mind, according to Duncan, to avoid the sin of art for art's sake. Instead, that labor leads us to Love: "The beauty of sound is, for Dante, first and last, the essence of his art. . . . Falling in love with the sound we revere the literal, and search out the excellence of the word as we would search out a beloved" (*Fictive* 152). We can see the moral implications of this falling in love with sound and with the literal enacted in "The Fire."

From the literalness of the signifiers on the page in "The Fire," we can abstract, or *sweeten*, the language and approach a love that does not distinguish between fiction/truth, word/reality, or self/body. In this poem, even the animal is sweetened, by taking on a human visage, as the figure of the face becomes pivotal in the characterization of demons and saviors (*Bending* 43). In using a quote from the Renaissance mystic, Ficino, who states that song and sound "strike the aerial spirit of the hearer, which is the junction of the soul and the body," Duncan makes poetry literal and implies that poetry raises our ethical conscience: "chords and melodies of the spell that binds / the many in conflict in contrasts of one mind" (*Bending* 42). Poetry literally (and in its literality) is the ob-ligation that binds person to person, individual to people (nation), Satan to Christ, and heaven to hell. Allow me to illustrate this poetic binding.

In "The Fire," each matrix, an inverse and rotated reflection of the other, acts as a bookend at either end of this sonata. True to the sonata form, the poem is divided in half by a pivot, a chord, a binding. Drawing on the musical aspect of Duncan's poetics, we can explain the change in the last matrix in terms of the sonata form, which "is the open modulatory plan of binary form, in which an initial modulation from the tonic to a new key" and back to the tonic, resulting to two large sections ("Sonata"). A change, which happens at the pivot, results in the alteration in the second matrix that returns to the main theme with a difference. The location of the "key change" or "turn" of the sonata, "The Fire," is ambiguous. One possibility aligns it approximately with the line, "the World-Ensouling?" As one will recall, the introduction to *Bending the Bow* defines this "World-Ensouling" as the embodiment of the poem in a healing of common humanity, an ethical aspiration indeed. However, if one counts all of the lines as they are paginated, then the line beginning "following the daily news" is the epicenter of the poem. If the latter possibility is the case, then the binding is the literal news, the quotidian details of day-to-day existence, many of which demand ethical responsibility: "the earthquakes, eruptions, flaming automobiles, enraged lovers, wars against communism, heroin addicts, police raids, race riots . . ." (*Bending* 42). One last possibility exists—by counting the prose sections as one poetic line, the midpoint of the poem becomes the space between the stanzas marked by "avidly" and "following the daily news" where the past meets the present, Hieronymous Bosch meets Walter Cronkite. This would mean that silence binds these elements, as well as us to them, in the present of the poem. Regardless of which of the three theories one chooses, the binding of "The Fire" is not an indicative statement, knowledge, or any other obvious form. Like the saying, the binding is itself absent, silent, the *para-* in paradox, the "beyond" (*Fictive* 87), the trace of the Other. This trace signifies an opportunity for love to manifest, to love as a verb. Duncan captures the strife in "The Fire" not in order to overcome it but to love it: "It is not in political right thinking or in political power that we come into the apprehension of a World Order but in falling in love" (*Fictive* 133). Only in this kind of love can we "see further than our own sense of what is good to the goods of our history at large, [and] we find them worked in darks as well as lights" (139).

Poethical Love

So far, I have only intimated that the testimony in Duncan's poetry, which true to "What Is" in all its linguistic and poetic indeterminacy, is loving. But a deeper understanding of this love can better reveal his ethics. Pervading Duncan's idea of "What Is," Love is nonjudgmental and sensual and opens the subject to the Other via the body. However, what distinguishes Duncan's use of "love" is that, although it is self-constituting, it is not self-serving. The 1960 poem "Come, Let Me Free Myself," explicitly articulates the theme of ethical love:

> Come, let me free myself from all that I love.
> Let me free what I love from me, let it go free.
> For I would obey without bound,
> serve only as served (Roots 3)

In order to "obey" the inner ethical law, which here means to love and care for another, I must let go of any claim or possession of what is loved, including self and others. This letting go that comprises the love in love Duncan frames in the language of service to an other, even if that service is reciprocal ("serve only as served"). The last stanza of the poem highlights this necessity of letting go of the Other:

> O let me be free now of my way, for all that I bind to me
> —and I bind what I love to me,
>   comforting chains and surroundings—
> let these loved things go and let me go with them.
> For I stand in the way, my destination stands in the way! (*Roots* 55)

In other words, in letting others go, I free myself. At the same time, my freedom abides in my service to others. Levinas understood love similarly. In his analysis of "The Subjectivity in Eros," Levinas writes that "[t]he freedom of the subject that posits itself is not like the freedom of a being free as the wind. It implies responsibility. . . . The coinciding of freedom with responsibility constitutes the I, doubled with itself, encumbered with itself. *Eros* delivers from this encumberment, arrests the return of the I to itself" (*Totality* 271). The poem issues love in terms of its freeing effect for the Other and not of its benefit for the self. In this freeing, Duncan, like Levinas, unsays what he has said about the binding elsewhere as a tie of love, but both sides of the binary, free/bind, presuppose the Other who is the transitive recipient of the action. This orientation toward the Other is accented in the tone of the poem, which is uttered much more like a prayer than it is in an active, imperative voice. This tone is necessary to invoke the beloved (things and people) that provoked love from me and the desire to "bind" them to me in the first place. From the beginning, I am bound to the Other, and even freeing is paradoxically a binding in that it serves and obliges. So the next lesson to learn is that letting go of claims of comfort and total possession (that love is about me) is what not only frees the Other (who is always already free before me) but also frees me who stands in my own way. The self needs the Other, in both Duncan's content and paradoxical form, in order to be free.

But love is ethical for Duncan precisely because it is *Eros*, a carnal desire, an incarnated desire, a poetic desire. The section titled "Love" in "The Propositions" from Duncan's *The Opening of the Field* (1960) explicitly connects erotic and ethical love. Love, described earlier in the poem as the "force that drove me to the ground prime reality," is inextricable from the life force of sexuality:

> The sexual drive, erect
> intention, is deep, is absolute.
> No more deep or absolute
>
> than tenderness. It is life
> that tenders   green shoots of
> hurt and healing   we name Love. (33)

In this poem, ethics, as the sexual love-responsibility for another, is embodied in both the love of a mother in childbirth and the love of Christ on the cross for humankind. Many of the figures of Christian sacrifice in Duncan's poems, his idea of the ultimate love,[14] are also sexual, like the intersection of the beams of the cross or of the lines of a woman's mouth and her genitals—"all maidens bear Christ's sign   with them" ("As In the Old Days, *Passages* 8, *Bending* 24).[15] In the juxtaposition of Christ to female genitalia, we see that both sex and sexuality are a critical component to the ethical relation that Duncan sees in Christ's act of love. In "Man's Fulfillment in Order and Strife" (1968), Duncan equates Christ in his passion to "Sappho who is the maker and sufferer of divine or immortal love songs: the wonder of their making and the pain of their feeling embodied are inseparable" (*Fictive* 124). But this union of sex and ethics is not a vile or dreadful marriage (like that of Sin and Satan in Milton's *Paradise Lost*) but an occasion of joy and loving. Love is expressed only through the body, the body of language, in relation to the Other. Such bodily contact does not devour the Other, as Levinas points out in his analysis of metaphors of love (*Totality* 254–73). Bodily contact, which literally and figuratively connotes sex, expresses for Duncan obligation for-the-other. The body, which is always sexual, expresses at once the linguistic and material obligation to the Other.

Returning to "The Torso," we can trace the confluence of this freeing binding of Love with erotic desire:

> a wave of need and desire over   taking me
>
> cried out my name
>
> (This was long ago.   It was another life)
> and said,
> What do you want of me? (*Bending* 64)

Duncan often employs vertical as well as horizontal syntax so that words above and below each other can be read as interconnected, as if in a web.[16] Note how the assonance of "desire" and "cried" is emphasized in the placement of words on the page, which reinforces the connection between language and the Other. The calling out of the speaker's name (either by the lover or the desire within the speaker himself) forges their bond. Although Duncan intended these spaces to signify breaths and pauses, they also have the effect of inviting alterity into the poem, here in the desire for another. As Levinas writes in "On Intersubjectivity: Notes on Merleau-Ponty" (first published in 1983), "Nor is the caress that bespeaks love the mere message and symbol of love, but rather, prior to that language, already that love itself" (*Outside* 101). The erotic desire for the Other is inseparable from the utterance, the way Duncan has written it on the page, and the saying of language itself. Thus, Duncan's inability to articulate this desire leads him to assign it to "another life," a pun encompassing both his life and the Other's. But what his cry lacks in clarity, it makes up for in the fact that it is exhaled from the body, expressed, and called forth from the mouth of the Other. The voice coincides with the chest, neck, diaphragm, and pubis that provide force for its passage into throat and poem. Ultimately, this love exposes a demand placed on the subject by the Other: "What do you want of me?" A question the subject cannot escape brings him to erotic love.

Duncan's homosexuality creates some interesting doublings and reflections within this ethical love that change figurations of the subject. The famous line near the end of the "The Torso"—"For my Other is not a woman but a man"—could believably refer to Beauvoir's introduction to *The Second Sex*, which rejects the historical tendency of patriarchal culture to "other" women and therefore identify itself as superior (Beauvoir xxii). In this way, "The Torso" is a critique of society's rejection of homosexuality. But the most interesting part about Duncan's use of this term, *Other*, is that it appears right below "Self" and, as Greg Hewett rightly points out, Duncan deconstructs this dichotomy by identifying the otherness in his own self and body. As was true for Dorn's I character in *Gunslinger*, the self is a subject because it remains other to itself. Quoting Julia Kristeva, Hewett points out that this Other is "the very space of metaphorical shifting" (543), a shifting I would call the binding of the poem. The subject itself is the navel, the center of ethical responsibility. However, this semiotic shifting does not merely result in identification with the Other and thus a reduction to the self-same. Instead, the shifting within the self echoes an alterity outside the self that cannot be known or named but only loved:

> I do not know, I said.   I have fallen in love.   He
>   has brought me into heights and depths my heart
>   would fear   without him.   His look (*Bending* 64)

Acting as turns (as in breath and in music), the spaces between phrases syntactically heighten the uncertainty the "I" feels when interposed by the lover. The spaces defer syntactic closure but also allow one to read the units as discrete, which often results in the part contradicting the whole of the sentence. If one reads the gaps as unsure pauses, "the heights and depths" raise fear at first, but then the fears only exist "without him." This fear and uncertainty do not change the love but urge it on: "In your falling / I have fallen from a high place. I have raised myself / from darkness in your rising" (64). In other words, the Self follows the Other, taking responsibility for the Other's risings and fallings. Furthermore, the fact that this section is single-spaced indicates that the lines come quickly and urgently after each other, as if Duncan were sputtering it out. Love does not persevere through the uncertainty in the face of the Other or the gaps and stutters, "seeking the locks, the keys"; those formal silences, seekings, and stumblings *are* love.

This love of what one cannot or does not understand is certainly something Duncan wants to experience in his own life, in the form of being able to erotically love any other one chooses. But this love is also what Duncan wants for the homophobic, sexist, and racist culture that he lives in beyond the outward show: "Tolerance could be no substitute for love" (*Fictive* 133). The kind of "falling in love" he describes in "The Torso" branches out from merely an individual, romantic act to a communal one: "It is in the very act of love, in the marital union, and then in the love-banquet of brotherhood —at once ideal and sexual—that the meaning of freedom and fulfillment is at work." As implied here, this love is bodily: "Only in the love-feast of the agape and in the love-wedding in which desire was liberated in sensual delight would the work be done" (*Fictive* 133). Beyond a social contract for Duncan, the binding of marriage frees through an ethical love that could counterbalance the monstrosity of war. Through his poetry, he hopes to fashion a new "world-ensouling" that would integrate the body and its sexual desires into the ethical fabric of the community and keep them in productive, rather than destructive, tension.

part 3

AN ETHICS OF SEXUAL ALTERITY

CELIA. Let us sit and mock the good housewife Fortune from her
   wheel, that her gifts may henceforth be bestowed equally.
ROSALIND. I would we could do so; for her benefits are mightily
   misplaced; and the bountiful blind woman doth most mistake in her gifts to women. (*As You Like It* I.ii)

The onset of Language poetry in the 1970s and 1980s, with its
self-reflexive exploration of language as an opaque medium, marks a shift in
American poetics from *what* a poem says to *how* a poem says. This shift—or
swerve, as Joan Retallack might call it (*Poethical* 1, 15–16)—is so extreme that
Language poetry could be said to concern itself with *that* a poem says anything at all. By examining not only what words mean but the very way
meaning is produced, the contemporary avant-garde, and its renowned sub-
set, Language poetry, is acutely aware of the *sociality* of language and focuses
more on the event of utterance/writing than on conceptual or subjective
content. This brief example from David Melnick's book-length poem, *Pcoet,*
perhaps the epitome of "the language poem," if such a thing exists, highlights this shift from said to saying:

11.

sadd bier
metapoif
lid   cift   ure,

hid tyer

As Melnick says himself, these poems are collection of letters "that seem to
be words but are not," and they at every turn thwart any reader's designs
toward coherent meaning ("Short" 13). What is left is the event of the poem
on the page, the poem's "metapoif" or metapoetic *saying,* without any discernible content, or *said.* But for many readers this shift obliterates any

ethical potential in the poem. As Tim Woods writes, "The persistent focus on the value of referentiality, the obscurity of reference in their poetry, and the general issue of semiosis have clouded the fact that the Language poets in particular have sought to make a significant intervention in the reconceptualization of contemporary ethics" (15). The ethical potential of the poem, we might say, can lie in the *attempt* at meaning, which signals to us simply that we are in a communal, social context. Through an analysis similar to my reading of George Oppen, one could easily foreground the saying of the Other and its implied obligation in language.

But without sifting through the contested gamut of Language poetry looking for examples of the ethical saying of language, a more important ethical challenge emerges concurrently with Language poetry in the late 1960s and early 1970s: the women's movement. For in the intersection of these two historical events, Language writing and feminism, we can see the trajectory of Robert Duncan's meditations on the embodiment of love taking on increasing significance in the context of sexual difference. Considering the changes involved in this historical confluence, I will look at two women Language poets, Susan Howe and Lyn Hejinian, in order to examine the difference being a woman can make in writing innovative poetry and thus to considerations of ethics.

According to Douglas Messerli's appendix of publication dates in his anthology *From the Other Side of the Century,* the year 1976 appears to be a watershed year for American women poets in the experimental strain, with first books by Hejinian, Fanny Howe, Leslie Scalapino, Fiona Templeton, and new books by Susan Howe, Lorine Niedecker (the posthumous *Blue Chicory*), Bernadette Mayer, Alice Notley, and Rosmarie Waldrop. Although most of these women had been writing and even publishing much earlier, 1976 marks at least a full flowering of this tradition and community of writers in the small-press publishing industry.

Over the next twenty years, however, only three critical works devoted strictly to Language poetry emerged, including Linda Reinfeld's *Language Poetry: Writing as Rescue* (1981), *Textual Politics and the Language Poets* by George Hartley (1989), and Bob Perelman's *The Marginalization of Poetry* (1996). Peter Quartermain's *Disjunctive Poetics* (1992), and Marjorie Perloff's *Poetic License* (1990) and *Radical Artifice* (1991) also deal with Language poetry in the larger context of experimental writing in America during the twentieth century. But a majority of the most recent books have strikingly focused on these women Language poets because their force and social relevance is so significant, especially as a community or group. The first full book devoted solely to the subject of sexual difference in Modernist and postmodern experimental poetry was *The Pink Guitar* (1990) by Rachel Blau DuPlessis. Although the book includes chapters on Beverly Dahlen and Susan Howe, it is not devoted exclusively to Language poetry as a phenomenon. In *Pink Guitar*, DuPlessis leaves the issue of ethics open as a question, which she never answers: "If one could retain that passionate, feeling ethics without the uniformities of telos . . . Is it possible? Which way do I turn? What do I turn?" (152–53). Since then, major works by Ann Vickery, Juliana Spahr, Rachel Tzvia Back, Lynn Keller, Megan Simpson, Elisabeth A. Frost, and Linda Kinnahan have mined the rich vein of gender issues in experimental poetry by women. However, these works only tangentially, if at all, address the ethics of the writing as it relates to the issues of gender, sex, and sexual difference. Only Joan Retallack's *Poethical Wager* (2003) deals in an extended way with the relation between ethics, gender, and experimental writing, colliding in what she calls *the experimental feminine* (90–101). "Feminist dyslogic," she writes in the context of the struggle between tradition and experiment in Western culture, "the need to operate outside official logics—is essential because official logics exist to erase any need to operate outside official logics, that is the feminine. If this seems circular it's because it is" (*Poethical* 92). To risk the wager of testing the vicious cycle of official limits, she says, is "an act of poethical courage" (*Poethical* 94). Yet even Retallack's incisive feminist analysis of the "wager" of experimental writing by women in the mode of the "Feminine" reifies the kind of dualistic, dialectical thinking that my project is trying to avoid. My question is, can we provide an ethical model that reads in the nondialectical mode of subject-Other, both-and, zero-two?

This lack of ethical discussion and of a model of ethical alterity motivates my choice to focus solely on women writers in Part 3. The other main reason is that these particular women Language poets—with their unique formal challenges to notions of subjectivity, the body, the sexes, and morality—introduce gender as a defining ethical problematic; this perhaps is the most important contribution Language poetry can offer to the ethics of this experimental strain of poetry. I would also like to enter the debate in terms of gender by proposing a feminist context to these Language poets that best illuminates their poetry and their challenge to conventional ways of thinking of sexual ethics. Because these poets, particularly Howe and Hejinian, see sexual difference as situated in the singularity of experience with otherness in the writing of poetry, their approach to gender could be called, using Julia Kristeva's term, *third-wave* feminism. Unlike other waves of feminism that either focus on women's political equality with men or rely on main-taining sexual difference as an inescapable mode of analysis, the feminism implied and expressed by these writers attempts to envision an ethics not dependent yet still contingent on gender, or, as I would prefer to call it, an ethics otherwise than gender. More precisely, I want to question universalizing ideas of sex or sexual difference because they are not appropriate to the interpretation of these female Language poets.

Aside from the lack of ethical criticism of Language poetry, the lack of awareness of feminist theory in ethical criticism is also a problem. The January 1999 special topic edition of the *PMLA* brought to the attention of the broader profession a recent development in literary criticism, what has been called the *New Ethical Criticism*. Curiously missing from this special issue is a representative essay from, or a brief discussion of, the feminist strain in ethical criticism and theory.[1] No Jane-come-lately, this strain dates back at least to Simone de Beauvoir, who explicitly discusses a feminist ethics, namely an existential ethics, first articulated in *An Ethics of Ambiguity* (1947) and placed into the service of feminist readings of myriad contexts, including literature, in *The Second Sex* (1949). Since then, ethics has been a major concern in many forms of feminist discourse. In poststructuralism since the early 1970s, ethics has been a main topic of discussion, resulting in major works by Luce Irigaray (*L'Ethique de la différance sexuelle* 1974 [*An Ethics of Sexual Difference* 1993]) and Julia Kristeva (*La Révolution du langage poé-tique* 1974 [*Revolution in Poetic Language* 1984] and *Desire In Language* 1980), just to name the most influential in the field of literary criticism. The publication of Carol Gilligan's *In a Different Voice* (1982), which espouses its famous "ethic of care," also marks the momentum ethics was gaining in Anglo-American feminism. These groundbreaking works have influenced many feminist scholars—Jill Robbins, Tina Chanter, Drucilla Cornell, Elizabeth Grosz, Kelly Oliver, Margaret A. Simons, Ewa Ziarek, Deborah Bergof-fen, and Ann Mellor, to name just a few—writing mainly in the decade leading up to the 1999 issue of *PMLA*. Shocking how a corpus this large and influential could be overlooked, but the reason may not be gender bias on the part of *PMLA* special issue editor, Lawrence Buell; more likely, it is because few feminist scholars choose to give ethical readings of literature. These writers often remain, instead, in the discipline of theory and philosophy as if those were the proper domains of ethics, not literary criticism.[2] This choice obfuscates, however, the rich contribution that women novelists, dramatists, and poets can make to this evolution of a "new" feminist ethical criticism.

In the absence of sustained discussion of sexual difference in the context of "the new ethical inquiry" and ethics in the criticism of Language poetry, the question arises of how to enter that critical debate and to stress the importance of the contexts of sex and ethics. If George Oppen and Charles Reznikoff reveal to us, the readers, how we come to make moral judgments, then the Language poets make apparent to us the language of those judgments— the language of judgment that composes and layers institutions that maintain, interpret, endorse, and enforce codes of morality. Embedded in a lyric full of words such as "regularities," "judging," "recognize," and "information," the following lines from Hejinian's *The Cell,* are the language of the moralist:

> Something into something, in increments,
>   perhaps viscous
> I am a moralist—there's
>   no substitute
> So temporal persons confront temporary
>   waves
> *   *   *
> I followed the sound but
>   the thing was gone
> For society I now have
>   you
>   *February 11, 1988* (129)

This lyric's emphasis on measuring and discerning, signified in the use of absolute adjectives such as "temporal," dramatizes a reaction to the uncertainty of everyday life, the "something" and the "temporary waves." This reaction belongs to the moralist who, like the "I" figure who tracks sound (for the subject is the site of ethics conventionally conceived, as Hejinian's focus reveals), must investigate phenomena not simply to find their meaning but to assign them value ("increments") within a moral system. Hejinian distances herself from the "I" of the poem in order to make such language visible. The last line, enacting the putting into rationality and the rationing of the burden of obligation always already there, foregrounds the very social basis of the language of judging and regulating found in the rest of the poem.

Challenging such moralizing logic, the women Language poets, such as Kathleen Fraser, Rae Armantrout, Rosmarie Waldrop, Carla Harryman, and Susan Howe, in addition to Hejinian, raise new questions about the ethics of poetry within the context of the emergence of feminist ethics in the 1980s.

Woods is correct in writing that "Hejinian's poetry has persistently main-tained that an openness to otherness is an ethical stance" (252), but that as-sertion does not account for the specificity of the ethical stance of these women.[3] Drawing on their avant-garde forebears (particularly Stein and Niedecker), they insist that sexual difference matters in the consideration of ethics but that sex is not the determining factor in the ethics of their poetry.[4] For instance, they are *for* writing as women poets and *for* challeng-ing traditions that exclude their voices based on sex, yet unlike poets such as H.D., they are *against* the idealization of the Feminine, as eternal and essential principle.[5] In the tradition of the avant-garde, these women usu-ally avoid idealization of any kind perhaps because as Kristeva warns, "we will never be able to defuse the violences mobilized through the counter-investment necessary to carrying out this phantasm [of relation to the mother without castration], unless one challenges precisely this myth of the archaic mother" ("Women's Time" 481).[6] This tendency not to idealize extends to issues of aesthetic form and literary history, including a feminine tradition, or an *écriture féminine.*[7] Instead of writing *like a woman,* whatever that vague notion might mean, these contemporary avant-garde poets write *as* women, which cannot be said of many of their male counterparts who mostly ignore the influence their sex has on their writing.

The problem remains that to universalize *like a woman* makes the phrase mean the *nothing* that it has meant in patriarchal history; instead, these poets allow the *lived experience* (a Sartrean term employed by Simone de Beauvoir), of being a woman to inform and deform their writing in histori-cally specific and aesthetically considered ways.[8] Thus, the mutable, subjec-tive, and wide-ranging realities of being a woman inform their poetics. But in the context of Beauvoir and Maurice Merleau-Ponty's phenomenological view of the body as a nexus of situations (including race, politics, religion, morality, nationality, and the like, in addition to gender), their critical and embodied view of language makes that experience of gender only a contin-gent, rather than a necessary, part of the situatedness of meaning in their ethics. In other words, the way a particular aspect of a life, such as gender, effects a person depends on the particular situation and the interrelation of other variables that can only be addressed through a detailed (poetic or an-alytic) investigation of that person's life. In Levinasian terms, the feminist perspective of these poets puts the ethical relationship to alterity before sex-ual politics.

These Language poets are among a handful of women poets since 1960 who reformulate "the body," the privileged site of sexual difference in much

feminist criticism and poetry, as a theme—particularly, as a theme in traditional and representational ways. And although my argument might work
just as well with the work of, say, Patricia Dienstfrey and Rosmarie Waldrop,
both of whom use the body as a major trope in their writing, Hejinian, and
Howe use the term "body" sparingly, which makes its use all the more effective. Like Duncan, they do not assume an understanding of the body because
it is what their phenomenological methods explore. Often due to sexual difference, the body is also for Howe and Hejinian what "gets in the way" or
filters the gaze of phenomenology. Regardless, all of these women use form
to explore the structural meaning of the body in its relation to the social and,
thus, to the alterity (in)(of) language. The body is not simply a substance
that can be separated from the mind and, thus, thematized because it exists
in relationship—in situation, that is, in language and interpretation—to
the world and to others in language. What "the body" can mean becomes
a major question in their work, and such questioning is the reason why this
signifier rarely turns up in their poems. When the word does appear, it appears under the severest of scrutiny and even suspicion, since its meaning
has so long been controlled by patriarchal discourses.

In order to more fully understand Language poetry's scrutiny of the gendered body, it is important to take up the poststructural problematic of the
body and subjective experience. Counter to the phenomenological mode
of Beauvoir, poststructuralist writers, particularly the feminists, locate the
body not simply in an identifiable existential realm but in a linguistic web
of interpolation that has been spun historically. In other words, they focus
more on what Merleau-Ponty calls "the body as sign," which I elucidated in
the context of Duncan's sexual poetics. For Howe and Hejinian the saying *is*
the body; there is no difference, even on the level of the signifier, because there
is no body without the saying of language. Thus, the body is linguistic and,
moreover, infused with alterity. To reiterate, any body is not, as Beauvoir
describes it (34–35), just my platform from which I perform, but constitutes
my saying to the Other. My very utterance. Although Duncan's notion of the
body is marked with the situation of sexuality and sexual orientation, it
does not engage sexual difference—he is not much concerned with writing
as a man, per se—but many women writers of this experimental American
strain of poetry take sexual difference into full consideration in their writing,
which thus alters their ethics.

In the following chapters, I will read long poems by Howe and Hejinian
that invoke the body thematically and figuratively in the context of ethical
feminist theory in order to bring into relief the critical role the body plays in

their ethics as a contested site of sexual difference. Later, in reading the work of Hejinian, I explore her notion of the sexed body as a more contextual and syntactic position in the social realm, which is permeated by language and its gestures of alterity. In fact, I proffer that none of the terms currently used in feminism—"gender," "sexual difference," or "identity politics"—can account for the social critique in experimental feminist poethics. Therefore, I have coined the term *sexual alterity* to describe not only the relations between self and other, reader and writer, in the poetry but also the relationship between the poets and their own bodies. By showing how language and bodily experience are intersected by sexual alterity, these poets can help us begin to elucidate an ethics in the poetry of avant-garde women writers.

The Nearness of Poetry
Susan Howe's *The Nonconformist's Memorial*

CORDELIA. [aside] What shall Cordelia speak? Love, and be silent.
(*King Lear* I.i)

In spite of recent critical work such as Peter Baker's *Obdurate Brilliance,* which explains "why experimental writing should not be marginalized by American feminist literary criticism" (165), Perloff's polemical charge in her 1987 essay, "Canon and Loaded Gun," still holds true: feminist and poetry establishments alike ignore postmodern experimental women poets because their poetry does not easily fit into an activist ideology or an accessible aesthetic. Attempts since 2000 by critics, such as Lynn Keller, "to encourage less sectarian and schismatic responses" to different poetries have failed when one looks at how rarely experimental writers like Susan Howe are addressed at profession-wide conferences, national awards, or in broader period anthologies (*Forms* 19). "Language writing," Ann Vickery writes of the experimental poetic community with which Howe is associated, "is still undervalued in its feminist potential" (12).

Despite being ignored by most feminist and literary critics, Howe undertakes unmistakably feminist work when she vociferously exposes the exclusion of women in literary and political history. Perhaps the most pressing issue throughout her work in the late 1970s through the mid-1990s, this critique of the exclusion of women in history alone makes her relevant for feminism. Howe's book *The Nonconformist's Memorial* was first published by Grenfell Press in 1992 and then as a New Directions Paperbook Original in 1993. In it, the title poem critically recontextualizes Mary Magdalene's discovery of the risen Jesus and rewrites perhaps the most dominant narrative of Western civilization—the resurrection of Christ. In her revision, Howe not only foregrounds the erasure and demotion of women in the story due to the exclusionary practices of patriarchal history—"The act of Uniformity / ejected her" (5),[1] but she also draws attention to the fact that more than one version of this narrative exists, opening a space for feminist retellings of the story. Not surprisingly, this subversion of culture and its "devaul[ation] of the female self" is where Rachel Blau DuPlessis centers the "ethical and moral position" of women's writing (*Pink Guitar* 17).

Despite the clear-cut mission of rescue in the poetry,[2] Howe's complex feminism and its ethics require more than a liberatory or redemptive narrative. As Kornelia Freitag puts it, Howe is skeptical of any discourse that presupposes a linear progress that assumes a unified subject, and/or that is not embedded in history (49). Furthermore, Howe's experimental poetics eschews the logic of identity, which I define as the ability of readers to identify with the content of the poem (and ostensibly the experiences of the female poet or persona) that marks the work of more mainstream feminist writers like Adrienne Rich. Such identification is demoted in favor of calling attention to the strangeness or indeterminacy within the common structures of language. According to much poststructuralist feminist ethics, the purpose of foregrounding otherness is to change the common and historically oppressive structures of language. Language poets, such as Howe, foreground the very language of the culture around them that replicates or resists the suffering, identity, oppression, or experiences of women.

Perhaps such complexity deters further feminist appropriation, particularly from Anglo-American feminisms focused on identity because difficult form, in the minds of many, dulls the edge of political allegiance. But Howe's critique of identity through alterity is precisely why we should look more closely at her. Much in the vein of the antinomian women—like Mary Magdalene and Anne Hutchinson, whom she inscribes into her poems—Howe's statements in her prose and interviews show exactly why she is often avoided in theoretical contexts. Take this example: "A poet is never just a woman or a man. Every poet is salted with fire" (*My Emily* 7). Or, commenting on Emily Dickinson's choice of isolation: "I think she may have chosen to enter the space of silence. A space where power is no longer an issue, gender is no longer an issue, voice is no longer an issue, where the idea of a printed book appears as a trap" (*Birth-Mark* 170).

What can first- and second-wave feminisms, invested in the ethical goals of either achieving political equality or investigating sexual difference, do with such statements? Keller, without acknowledging the potential theoretical and political snags of such transcendence of gender, wholly endorses Howe's remarks (*Forms* 202). Even DuPlessis, a feminist critic who is one of the most vocal proponents of Howe's "anti-authoritarian ethics" (*Pink Guitar* 9, 17), acknowledges Howe's impulse toward transcendence, calling "[t]his project colossal in its hubris . . . In its unsettling" (126). Neither DuPlessis nor Keller, however, explores the implications of such an ethical project of transcendence. Megan Simpson, on the other hand, suggests a possible practical effect of language-oriented writing by women, including Howe: "If gender is no longer seen as an essential characteristic of a core identity but as relationally and discursively constructed in a social context, a broader range of subject positions might become available for people gendered female . . . for greater agency and active participation in the making of meaning and the processes by which knowledge is constructed" (xii). As we will see, though, Howe's ethics does more than "rescue" lost voices or expand "identity" and "knowledge"; it brings us to the very limit of those signifiers and explores the conditions of ethics itself.

Further complicating any facile translation of Howe's feminist poetic practice into an ethics is the way in which she questions her own belief. In a 1990 interview with Edward Foster, Howe expresses her exasperation at how women are still left out of the canon: "So here while I am trying to believe and think I do believe that genius transcends gender, sometimes I honestly wonder" (*Birth-Mark* 168). Germanely, this questioning occurs in the context of her identification with other women poets, including Objectivist Lorine Niedecker, whose work has been ignored like many others in favor of "juicy" biography relating to her love life. In this interview, though, after disclaimers admitting she doesn't know the answer to the problem of sex and sexual difference in poetry, Howe inevitably returns to the notion of transcending gender:

> And that's where I disagree with a good many feminist critics. I think when you write a poem you use sounds and words outside time. You use timeless articulations. I mean the ineluctable mystery of language is something . . . it really doesn't matter if you are a man or a woman. We are all both genders. There is nothing more boring than stridently male poetry and stridently female poetry. (*Birth-Mark* 172)

Clearly, Howe's feminism remains conflicted not only, as Freitag points out, between second-wave feminism and poststructuralism (56) but also because of her precarious vision of a place-time beyond gender.

Some might reject as reactionary Howe's debate with herself on the transcending of gender, but I see such enigmatic statements as the beginnings of a feminist ethics that not only shares practical and theoretical concerns for women but readies us for a move beyond dependence on epistemological categories, into what Julia Kristeva calls *Woman's Time*.[3] This postmodern space/time envisions women and men engaged in aesthetic practice not necessarily determined by sexual difference but first by an ethical relationship with the Other.

Although Howe does indeed attack what she sees as the proscriptive force of some feminisms, there are certain theorists, such as Luce Irigaray and Alice Jardine, whom Howe admires (*Birth-Mark* 170). At the same time, we must be careful, as Language poet Bob Perelman points out, to avoid categories of gender that "obliterate the complexities of the writing" (127). Therefore, I would like to selectively appropriate some theoretical frames that I think will help us understand Howe's feminist ethics, rather than simply support theoretical arguments. In her long poem, "The Nonconformist's Memorial" (1993) and in her book-length study *My Emily Dickinson* (1985), Howe explores a woman's time that transcends judgmental categories by rigorously investigating the relation of the sexed body and language to alterity. In this quest, Howe shares a visionary, utopian power of a nonprescriptive ethics, and in this context her desire to transcend gender norms can best be understood.

Proximity and Transcendence

From the perspective of Kristeva's and Irigaray's work, we can see how poets such as Howe alter the rendering of (female) subjectivity locked in an excluding dialectic where the Other (woman) is a negative construct of masculine ideology. Howe constructs sexual difference in a more nonrepresentational way that evokes otherness without the necessity of dialectical categories. This is not to say that Howe thinks that no oppression or hierarchy has transpired in the historical relations between men and women. On the contrary, Howe uses innovation with language and form, for example, to bring forth a gendered code inscribed in language. Take this poem from Howe's experimental book-length piece, *The Liberties* (1980):

> We are
> in a sandheap
>
> We are
> discovered
> not solid
>
> the floor
> based
> on misunderstanding. (*Europe* 210–11)

In a sense, we see dramatized here Irigaray's belief from *This Sex Which Is Not One* that philosophy has founded its own assumptions by othering woman as lack or volume. In particular, Howe echoes in her poetry the cultural myth that the female body has been "discovered," especially as a lack or space, a "misunderstanding" that has prevented sexual difference from being considered as relevant to ethics. The "floor" of judgment, which provides the ground for hierarchies of the sexes, is "based on misunderstanding." But for Howe, identification of sexual difference must be historicized (as she does with Swift's relationship to his lover, Stella, in the first two parts of *The Liberties*) and then overcome in order not to reify the boundaries determined by patriarchal civilization and not to repeat the "misunderstanding." Supporting all of this feminist historiography is the form of the poem: the words describing "we" are literally excluded to the right margin, while at the center, the ostensible position of masculine discourse like Swift's, is firmly planted the "misunderstanding."

But the transcendence of gender norms that Howe seeks cannot arise from purely negative critiques of patriarchy. Contrary to more dialectical philosophies, where the subject is separate from and opposed to the Other, Irigaray also claims that the two sexes merge and divide, mingling ("not solid" as Howe says) like the lips of lovers or of a woman's vulva. (The confluence of the body with such abstract philosophical realms is not a simile for Howe or Irigaray). The freedom to be ethical, as in Robert Duncan's poethics, comes only through bodily contact with the Other. In "Thorow" (1990), Howe echoes this almost word for word: "You are of me & I of you, I cannot tell / Where you leave off and I begin" (*Singularities* 58). Instead of revealing social oppression or alienation, the role of the signifier "body" in Howe's writing is primarily ethical. The paradox in Howe's work that Simpson identifies—that the poetry "rides the rift between empiricism and textuality" (165)—remains true for the body in the texts as well. The body is both the experience of reality and formed by language—in fact, the two are inseparable for Howe because language for her is material reality. Thus, to ask whether, as a language-oriented poet, Howe intends the signifier "body" to point to a reality outside of language where women suffer is a misleading question. Beyond this dichotomy, a third way foregrounds the ethical imperative behind all language: In Howe's poetry, the woman's "body" places her at the call of or in proximity to the otherness inherent in the text's gaps and ambiguities, an otherness that points to the Other, the other person. Howe's "body" does not just function, as Simpson's analysis would imply (169), as the other that enables patriarchal epistemologies; Howe's relation with "otherness," like Irigaray's, has a much less negative or dialectical valence. Echoing Duncan's notion from *Passages* of an "under side turning," she writes elsewhere in "Thorow," "Original of the Otherside / understory of anotherworld" (*Singularities* 50). Such gaps, which mark the demand of the Other as well as the erasure of women from history, become the productive field for Howe's ethics of alterity.

In the vein of poems by previous experimental women writers like Dickinson, Niedecker, and Gertrude Stein, poems such as "The Nonconformist's Memorial" clearly demonstrate that Howe's move toward transcendence still includes deconstruction of sexual difference; but such analysis need not involve a proscriptive program. For Howe it involves instead an ethics that does not dictate "rules of engagement." She speaks of the importance of sexual difference as she distances herself from feminists like Hélène Cixous, Sandra Gilbert, and Susan Gubar:

> Yes, gender difference does affect our use of language, and we constantly confront issues of difference, distance, and absence, when we write. That doesn't mean I can relegate women to what we "should" or "must" be doing. Orders suggest hierarchy and category. Categories and hierarchies suggest property. My voice formed from my life belongs to no one else. What I put into words is no longer my possession. Possibility has opened. (*My Emily* 13)

Instead of being about normative control of writing practice or of judgment and definition, as in determining a proper *écriture féminine*, Howe's feminism is one of the opening of writing to possibility, to what is other and unknowable. As such, she eschews an ethics of proscription in favor of one of singularity and nonidentity.

"Givens of Dickinson's life," Howe writes, "her sex, class, education, inherited character traits, all influences, all chance events—all carry the condition for her work in their wake" (*My Emily* 13). In Howe's emphasis on "conditions," we see an almost existential analysis of Dickinson's situation, but the body serves not an end in itself, nor does it act as a symbol for group oppression. As the passage from "The Nonconformist's Memorial" quoted earlier indicates, sexual difference makes a difference particularly in the writing of history:

> The act of Uniformity
> ejected her
> and informers at her heels
> Citations remain abbreviated
> Often a shortcut
> stands for Chapter (5)

Crucial to the poetic deconstruction of the resurrection narrative in which Howe is engaged, sexual difference justifies the "abbreviations" and "short-cuts" that leave women out of history. This example, however, does stand as a universal memorial for all women who have been excluded. It is a non-conformist's memorial, specifically, Mary Magdalene's. True, others are mentioned—Christ, St. John—or alluded to—St. Joan of Arc, Anne Hutchin-son (27)—but they too are properly contextualized, not immortalized. The poem is also a *nonconformist* memorial in that the form of the poem itself refuses to conform to lyrical decorum.

In responding to this universalizing tendency in some feminist poetics, Howe could easily focus on the differences that make particular women who they are, and she does this to an extent. However, she does not stop there. As Lew Daly claims, Howe infuses this examination of difference, in addition to all textual critique, with an inflection of alterity. Alterity, which Daly defines through the work of Emmanuel Levinas as what in another person escapes knowledge and definition, plays a preeminent role in Howe's work through-out her career. However, what Daly does not point out, is that for Levinas the Other is always already the very saying of language and is not limited to the other of the subject, contaminated with what Jacques Derrida would call "a metaphysics of presence." In other words, the ethical demand that the Other places on the subject inf(l)ects language at the very moment of its utterance. The ethical turn and the linguistic turn here coincide.

This formulation of the ethical relation as language fits nicely with Howe's Language poetics that foregrounds and documents *texts* rather than relating authentic experiences. I agree with Simpson, who states that we "meet the other with writing" in Howe's texts (194), but this "meeting" is in a sense more dramatic and terrifying than that. As Rachel Tzvia Back articulates it, Howe's poetry takes the reader captive, requiring "a surrender to the un-familiar and the unknown, which is also a surrender to the Other" (7). But ultimately, Back sees the surrender to the Other as a journey toward the self and freedom (173). I argue that the Other in Howe, rather than becoming opposite or subject, *stays other*. Going a step further, I want to emphasize the demand implied in Howe's captivity trope: Howe's poetics shows us that the alterity (i.e., Mary Magdalene's story) within the language of those texts (the Gnostic Gospels) *obligates* us to the Other. In other words, ethics as inescapable obligation arises when the Other remains other in and through poetic form.

In *My Emily Dickinson,* Howe points specifically to the devices— "Repetition, surprise, alliteration, odd rhyme and rhythm, dislocation, deconstruction" (11)[4]—these women used to open language to the ethics of alterity:

> Emily Dickinson and Gertrude Stein also conducted a skillful and ironic investigation of patriarchal authority over literary history. Who polices questions of grammar, parts of speech, connection, and connotation? Whose order is shut inside the structure of a sentence? What inner articulation releases the coils and complications of Saying's assertion? In very different ways the countermovement of these two women's work penetrates to the indefinite limits of written communication. (11–12)

This passage begins with questions that resonate with most "second-wave" feminisms, namely critiques of literary history and the patriarchal hegemony that is "shut inside" language itself. But then it moves to a different type of question, one that involves not the relation of a sexed subject to external power relations but of the subject's articulation of the urgency of *Saying* itself. Howe's use of this term can be traced to her readings of Heidegger and Levinas later in the book and also in her journals and letters (Susan Howe Papers, UCSD 11.16.18, 74.4.18, 201.14). Hence, I give her use of the term an ethical reading, equating her *Saying* with my "saying." In the passage I quote above, my equation is confirmed because the saying works in tandem with the final statement concerning "the indefinite limits of written communication." For Howe, the saying works in tandem with the final statement concerning "the indefinite limits of written communication." For Levinas, the saying of language (in crude terms, the event of the face of the Other speaking) beyond what is said (the content and form) opens all ethics. In Howe's terms, the very saying, or utterance, of language asserts or demands something of the subject that language uncoils, and that something is the precinct of her ethics.

In the following passage from "Articulations of Sound Forms in Time," (1990)—Howe's poem written prior to "The Nonconformist's Memorial"— alterity, as the Other "beyond thought," unfolds in the context of notions of truth, the trace, and language:

> sand track wind scatter

> Inarticulate true meaning
> lives beyond thought
> linked from beginning (*Singularities* 30)

These tracks in the sand, susceptible to the slightest wind, are the trace of an "inarticulate true meaning [that] lives beyond thought." This passage can be read as a description of Howe's poem itself, which borders on inarticulate and scattered. These self-reflexive formal moments, in addition to the content, are the trace of the Other in a poem. For in self-reflexivity, the author reaches out to the reader by leaving a trace of herself in the text, a trace that the reader must respond to as the trace of the Other. What is more, these self-reflexive moments, as a self-conscious gesture, link the poem to the most primordial element of language, the saying, or the call of the Other. Through them, the writer insists, "I am speaking, respond." In Howe's language, ethics weighs on us even before the event, before time, "linked from beginning."

Moreover, the questions Howe poses above are the beginnings of a *feminist* response to that alterity, not merely a universal response to a genderless *Saying*. In this context, feminism—which Daly unfortunately rejects as a blockade to this task of welcoming the Other into her poetry (40–41)— fulfills, as much as any critical/political movement, Howe's project to heed the call of the Other.

In order to understand the feminist role such alterity plays in Howe's poetry, I would like to invoke what I see as a problematic yet germane moment in Irigaray's writing when she describes the relation of the sexed self to the Other in terms of *proximité*, or nearness. Unlike an ordinary notion of bodily presence, nearness for Irigaray means far more than physical closeness because of the alterity involved. Howe seems to understand the relationship with alterity in a similar way. Judging from early manuscripts, the nearness to alterity has also been an issue in her poetry for some time, as it has with Irigaray. One manuscript of section 5 of Howe's "Speech at the Barriers," from *Defenestration of Prague*, written in the early 1980s, at the same time Irigaray was first being translated into English, contains two lines that both suggest proximity and its opposite: the lines are "never touching" and "Reaching across alone in words oh." The lines remain in the published version, but in the manuscript they are in the same stanza at the end of the poem, which suggests to me that Howe sees them as connected in that there is an inherent separation in the intentionality and desire of language, "in words oh" (Susan Howe Papers, UCSD 201.5.1). In other words, proximity is a function of language and contains its other, separation or distance, within its signification. Because many feminists, such as Beauvoir, have a dialectical conceptualization of the relation between (male) self and (female) Other,[5] they can only see interpersonal relations in terms of antagonism and synthesis. Howe's poetry, in its complex invocations of alterity in the world of objects as well as the human community, requires a more nuanced approach, one that neither reifies Hegelian categories nor perpetuates a metaphysics of presence.[6] But if not founded on presence or on dialectics, what does Irigaray mean by *nearness?* This term is very vague, yet it seems to have many far-reaching implications for feminist negotiations of the body. I'll flesh out four of them relevant to Howe's poethics in the 1980s and 1990s.

The first implication of Irigaray's notion of proximity is that it critiques identity as the ground for feminist reclamations of subjectivity. She defines it as a "[n]earness so pronounced that it makes all discrimination of identity, and thus all forms of property, impossible" (*This Sex* 31). Clearly, Irigaray's category of "the feminine" is not necessarily tied to the biological body because "[s]he resists all adequate definition" (26), including biological ones. Howe writes similarly of Emily Dickinson's subjectivity, which Howe describes as "a mapless dominion, valueless value, sovereign and feminine, outside the realm of dictionary definition, the selflessness of filial benediction swelling forever under human uprootedness in fiction, the love beyond words to tell" (*My Emily* 111). Here we have the same attempt to identify the impossibility of identification in Irigaray's model of the subject. Thus, the experience of being a woman, more precisely of being a subject, is to *lose* identity, especially identity found in categories of gender that divide and exclude. According to Irigaray, "She herself enters into a ceaseless exchange of herself with the other without any possibility of identifying either" (*This Sex* 31).

Second, Irigaray's notion of proximity presents a different model of otherness. Unlike prior feminists like Beauvoir, Irigaray does not view the woman as Other determined as victim within a masculine economy; note the woman is the *subject* in her analysis. The term *the Other* for Irigaray has a more positive, or at least androgynous, valence because the Other facilitates and demands the loss of identity that constitutes the woman as subject. In proximity the self and the Other lose identity, and this very loss of identity constitutes the ethical because it prevents the reduction of women to property. Nearness, then, is not the determination of common ground based on identification (or of exclusion based on difference) but of the way proximity to the Other emphasizes the alterity disturbing representation, economy, the relation between people, and the difference between men and women. The freedom to be ethical, then, comes only through contact with the Other. Contrary to more dialectical philosophies, in proximity the Other is not my enemy.

Third, proximity also has much to do not only with subjectivity and ownership but with the body. The lips of a woman, as Irigaray says we must remember, speak and are always touching themselves/each other, so proximity is about the subject's relation to her own body (*This Sex* 209). If subjectivity is experience in a body, so then is the relation to the Other only experienced in a body. Facilitated, Irigaray argues, by the mucous membranes of the body, proximity is the lubricated encounter with an Other (*Ethics* 48, 109–11). This body, this lubrication, is the ground for an ethics of sexual alterity.

Fourth, this notion of embodied nearness dislocates sexual difference from the mode of agonism, and as Irigaray says elsewhere, returns it to the first realm, that of "wonder": "Who or what the other is, I never know. But the other who is forever unknowable is the one who differs from me sexually. This feeling of surprise, astonishment, and wonder in the face of the unknowable ought to be returned to its locus: that of sexual difference" (*Ethics* 13). What I want to highlight in this passage is Irigaray's inscription of a radical alterity, much like Levinas's, which she uses to emphasize the wonder of relationship with a sexed being. In the context of Saint-John Perse's poetry, which Baker calls "a meditation, probably unresolvable, on the very nature of these differences," Baker describes a similar sexual relation with radical alterity, "[no]t rational explanation, but wonder; not empty amazement, but rather a profoundly unsettling experience that challenges the very system of oppositions that organizes our mental and social structures" (*Obdurate* 37). In order to understand Susan Howe's work, it is also crucial to situate sexual difference in the context of such an infinite and irreducible alterity, and this slight emphasis of Irigaray's work can help us better to understand Howe's feminism, which can be summed up in the following maxim: *Every other—regardless and because of sex, gender, and orientation—differs from me sexually to an infinite degree.* This sexual alterity preempts any discrimination of difference based on identity, be it sexual or otherwise. In Howe's poetry, the woman's body—not other itself as in Baker's analysis, which risks replicating the subordinate position of women (*Obdurate* 39)— places herself at the call of or in proximity to the otherness inherent in the text's gaps and ambiguities. It is here we may find the ethics of Howe's poetics.

Bodily Rigorism

Considering the theoretical problems presented by proximity and alterity, it is no wonder that the touch of bodies is very touchy in Howe's poem, "The Nonconformist's Memorial," which Back cleverly calls "The Gospel According to Mary Magdalene" (123). One reason the word *touch* is a problem for Howe is because it is essential to the scene of Mary Magdalene and the not-yet-ascended Christ. In this particular work, Howe presents an encounter with the sexual alterity of another person, as an encounter with the trace of divinity. Mary Magdalene, it seems, is a perfect figure for an ethical exploration of the body. As a prostitute, she is by her trade pejoratively associated with her body, and, in the fourteenth chapter of Mark, Jesus defends her from criticism by the disciples because she has come to anoint his body for burial. Drawing on this context, Howe's poem is marked not only by alterity, in content and form, but also by the presence of words and figures of the body, which anchor alterity in sexuality. Many of the poems in fact constellate these terms as contingent on each other so that the body becomes the space of nearness to the Other:

Arranges and utters
words to themselves
Of how and first she
was possible body
Pamphlets on that side
the author of them
Parallel to the mind
a reprobate mind clings
close
inner outlaw impenitent
Over-againstness at least
Rigorism (*Nonconformist's* 24)

If we follow the convoluted web of this poem, we see intimately entwined the elements of body, textuality, and nearness; and, as in the poetry of Duncan, whom Howe evokes as one of the first poets in America to publicly acknowledge his homosexuality, Howe employs nearness to elide long-held boundaries. In fact, the "close / inner outlaw," in which inside touches outside, comprises the "impenitent /Over-againstness" of the nonconformity of Mary Magdalene, St. John, John Milton, Anne Hutchinson, Edward Calamy, Robert Duncan,[7] and other "reprobate minds." Howe, in the context of analyzing Dickinson's relation to the Civil War, couches rebellion in terms of crossing and mixing: "In Civil War we are all mutually entangled. To be rebellious but to distrust rebellion comes easily to women who may lose their husbands and children. To be rebellious and to distrust rebellion is the plight of the tragic artist. Daring is dangerous" (*My Emily* 114).

Yet the bodily touching of inside and out, through which a person is "in touch" with her or his unique inner spirit, is not the only form of nearness in the poem. In the context here of the redaction of King Charles's book, *Eikon Basilike,* the very icon of patriarchal power, "rigorism," as a form of "over-againstness" is the textual mode of rebellion and transcendence that Howe admires and is borrowing from her source texts. The poem itself forms an "over-againstness" with its splicing together of different contexts, from the gospels to *Eikon* to philosophy to Duncan's poetry to Howe's own biography and personal journals. The rigorous examination and juxtaposition of this material is not a form of argument or exclusion. Rigor leads ultimately to complication, uncertainty, and otherness. As Keller notes, Howe's open-ended poetics "precludes her assuming a dictatorial role or imposing a totalizing vision" (206). Thus without total overview, rigor is only possible in the many forms of nearness in the poem: the nearness of self to Other (Mary Magdalene and Christ), the nearness of "words to themselves," "Word and words together" (17), and bodies clinging to bodies.

All of these contexts, often portrayed in culture as separate, begin to blend in Howe's writing. For the gravity of bodies, "Don't cling to me . . . Literally stop touching me," is not only the pivot of sincerity/security around which bodies move, but for Howe is literally speech itself: "*We* plural are the speaker" (*Nonconformist's* 11). Only through the proximity of self and Other can language arise, blurring individual boundaries of authorship and ownership. Mary Magdalene, impetuous but uniquely privileged, has already touched the Word, the body of the unrisen Lord, the physiological counterpart to the many other boundaries—political, apostolic, and patriarchal—that Mary Magdalene crosses. In a poem two pages earlier, Howe writes of an "intractable ethical paradox" that involves not only "uprightness" but also the confusion of pronouns and names. As for Irigaray, the crossing of boundaries in nearness marks Howe's ethics as paradoxical. Or to restate, this bodily touching, which at once crosses and separates, models the sexual alterity that marks the ethical turn of the 1980s and 1990s.

The following poem accents this nearness to the divine not as the secretive affiliation that would mark membership to an exclusive order—as Howe portrays the disciples—but as an encounter of obligation to otherness:

As though beside herself
I want to accuse myself
would say to her confessor
Confessions implode into otherness
lay at night on thorns
For the purpose of self-concealment

would have consumed iron
And she fled her ecstasies
many occasions (*Nonconformist's* 25)

As we see in Irigaray's work, the ecstatic relation of self to self is a relation to an otherness just as is the self-concealment of confession. Howe writes, "Reader I do not wish to hide / in you to hide from you" (30). This confession, in its very utterance, opens the subject, "as though beside herself," to the Other and to language. Language, as Howe describes it, as "implode[d] into otherness," resists interpretation and communication, prevents a pure purging of sin and responsibility, and, in a far more puritanical mode than Edward Dorn or Robert Duncan's ethics, continually turns us away from our "ecstasies" and toward the Other through the experience of sexual alterity. As Howe points out later in the poem, "I wander about as an exile / as a body does a shadow," where, counter to *Gunslinger's* revelry, exile is a silent and ghostly position that also opens her (body) to the Other who (is) (in) language: "It is the Word to whom she turns / True submission and subjection" (*Nonconformist's* 30). The turning to the Word, the act of writing a poem, the saying of language, and so forth, is a bodily state and takes on even more significance when enacted by a female body. This submission is not necessarily the victimization of woman in patriarchy, nor can it be separated from it, as Howe herself talks on the one hand of her own "Slavery," which could be read as being subject to or complicit in patriarchy. But the subject is not as one excluded but as one subjected to (etymologically from the Latin meaning *thrown under*) the Other in a way that is similar to Irigaray's notion of identity as loss, described above, and to Levinas's notion from the 1970s of obligation as a pure loss of the one-for-the-other ("Trace" 348–49). Howe re-includes Mary Magdalene into the story in order to stress her importance, not merely to bemoan her exclusion. At the same time, Howe stresses Mary Madgalene's devotion to Christ in ways not recognized by tradition (theological or feminist). Mary Magdalene is remarkably obligated to Christ in Howe's account. This one-for-the-other of obligation ultimately leads Howe to self-realization and freedom (*My Emily* 117–18).

But such freedom does not come in leaving the material realm; freedom would not come in transcending the body itself. Take this poem for example:

She saw herself bereft
of body
would only seem to sleep
If I could go back

> Recollectedly into biblical
> fierce grace (*Nonconformist's* 32)

This vision of being bereft of body, perhaps a dream since the poem is "set" at night, is only a semblance of sleep, a fantasy of time travel. But the body, whether within it in life or without it in death, keeps one from going back to witness the event of the resurrection. Thus the body is necessary for history itself and becomes, as for Duncan, the site of the call to ethical obligation. The last line of the entire series enigmatically unites body and obligation: "Her love once said in her mind / Enlightenedly to do" (33). The enactment of "enlightened," or I would gloss perhaps, "ethical," acts does not occur by leaving the body but by resurrecting it, reconnecting it in nearness to the mind and heart, informed in the ear by the Word. These bodily experiences with sexual alterity in Howe's work lead not to ecstatic transcendence of the body but to the transcendence of traditional notions of gender through obligation to the Other.

But this obligation also takes on a larger social imperative. Commenting on the passage from Mary Rowlandson's capativity narrative in which her six-year-old daughter dies in her arms, Howe analogizes America's history, past and present, to this fecund moment of shattering Love and inescapable culpability:

> What redemptive vision can transform the radical chaos of one wounded child's slow and agonizing death in the ahuman continuousness of a virgin forest? Where is the warm hearth Heidegger finds through Hölderlin's perception of what lies waiting at the summit of the central Self? Before World War II could any work of European imagining exceed the rough-hewn intensity of this American Puritan mother's prophesy? (*My Emily* 112)

The figure of the mother holding her dying child or of a woman poet writing emblematizes, for Howe, an inescapable obligation that can only be laid bare through the "rough-hewn intensity" of living (and writing) in the wilderness, on the borders between worlds, white and native. This living, Howe suggests, could not have been conceived in European understanding until the Holocaust in which the Will of Self comes face to face with the seeming threat of otherness and is exposed. Sensing the same problem with "the summit of the central Self," Howe's response to Heidegger echoes Levinas's indictment of the anonymity of Heideggerian Being: Hominess and domesticity are replaced with insufferable weight, exile, and wilderness (Levinas,

"Trace" 345–48). In this critique of a conformist Self, however, Howe does not advocate an ethics of blame in which the poet hands down sentences, literally, to a collective of convicted perpetrators. In other words, she does not judgmentally condemn America, or men, or Europeans. Nor does she champion women as victims. This invocation of alterity—"[t]he persistent ground of 'alterity, anonymity, darkness'" (*My Emily* 113)—is not simply about legitimizing concepts traditionally coded feminine, as DuPlessis suggests (*Pink Guitar* 126–27), nor is obligation a noblesse oblige about what one powerful group (men) owes to another underprivileged group (women, natives). Most of all, Howe's poethics takes singular responsibility not only for her own but a nation's debt to the Other, above and beyond the politics of gender and power. Obligation's anarchy rends all orders.

In such a relation between the body, the text, and the Other, Howe creates a subject "without any real subject" (*Nonconformist's* 10) who is decentered, fragmented, and nonhierarchical, whose mode of being, like language, is expression. Howe underscores this emphasis on the saying of language rather than what is said when she adds emphasis to John 20:18: "Mary Magdalene came and told the disciples that she had seen the Lord, and *that* he had spoken these things to her" (*Nonconformist's* 3). In italicizing *that,* Howe emphasizes the importance of the event of speaking. What was said by the risen Christ defers to the utterance itself, which Howe cites as the opening of an alternate, antinomian tradition—carried on by Anne Hutchinson—that parallels the patriarchal and pronominal tradition of the Church founded by the Apostles. Ultimately, as Daly has pointed out, what is expressed is an infinite obligation to the Other to carry out the saying word of the Word. For Howe, the emphasis on the utterance—the struggle of language against patriarchal authority, the breaking out of wilderness into civilization—brings us up rigorously against alterity.

An Other Grammar

Obligation in Howe's work involves not only theme or content but also form. And this formal working of obligation, Howe points out, has particular resonance for feminism: "For these two feminist scholars [Gilbert and Gubar] a writer may conceal or confess all, if she does it in a logical syntax. Emily Dickinson suggests that the language of the heart has quite another grammar" (*My Emily* 13). In other words, feminist criticism of poetry has been blind to an ethical verse that rejects overt, conventional pronouncement in favor of a grammar of the "heart," otherwise known as the saying of language. As DuPlessis says, "The deepest effect of this experience of otherness is the dissolution of language" (*Pink Guitar* 138), which means a dissolution of form in particular, but this dissolution is not only about catharsis and the construction of female identity. Formal experimentation enhances Howe's feminism that consists in finding, outside of logical syntax, "another grammar" of the Other. It must be stressed, however, that this is not a separate but equal grammar, which resides outside yet works like the symbolic order, that only women can speak; ths other grammar is an ethical posture toward another person regardless of (yet obliged to bodily) sex. Through this other grammar, obligation can speak to the Other without being demoted in favor of order or rule.

Throughout *My Emily Dickinson,* Howe praises a form full of "rupture and parataxis" as the exploration of terror (116) and "stammering" as a humility and openness to uncertainty (21–22). "Stammering," which can only happen in a body, has been a staple in Howe's career. It also pervades the poems that comprise the anthology of her early 1980s work, *The Europe of Trusts,* especially "Speech at the Barricades." In manuscript versions of the poem, the word *stumbling* is also prevalent but seems to have been excised. The lines "Omen of stumbling unknown Captaincy" and "stumbling phenomenology" were cut from the "Corruptible first figure" poem (Susan Howe Papers, UCSD 201.5.1). She takes the motif up, however, in her later work: The "stammering" takes place literally and figuratively in "The Nonconformist's Memorial" around the Word itself:

Is that the same as Hell
Theologians in that fire
As to her physical health
and the fire
As night to understanding
or truth to fiction
stammering to a redaction
the quick and simplicity
Believing unbelieving reader
there is now no rest
She confessed to a Confessor
tell lies and I will tell (*Nonconformists's* 29)

The striking thematic of this poem includes figures of blackmailing Confessors and Theologians in Hell, echoing the figures that people Dante's Hell in Pound's Canto xiv; these images seem to place Howe's savaging of male tradition against the "stammering" of Mary Magdalene's truth. The relation

of gender to this stammering is illuminated by one of Howe's most important statement on her feminism, which includes the passage: "Promethean
aspiration: To be a woman and a Pythagorean. What is the communal vision of poetry if you are curved, odd, indefinite, irregular, feminine? I go
in disguise" (*My Emily* 117–18). Howe desires to think through dualisms
(Pythagoreanism) without falling prey to the traditional alignment that
woman=evil. That is her "Promethean aspiration." Freedom from the patriarchal vision, in this passage for instance, comes from her understanding of
the difference between slavery and obligation.

But even more stammering occurs in the above passage from "The Nonconformist's Memorial" on the formal level. The poem sets up a series of
analogous, if oxymoronic, relationships—between health and fire, night
and understanding, truth and fiction, and stammering and redaction—but
what is important in this particular lyric are the moments when the relationships slip, as in the pun on "Hell" and "health" suggests. The first "As" in
the third line does not seem to have a clear relation to the previous two lines,
and the line break after "health" makes it questionable whether the next line
completes a grammatical unit. But with lines 5–7, the poem presents us
with what appear to be oppositions, with stammering being the opposite of
redaction—to put into writing, to frame, to edit, to publish. But are they
opposite for Howe? Or does the form of stammering, Howe's brand of editing—where the word *to* both binds and divides—itself bring stammer and
redaction together and thus truth and fiction? And after the stammering line,
the syntactical relationships between the lines seem to dissolve. Stammering.

This stammering is textual, and with the word made flesh it is also corporeal: "word flesh crumbled page edge" (*Nonconformist's* 13). As Daly writes,
"Howe laboriously reclaims the mechanism of meaning in its primacy as a
metaphysics to which language extends the possibility of bodily contact, a
metaphysics giving-way to rather than weighing-in against affection and ecstasy in language" (45). In the conflict between ecstasy and exile, the body
too has its own alterity. In the several poems following "Is that the same as
Hell," toward the end of the series, formal stammers coincide with the very
function of language and thus of the body. In the following poem, names
are not enough to encapsulate the relationship of the body to the Other:

I remember the strangers
Not finding names there
Immanence is white with this
Where to find charges

A hymn was contesting a claim
Court of interior recollection
Map of a wilderness of sin
There I cannot find there
I cannot hear your wandering prayer
of quiet (31)

What replaces the certainty of naming is deixis. Three of these lines end in deictic pronouns that point to nothing but the inability of words to name. "Immanence is white with this." With what? The *not* finding of names? Immanence, perhaps the body of Christ himself, is white with Death? Who knows. Even the places that control meaning, churches and governments with their "charges," and the memory of dissenters and the moral "map" of doxology, cannot contain this signified: "There I cannot find there." Echoing Stein's infamous phrase, "there is no there there," Howe self-reflexively points to deixis itself as the mechanism of all language: words point only toward the abyss, "wandering prayer / of quiet," more silent than silence. Although I have stated that for Howe the saying of language opens one up to the Other, this opening consists not in a connection of identity or understanding: "even language never truly connects me to another" (*My Emily* 107–8). Howe gives us the language not of knowledge and claim but of the finding, the walking, the praying, the recollecting, the stumbling, the stammering, the wandering, the exile, and the stranger.

This change of emphasis has everything to do with escaping a tradition based on claim, hierarchy, and exclusion, which was constructed mostly by men. For Howe, as for Kristeva, constructing a feminine logic that simply turned the tables and used the same tradition of logic to exclude men would not facilitate escape. Hence, Howe relies on the saying to situate gender— obligation both allows for norms to arise but its infinite character calls those norms into question—avoiding the pitfalls of the replication of history. Under obligation, sexual difference cannot collapse into norms founded on identity. In the 1994 *Talisman* interview, Howe explains the intention of such devices in her own poetics: "So I start in a place with fragments, lines and marks, stops and gaps, and then I have more ordered sections, and then things break up again. That's how I begin most of my books. I think it's what we were talking about in history as well—that the outsidedness . . . These sounds, these pieces of words come into the chaos of life, and then you try to order them and to explain something and the explanation breaks free of itself. I think a lot of my work is about breaking free" (*Birth-Mark* 166). In her poetry, it seems, Howe takes pieces of "outsidedness," traces of the Other, and tries to "order them" knowing full well and welcoming the inevitable breaking free of the Other in and from the poem. Freedom then comes after a response to the Other in language, in the lyric not as a reaction against patriarchal tradition, which would simply, in opposing it, reify its power. For Howe, the lyric is the "highest form. And in this form I hope that sexed differences are translated, transformed, and vanish" (*Birth-Mark* 171). This event, the "goal" of Howe's feminism perhaps, occurs for the briefest moment in one of the more radically typographical poems in the series (see Fig. 3). How are we to read this poem? What are we to make of the upside-down passages and the words written over or too close to each other? Is this compression and overwriting of words in a palimpsest a literalizing of rigorous proximity, the words being as close to each other as they can be on the page? Perhaps there is no key, in this poem or in this series, which would provide a legend from which this poem may be deciphered. Not that there is no way to read it, but that any interpretation must remain contaminated with uncertainty, with an alterity that escapes category. Any way we decide to read it, we must respond to that alterity. We cannot pretend the poem is final or ordered.

What I see in this poem is a metamorphosis narrated in each direction the poem can be read. If we start from the first "right-side up" words, we begin with the call to transcend the world, which thematically fits with Howe's interest both in the transcendence of the Other and of gender. Here, the subject writing is neither named nor gendered, as the poem remains in first or second person, but we are constantly reminded of the material body that causes us to "stumble" our "feet wrapped in hay." The references to the nativity here bring the idea of incarnation to bear on the poem not as mythology but as phenomenology. The stanza ends in what civilized man has always considered the ultimate straying from the Word, a lack of knowledge. Such a conclusion is immediately ironized in the proximity of this ignorance to the phrase *Happy to be in peace*. Suddenly, the stumbling and straying from knowledge brings happiness and peace to the "Hearers of the Face Discourse," which, as Howe is perhaps pointing out by running the words together on the page, is peace itself. The singing jubilation of this peace, however, is tempered by the trembling of a woman's (Her, Mary Magdalene's, Susan's?) body "like a leaf" (of a tree, of paper?). This trembling, along with the simple act of drinking a tumbler full of water, brings us back to the impingement of the body. This act of drinking, the transfiguration of blood in the Eucharist, leads again to transcendence: "Out of enclosure She /

was out of enclosure

Transfiguration

Out of enclosure She

So many stumble

going out of the world

Come then!

Feet wrapped in hay

I stray to stray

her knowledge of Me

Hearers of the Face Discourse

Happy to be in peace

know next to nothing

She drank a tumbler-full of water

Often singing

Her body trembled like a leaf

3. Page 16 of *The Nonconformist's Memorial*.

was out of enclosure." The vicious cycle of the tautology of this last (first?) line, from which the word *Transfiguration* bursts forth in italics, mimicking the act of transcendence, has the same structure as the poem itself, if read as I have suggested. In a two-way flow, we begin in the body that is transcended only to oscillate back to the body, which leads us again to transcendence. Thus, there is no transcendence without the proximity of the body. In the context of gender, the simple acts of stumbling, singing, drinking, or writing prefigure the transfigurations that move us beyond the sexed definition inherent in pronouns. Although critics like Back present convincing readings foregrounding the meaning of transcendence, the best gloss on this poem comes from Howe herself in *My Emily Dickinson:* "Poetry leads past possession of self to transfiguration beyond gender" (138). Being sexed does not mean owning or identifying oneself; it means opening to the changes alterity can bring, especially in the context of the way "being sexed" comes to mean for us. Such sexual alterity, which moves us beyond the gender of pronominal distinction, a distinction that is often used to reinforce inequality, is not a result of the form; rather, Howe's formal experimentation invites the wilderness into the enclosure of the page.

Although the form of "The Nonconformist's Memorial" is relatively conventional, the poem deals more explicitly than any other in Howe's published corpus with the body and its relation to sexual alterity. But it is no wonder that many of Howe's poems—such as "A Bibliography of the King's Book," "Scattering as a Behavior Toward Risk," and "The Liberties," which deal explicitly with the theme of sexual difference—explode traditional lyric form and scatter the body of the poem across the page. More than just an aesthetic act, this formal scattering enacts the transformation, re-situation, and transcendence of sexual difference through the body of/and language itself. These poems, which like nets multiply empty spaces or like acoustic rooms cultivate silences, open themselves to the Other in their very bodies that are the bodies of expression. This nondidactic ethics, which does not tell us how to behave as sexed beings, affords us the liberty to live without boundaries of sexual difference determining our fate. Unique to Howe's ethics, this bodily freedom ironically leads us to an ethical obligation to the Other: Mary Magdalene's freedom through the poem returns her to Jesus, the sexual alterity of the Other.

Although Mary Magdalene's experience as a woman is important in the context of her nonconformity in a male tradition, the division of sexual difference is an enclosure enforced by that same male tradition to which women writing, or men writing, are in no way obligated to adhere. Ethics for Howe therefore does not consist in a woman using her body—whether in child-birth, mourning, captivity, or restoration—to perpetuate a male-writ law, but to be on call to the Other whose alterity eclipses rational categories, including sex and gender. Although Howe's ethics is not proscriptive, she does, as Freitag points out, continually call for responsibility in reading as a subversion of Western civilization (56). Yet as Language poet Steve McCaffery points out, reading is not always subversive (*North* 123–24). What those possible meanings could be is not as important, in my estimation, as the structural device of emphasizing responsibility to sexual alterity in reading. I do agree, though, that Howe opens the text to possibility, but her de–construction is more literally a de–struction, de–structuring (à la Nietzsche and Heidegger) that takes apart the language while at the same time returning to order. As Howe says, she's "in disguise" (*My Emily* 118). Thus Howe emphasizes not a particular reading and its skeptical politics, but that reading itself bears a responsibility in and from language.

On the other hand, the poet's "ethical obligation," according to Howe in an interview, is to express her "deepest necessity" (Keller, "Interview" 30–34), which for her is a dual responsibility: (1) to a sexed Other (e.g., in the figure of Mary Magdalene) who has been excluded from history; and (2) to the Other whose sexual alterity pervades the body/text and brings us in closer to wonder and joy. Howe exemplifies this responsibility in her writing, for one, by writing in proximity to Dickinson. And by writing in proximity to, not about, her own body, Howe broadens feminist notions of ethical and political practice. She places herself firmly against any system, poetic, or mode of thought that operates by excluding the Other. What takes priority in Howe's poetry is not the shape or definition of a body according to some pre-given categories or norms, be they patriarchal or feminist, but of a particular body's orientation to the obligation cast upon it (as a spell or curse or an imperative not to touch) by the sexual alterity of the Other.

6 Permeable Ethics Lyn Hejinian's *The Cell*

PROSPERO. If you be pleas'd, retire into my cell
    And there repose; a turn or two I'll walk
    To still my beating mind. (*The Tempest* IV.i)

ROMEO. Bid her devise
    Some means to come to shrift this afternoon;
    And there she shall at Friar Laurence' cell
    Be shriv'd and married. (*Romeo and Juliet* IV.iv)

PROSPERO. Welcome, sir;
    This cell's my court; here have I few attendants,
    And subjects non abroad; pray you, look in. (*The Tempest* V.i)

GUDERIUS. But unto us it is
    A cell of ignorance, travelling abed,
    A prison for a debtor that not dares
    To stride a limit. (*Cymbeline* III.iii)

TITUS. There greet in silence, as the dead are wont,
    And sleep in peace, slain in your country's wars.
    O sacred receptacle of my joys,
    Sweet cell of virtue and nobility,
    How many sons hast thou of mine in store
    That thou wilt never render to me more! (*Titus Andronicus* I.i)

There are myriad similarities between Susan Howe and Lyn Hejinian, but I'll begin by naming just a few: First, as lifelong correspondents, they are often associated with the group of Language poets who began writing and collaborating in the 1970s, and they are often read in the same terms by critics. Using a similar avant-garde poetics, both poets invoke and question the binary relation of totality/infinity, desire/separation, masculine/feminine, part/whole, sex/gender, and sameness/alterity, which is why I think they fit nicely with this ethical trajectory coming out of the 1960s in experimental American poetry. They also both question, through their use of innovative forms, the view that the author authorizes meaning in lyric poetry (Mix). Like Howe's, Hejinian's poems, such as those found in *My Life*,

Writing as an Aid to Memory, Oxota: A Short Russian Novel, and *A Border Comedy,* are best *enciphered,* to use Steve McCaffery's terms, rather than *deciphered* (Hartley 67–68). That is, they require the reader to actively participate in "making sense" by bringing external contexts to bear on the poem because there is no unified "message" within the text itself. This mode of enciphering, incidentally, is another way of inviting the Other, as the unknowable reader, into the poem. In a poetics statement published in 2000, Hejinian refers to this cooperative relationship as one between "guest and host," highlighting its ethical import ("Some Notes" 235). Finally, both poets focus thematically on non-identity and use experimental structures that invite nonsense, strangeness, and alterity into the poetry.

In spite of such similarities, each poet approaches the problem of relating to alterity differently. For Howe, on the one hand, poetry is fragmentary at the level of the line (and even signifier) and rarely stays within its own bounds of reference, continually pointing to other texts, otherness, and others "outside" the text. In Howe's documentary style—as exemplified in "The Noncomformist's Memorial," "A Bibliography of the King's Book or, *Eikon Basilike,*" even her critical *My Emily Dickinson*—the writing takes on a certain encyclopedic feel that gestures toward the supposed totality of Western literature, perhaps because Howe is responding to the postmodernist challenge presented by the scope of the long poems of Charles Olson, George Oppen, and Robert Duncan. On the other hand, Hejinian's long poems (*The Cell, My Life*) do not make such grand gestures because they are not documentary, except in more subjective ways that document her own perceptual process ("Strangeness" 35–36). Rarely referring beyond their own thematic web of signifiers (which are often those of a Wittgensteinian philosophical text: "tree," "blue," "water," etc.) and their often abstract referents (that is, without specific signifieds), *The Cell* feels claustrophobic, closed-in, total. There may not be any literal reference outside the text or even outside Hejinian's perception itself, let alone any historical "source" for those signifiers; they are admittedly limited to the perception through time of the writer (and reader). Despite this seemingly total form, *The Cell* is unexpectedly permeable for two reasons: (1) the shifting syntax within sentence and lyric opens the poem to syntactic frames "outside" the poem, to different contexts or "language games" that attempt to control meaning; and (2) the lack of tight reference (as opposed to Howe's sometimes labyrinthine allusions and quotations) allows the saying of ethical responsibility to enter the text on the levels of grammar, syntax, punctuation, line, section, and whole poem much more readily. Now, these distinctions vary along a continuum between the two writers depending on the particular poems, but such differentiations serve as workable boundaries between the works at hand by Howe and Hejinian to show the broad range of responses to the problems that mark the ethics of contemporary women's poetry and the American avant-garde as a whole.

Since *The Cell* explicitly explores totality, we return in a sense to the beginning of this project and Louis Zukofsky's Objectivist "rested totality," which presented us with the problem *and* the potential of an ethics involving exclusion of the Other through poetic measure and the subsequent failure of that measure. In fact, this notion of measure recurs again and again in Hejinian's work. In 1985, for instance, she composes in her journals what I like to think of as a virtual *ars legendi* for *The Cell,* explaining what she sees as the elements of the content and form of her work. In this "legend," she calls form the "measure . . . of perception," but like Duncan she also claims to be interested in the "deformation of patterns," which immediately makes difficult any speculation of what the ethical impact of such totalizing measure could be (Lyn Hejinian Papers, UCSD 74.47.6). The essays she was writing at the same time support this; when she writes of Gertrude Stein's use of container motifs, like the carafe in *Tender Buttons,* she is also speaking of her own writing: "Across the motif of containment, there is a series of words relative to destruction, or, at least, change" ("Two Stein Talks" 133). Needless to say, a strong debt to Zukofsky and the notions of totalizing measure are at work here. However, Hejinian returns to Zukofsky with a difference: Her "totality" is a permeable one in which alterity pervades, without fear, the very fibers (lines and sentences and phrases and words) of the poem's measure. Hejinian's poetics invites the Other to such an extent that the very fabric of language seems to tear. But this tearing is not a curse but an ethical opportunity because, as she writes in the poem "The Person," "closure is misanthropic" (*Cold* 170). In "The Rejection of Closure," she details a poetics of openness that privileges devices that open the text not first to sexual difference but to alterity in language. In the wake of this paradox, we are left with a negative totality, a cell turned inside out and exposed to the Other, as both men and women are exposed in their sex. In Hejinian's poetry, we see that exposing the ethical saying of language "predates" the closure of the sentence, of the subject, of the cell, of totality, and of gender structures. From this holy/whole-y/holey ground of the relation to the Other, totality and hegemony lose their fearful countenance as the invincible domination of the transcendental signifier, the signifier-in-power.[1]

Ethics and Morality: Releasing Judgment

This loss of power, so pervasive in Hejinian's poem, lends it ethical potential, but it does not immediately answer the question: What can be said about the ethics at work (or at "fail") in *The Cell?* What cannot be said of the ethics of this poem, unlike some of the other poems in my project, is that it is virtually impossible to distill any unified and coherent moral themes, pronouncements, or judgments, even when Hejinian claims to be a moral philosopher.[2] In this way she most closely resembles Charles Reznikoff. That is not to say, however, that the poem does not engage the discourse of morality and ethics. In "Two Stein Talks," Hejinian repeatedly engages the ethical impulse of realism as she distinguishes the kind that Stein was developing (128–30). Of detective fiction, Hejinian asserts that its foregrounding of details "forces the trivial to become moral," a phrase that aptly describes her own poetry because the very words of moral philosophy themselves become the "details" in the poems (129). *The Cell,* too, engages the context of moral discourse explicitly in many instances (18, 19, 53, 82, 129, 150)— something that is even more apparent than in the poetry of Howe.

Though Hejinian herself sees this as a moral poem and herself as a moral philosopher, she cannot see the conflict in her own thinking of morality between form and content, the same conflict she points out in Francis Ponge's work in her journals from 1988 (Lyn Hejinian Papers, UCSD 74.47.7). At this point in her career, Hejinian's view of the poem's morality revolves around her own failure to cast the ethical workings of the poem in a context other than that of moral philosophy, which by definition must lay down judgments as a purely thematic rather than formal gesture. In some of her journal entries written contemporaneously with *The Cell,* much of her thinking about ethics remains in the mode of morality, especially in instances like a discussion of the ethics of some in the Language poetry group not wanting to interact with poets who disagree with them. Hejinian's response is that it would be "unethical" if we did not (Lyn Hejinian Papers, UCSD 74.47.7). But in choosing a form that, as she says later in the journals, "doesn't withhold judgment, releases judging" (Lyn Hejinian Papers, UCSD 74.47.7), which at the same time judges and does not judge, she irreparably alters the potential for such certainty and pronouncement, even if it is inclusive. Furthermore, as suggested by this passage together with her comments on French feminism in "The Rejection of Closure" (283), Hejinian thinks morality must be more than personal opinions and behaviors due to her emphasis on language and its social basis. These pressures make the distinction between ethics and morality a fruitful way of approaching her poetry that does not rely on systematic judgment.

This releasing of judgment happens mostly when she makes statements about morality in her journals in the context of her thinking about the form of her poetry. Because of her prose emphasis on the "formation (and deformation) of patterns" (Lyn Hejinian Papers, UCSD 74.47.6), the pronouncement of morality often gets qualified in the ambiguity of her poetry through what she calls "the language of inquiry" ("Strangeness" 38; Lyn Hejinian Papers, USCD 74.47.7). "But all my judgments," Hejinian writes in *The Cell*, "are / threaded / I don't think I'd know" (182). This inquiry questions not only epistemological bases of words but their ideological and social framing. Another poem from *The Cell*, one of the only in the series written over three separate days and in the wake of many of her moral reflections in the journals, captures this nonjudgmental ethics very clearly. Seeking an alternative, she frames her ethics as the obligation inherent in language and perception. I quote the poem in its entire published form:

> Unorganized octave ashes scattered in
>   the humid light
> The unblinking ears are their
>   damp confidant
> The poem is not natural,
>   unnaturally desired and saturated
> The relentless obligation of seductive,
>   descriptive, and corrupting perceptions
> Of some eternal, never-ending, everyday
>   task
>
> > *December 13 & 14, 1986*
> > *January 6, 1987 (53)*

This poem, explicitly about obligation in the poem itself, has several important intertexts that shed light on her inquiries into morality and ethics. As her journals show, Hejinian was reading Mauriece Merleau-Ponty on perception in April 1985, suggesting that Hejinian was thinking of the body as ethical in ways akin to what I discussed with Robert Duncan in chapter 4. (Lyn Hejinian Papers, UCSD 74.47.6). Not surprisingly, she quotes Merleau-Ponty in "Two Stein Talks," which she had begun writing in late 1985 (Lyn Hejinian Papers, UCSD 74.47.6 23 Dec 84), to make the point that *Tender Buttons* could be "a masterpiece of phenomenological literature" (131). She later refers to the integration of mind and body in "Strangeness" that is indicative of Merleau-Ponty's phenomenology (32). In addition, this notion of "relentless obligation" comes from a key connection she has with Emmanuel Levinas—Fyodor Dostoevsky. She takes much of what she knows about Dostoevsky's sense of obligation from Joseph Franks's biography (Lyn Hejinian Papers, UCSD 74.47.7: 26–28 Dec 86). In the 1970s, Levinas was fond of quoting from Dostoevsky's *The Brothers Karamazov* where a character claims that he is responsible for everything in the world.[3]

Even more than this genealogy of morals, the journals reveal that Hejinian extracted a line from this poem that reveals her abiding concern for ethics over morality. Between the fourth and fifth the extracted line reads, "adult, neurotic, responsible," which could modify either "confidant" or "the poem" (Lyn Heijinian Papers, UCSD 74.47.7). In the context of the other uses in the poem at large of "responsibility," which several times occurs in conjunction with an Objectivist-flavored "sincerity," this line takes on new meaning (*The Cell* 121–22, 133–34). I suggest that she means by this term, *responsibility,* not simply moral duty but an obligation before the law. The above poem suggests that morality is a not a given but a deep questioning that relates to the poem's very structure. Moreover, this obligation does not come from some general Logos from which flows a didactic moral system; instead, it arises from "some eternal, never-ending, everyday task." A far cry from a morality of pronouncement.

In another poem, Hejinian employs a near rhyme that I interpret as giving an alternative to the morality of pronouncement, in which a "cell" coincides with a "call":

A cell cannot boast stable
    achievements
If one can say (if
    one can) that the wind
    has a stitch, the leaf
    is without one
Sleep without opposite
A call (*The Cell* 67)

This poem gives us several more structural images analogous to the closed form of a cell—a person, a baby, a bulb, a honeycomb, confines, skin—but "call" shifts the metonymic structure that elides the difference between image and motion. *The Cell* is as much about "*if* one can say" anything at all, a call, the very utterance of language, which comes before and through form. This form, as with the call of the Other, is not necessarily "stable" in its "achievements," an instability that is literalized in saying "the wind has a stitch." The slip of the stitch calls attention to the call of language. In consideration of her concomitant emphasis on form and the "rejection of closure," we might consider the ethics of Hejinian's poem as a formal response to what morality cannot bring into its systematized context—the very relation to the call of the Other, language, sociality. An opening of the cell in its very closure.

Form: The Real Question

Hejinian's ethics of sexual difference has mostly to do with form, as in the structure of a cell and the relation between cells in tissues and the relation between subjects in language. Aside from the number of poems in the series that deal explicitly with the word "form" indicates (88, 103, 169, 199), many other poems deal self-consciously with more specific elements of form, such as "metonymy" and "discontinuity," which I will discuss momentarily. First, I would like to explain what an ethical openness means to Hejinian in terms of form. In a journal entry dated March 17, 1987, in the middle of writing *The Cell,* as well as the essay "Strangeness," she writes: "It is odd to think of my*self* as a 'moral philosopher'—odd because the thought of such a possibility strikes me and I feel a rush of 'rightness,' and outward feeling toward it as toward something that is properly mine." Hejinian then qualifies that thought, doubting that she could be a philosopher because "I have no system." But she ends by returning to her concern with form as "the philosophical (or moral) basis" for the poem: "Could I say that for me form is the ethical background or context of the poem?" She prefers this measure of form because it is "outside *me*" (Lyn Hejinian Papers, UCSD 74.47.7: 17 Mar 87). In her essay, "Rejection of Closure," Hejinian offers several devices through which openness can be achieved. When Ron Silliman in his question during the discussion session suggests that openness can deliver a "tremendous sense of liberation" (287), Hejinian does not disagree. The writing of many French feminists, Hejinian points out, uses formal devices very similar to the poetry of the contemporary avant-garde, such as "syntactic disjunctures," which in effect liberate desire, particularly that of women (283). But her work goes beyond what Andrews would call the libidinal model of language to the social model.

For Hejinian, ethics derives not from the deconstructive/emancipatory potential of an *écriture féminine.*[4] In fact, she rejects the notion of such a "woman's writing" as "narrow" because it fails to see the desire located in language itself, which is thus "androgynous" (283). Such a label may be applied to her own writing because her writing practice debilitates the coherent relation between sentences that is implied in discourse and is the very glue of judgment; thus the sociolinguistic mechanisms of determining writing's gender (or the gender of the writer) are also rendered unworkable. This unworking occurs in Hejinian's writing for the sake of the social potential of language. In "The Rejection of Closure," Hejinian identifies several poetic devices—such as gaps, invitations to the reader to produce meaning, "explosion of the subject," uncertainty, and repetition, some of which I have already discussed in an ethical context—that open a text up to the reader, the word, and the world. In her rather paratactic quotations of Luce Irigaray and even Gertrude Stein, Hejinian tacitly places her idea of openness in the domain of equality and trust between the sexes, particularly in the context of psychoanalytic investigations of language and desire (272–73, 275–76, 282–83).

In *The Cell*, this ethics, like closure, is primarily a formal problem.[5] For instance, the structure of metonymy is often used to explain Hejinian's poetry and its epistemology of sexual difference,[6] but the poem proceeds from that point of departure to other poetic practices, such as accident and parataxis, which provide a much more permeable model that resonate with her rejection of closure. What is more, syntax itself becomes the mode as well as the object of Hejinian's play on sexual difference because syntax for her is essentially social: "Citizens are milling in the / public grammar" (*The Cell* 182). This notion of the social as syntax—as "public grammar," the syntax as social in all its myriad and fluctuating forms—permeates Hejinian's texts and makes them permeable. In this permeability, found at all levels of her poetics, we may find an ethical relation to the Other.

Line Sentence Lyric

The Cell, as then unnamed, begins in 1985 when Hejinian resolves to write one sentence a day "without punctuation." This discipline, arbitrary yet difficult to maintain on one's own, eventually turns into a correspondence with Kit Robinson, in which they agree to write one 10–12 line lyric per day, mainly in response to the other's poems. According to the journals, the number of lines seems to have been taken from "Webster's Ninth" dictionary, which has an illustration of an animal cell with twelve parts. By January 1987, after a trip to Rome and a visit to the catacombs, these exercises become embroiled in definitions of the word *cell*, which guides her writing, and by mid-1987, it becomes the series called *The Cell* (Lyn Hejinian Papers, USCD 74.47.7). On the formal level, this poem acts as a deep interrogation of the relation between units, "cells," of the poem: the word, the line, the sentence, the stanza, and the lyric. As we will see, these formal elements have analogous biological "cells," which include individual persons. From this interrogation we may observe how Hejinian opens language to difference and multiplicity of meaning but also invites the influx of alterity, the unknown and unknowable.

The poem as a whole has some unique characteristics: left justified lines, no periods, quasi-stanzas that include one or more line breaks, stanzas in which lines after the first are indented half an inch, and what would traditinally be called stanzas because they are groups of lines with spaces between each group. This construction puts word, line, and sentence in tension. In fact, Hejinian's journal reveals that she added much to the poem in later drafts, especially most of the line breaks and indentations that create the quasi-stanzas. Notably, these stanzas do not always coincide with what would be a complete sentence, even if there were punctuation. One of the many examples of this quasi-stanzaic form comes early in the poem and not incidentally includes a reference to morality. In order to show the sense of unity in these stanzas, I begin with the stanza right before it that contains all the elements of a complete sentence:

> I can't say comprehensively that
>> it's dark
> There's been some communication—not
>> a storm—a person pitying
>> itself having identified with a
>> storm
> With eyeing the median lines
>> with the telephone lines
> With moralities—one mental space
>> capable of holding two contents (*The Cell* 18)

The units of line, sentence, and stanza are not discrete. If a complete sentence ends with "dark," then a new sentence starts with "There's." But where does that sentence end? At the end of the stanza at the word "storm"? Or does it go to "contents," in which case, the following two stanzas would be parallel in the sentence to the construction "with a storm." In that case, a person not only identifies with a storm but the eyeing lines and with moralities. But perhaps the last two stanzas should be read alone, as discrete thoughts, one about lines and the other about morality so that the expectation of the final line—that one space holds two contents—would be realized.

Any way you read it, the potential meaning is changed and even augmented if all readings are taken at once (a moral act).

Like these quasi-stanzas, almost every line, a cell in itself, can be read independently or in context of the sentence of which it is a part (or supposedly a part). Take the line "a storm—a person pitying." It can be read alone, with the elements in apposition, serving as figures for one another. Metaphorically or metonymically, a person pitying another is a storm, perhaps in the sense of tears, but also in the moral dilemma pitying creates by conflicting self-interest with altruism. Morality itself, the poem seems to be saying, balances such contradiction, as "one mental space capable of holding two contents." The contents of pity are perhaps paradoxical, at the very least, but even more importantly, those moral knots might best be perceived when "eyeing" lines of poetry and keeping tuned to the networks of lines, like telephone wires, that connect people across time and space. Again the sociality and the linguistics of morality are emphasized.

Not every sentence, however, internally coheres like the example above. This leads me to believe that Hejnian does not take for granted the sentence as a unit, which an equation of her poetics with Silliman's "New Sentence" might suggest (Shoptaw). Instead, the sentence is being opened to new semantic and syntactic possibilities.

> Firefighters—conventional devices—passing in
>   a hurry, the whole sky
>   wet
> The entire green
> To read it requires a
>   magnifying glass from the *OED*
> Words organized and more than
>   likely (*The Cell* 208)

Often in the whole series, each stanza can be read as a complete sentence on its own, but the line breaks literally break open the sentences in this poem and many other places. The first two lines form a complete sentence, but the appositives and modifiers interrupt and render almost unintelligible the mini-narrative of the firefighters. The next line, "The entire green," does not seem to fit in either of the more complete sentences before or after, and the ambiguous pronoun reference of "it" makes the coherence of that phrase to other stanzas virtually insoluble. The last line, "Words organized and more than," is almost a complete sentence, but the passive construction of the verb without the subject phrase "by ____" makes this line seem to not read as a sentence, particularly because the next line "likely," may or may not belong to the sentence. Unlike Ron Silliman and his New Sentence and even, we might add, Gertrude Stein and her sentences in meditation, Hejinian wants to expose the way sentences work, not as a whole but internally, particularly as moral phenomena.

The poem continues with a scene of conventional moral action and its problems:

> Not looking at the homeless
>   person to whom I've given
>   money
> Not asking him to know
>   me in addition to taking
>   money (*The Cell* 208)

The incomplete but parallel construction of these quasi-stanzas uncovers the analogous incompleteness and ultimate dissatisfaction of defining ethics in terms of action. The poem renders problematic the philanthropic act of giving money to a stranger in need through the use of negatives that reflect inner turmoil. But absent is the part that would complete the sentence, so Hejinian's form performs a syntactic shift on the level of the sentence. The lines invite the reader, the Other in a sense, to complete the sentence perhaps with the construction, "Not doing x . . . is bad or wrong." The reader must fill in the variables that are not provided in the poem. What x is might just indeed be filled in another frame, say, by the phrase, "the best thing to do for a homeless person." By inviting the reader's participation in the form, Hejinian—like Oppen and Reznikoff, who reveal their own complicity in violence—brings into awareness the way moral judgments are completed by the moral subject. More precisely, she can make the reader examine *the language* used to complete moral judgment. This judgment, also used to complete the meaning of other figures of speech, such as metonymy, will ultimately take us to the dismantling of judgment in the discernment of sexual difference. In this exposure of (moral) judgment lies Hejinian's poethics.

Metonymy

As the sentences, lines, and stanzas would indicate, the problem with this book-length poem is that no isolated lyric coheres internally in a thematic sense, yet each one serves as a figure for the whole. That is not to say that there aren't, as Joseph Conte says in his discussion of metonymy in Oppen, thematic threads that weave in and out of the poem (179). For example, the signifier "blue" in all of its meanings appears and reappears throughout the poem, but so do words related to sex/gender, the body, morality, and notions of totality. Even "metonymy" itself is a theme, which leads me to believe that it becomes compromised as a way of achieving critical distance from these poems. The fact that she was preoccupied with the idea of metonymy in her journal as well as in the two critical pieces she was writing at the time, "Strangeness" (1987) and "Two Stein Talks" (1984), gives credence to that assumption. Keep in mind that in these essays Hejinian is looking for a language of description that is more of a "language of inquiry" than some facile notion of realism or definition: "I propose description as a method of invention and of composition. Description, in my sense of that term, is phenomenal rather than epiphenomenal, original, with a marked tendency toward effecting isolation and displacement, that is toward objectifying all that's described and making it strange" ("Strangeness" 32). If we take this method to heart, then we cannot assume that the "object" of Hejinian's poem is some assumed signified of the poem's signifiers like "metonymy." In other words, if we think metonymically, then "metonym" means something other than its conventional definition.

As an alternative to the traditional part/whole binary of metonymy, I propose employing the dichotomies totality/infinity or continuity/discontinuity, which turn the poem toward the outside, the Other, for getting at the ethics of this poem. In other words, *Hejinian attempts a metonymy of the infinite, even as she is invoking notions of totality.* For example, her use of the *Oxford English Dictionary,* a figure in the poem that supposedly contains the totality of the English language and its history, serves only as a storehouse for innumerable texts yet to come: "Words organized and more than / likely," is the way *The Cell* puts it, suggesting that these unwritten texts are "more," in excess of what is known and conventional, the "likely" (208).[7] As others have pointed out, Hejinian's poetics use a metonymic logic, but rather than this logic serving simply an aesthetic or epistemological end, I suggest that it has an ethical trajectory. In fact, metonymy, as opposed to contemporary culture's preferred method of metaphor in the form of synecdoche, serves for Hejinian as the very structure of gender—each subject male or female internally is associated with but not limited to the (confused, contradictory, regulatory, conflicted) larger context of gender roles and relations but not reducible "below" them in a hierarchical or derogatory logic.

First, I must make clear that metonymy is a logic of continuity, hence the many references to film and other synonyms of contiguity throughout the book.[8] "This word in a flow," Hejinian states in *The Cell*, "is the metonym" (133). She discusses flow in "Two Stein Talks" as consciousness that is both continuous and discontinuous (133). We can see the power of this continuity almost everywhere in the poem:

> The mouth opens on an
> > agate
> The beach is named of
> > it

Like the many poems in this book that refer specifically to "metonymy," this passage gives us the metonymic figure of the agate, a precious mineral that comprises one of the elements of ubiquitous sand, as on a beach; for sand serves normally as a metonymy for time. Intriguingly, though, the agate—sand or time—is what the mouth opens upon, and in the figure of the mouth we have the metonym for not only the human body (which is more of a synecdoche) but for the human desire of expression itself. The next set of lines underscore that direction:

> A person could make a
> > movie of it, everyone with
> > its twin in sufferance
> There is that in poetry

The deictic pronoun "it" confuses these elements (body, material, representation) because it could refer to "agate," "mouth," or the opening act of representation (naming) itself. But the single "everyone," as opposed to the compound "every one," even suggests that the "it" refers back to "person," punningly as a grammatical term. Many instances throughout *The Cell* use the neuter third-person pronoun to refer to human beings, and if we don't just write them off as whim, then we might have the beginnings of a different kind of response to the gender encodings inscribed in language.

Using "it" to refer to sexed beings, rather than "he" or "she," poses both a solution and a problem, not only in this poem but elsewhere in *The Cell* (172–73). In the first place, "it" calls attention to the way we use pronouns (which we use almost unthinkingly, as we once did with the universal masculine, "he," to stand for all humans) to inflict/inflect gender. "He" and "she" work in grammar as a kind of metonymy/synecdoche in which the referent serves as the "part" of the general, gendered "whole," a category being either all male or all female, and ultimately the "whole" is gendered male because the general has been conventionally coded masculine. Second, the error of using the neuter pronoun to refer to people gives us a way not to pin gender on phenomena with judgment. Although not a strategy new to American verse,[9] using "it" to refer to a sexed human attempts in a sense to bypass or short-circuit the part-whole relation and to leave reference as loose as possible. In some contexts, Hejinian seems to say, what does it matter if a person is male or female?[10] On the other hand, despite presenting liberatory possibilities, the third-person neuter tends to objectify. The body, as an "it" is still an object, to be predicated in a sentence, acted on by social forces, and even physically violated, so such use of pronouns does not gloss over the objective reality/risk presented by the body.[11] Finally, "it" is marked by the attempt to step out of metonymic logic, because "it" too is tainted by the stink of reason and totalization. Yet at the same time, "it" ignores the difference genitals (or language—biology as a separate kind of discourse and experience) make by effacing difference altogether. At best, the effects of the neuter pronoun "it" jar and disrupt, yet do not necessarily offer a way out of the gender coding of the English language.

This same poem from "December 10, 1986" continues its weaving together of body and representation through the antimetonymic function of "it":

A fiction of factors on
      a film
The animals (not dogs) stampeding
      backwards to laughter
It's not in their eyes
Writing by putting a leg
      over a knee is animal
And again it is also
      mineral
It is anatomical to repeat
      but the time isn't right
The times aren't the same
So poetry isn't a reminder (*The Cell* 50)

Each "it" functions in this passage in a different way, with a completely different type of (non)referent each time. The first pronoun could refer to "a fiction" or to "laughter," but its position in the poem could connect it to "writing," which is placed right below "it." Either way, what is called into question is the ability of representation to capture what's "not in their eyes," to capture the body, to capture "it," as a strict correspondence of word to thing, the essence of what Hejinian calls *description*. The second "it" in line 8, could have the same referential possibilities as the first "it," but it also could refer to "putting a leg / over a knee," which "is animal" and also a neuter "mineral." The third "it" seems simply to be an empty subject, without specific referent. At any rate, each "it" could possibly refer to movements of or by bodies, but the ambiguous reference undercuts any clear representation of those bodies and/or parts. This ambiguity arises because representation, a total representation, needs the stability of reference through pronouns in order to work properly. Hejinian calls attention to this linguistic mechanism of representation by deforming it. Not the least of these deforming results breaks contiguous metonymic chains, exemplified by the pronoun. Metonymy as pronoun, like the "is" of metaphor (also under fire in this poem), does not provide a reliable mode of representation, of gender or of neutrality.

Also in this passage, besides the problems of representation (in film and in writing), Hejinian invokes the bedrock discourse describing the body, anatomy, in which "sex" does matter quite a bit. But Hejinian decontextualizes anatomy to such an extent that one cannot take "anatomical" at its usual value. First of all, this is the case because we don't know what "it" is. What is anatomical? Putting a leg over a knee to write? Is leg crossing, a particularly feminine gesture, being called to our attention? If so, then it also calls attention to the culture that defines it as feminine. This decontextualization of "anatomy" exposes the metonymic and metaphoric structure of anatomy itself. Anatomy works by repeating the imposition of the whole (general, scientific principles of the bodies in a species acquired through inductive reasoning) on the part, a single body. Furthermore, the discourse of anatomy, particularly that of sexual difference, seeks the lowest-common denominator of the production of sex in culture, a discourse so "natural" that it is almost unquestioned. Hejinian's poem subtly alerts us to this fact. Later in *The Cell* she muses:

> I was walking on the
> sides of my feet in
> the sand, trying not to
> make tracks identifiable as those
> of female feet (179)

This image hinges on the assumption that footprints have the mark of sexual difference, but the obviousness of the assumption reveals a frame in which all body parts act as figures for the whole and thereby carry the mark of sexual difference. What is worse is the gesture that indicates a woman would want to conceal, or is embarrassed by, her sex. This frame of seeing all female body parts as bearing the mark of some essential femininity, which works off the logic of synecdoche, is savaged again and again in the poem in many specific contexts. Much like Howe's poetry, Hejinian's satire works to remind us that the lived experience of sexual difference is singular, like finger- or footprints, and resists the universalizing tendency of anatomy.

Another related frame taken to task in her poem is the objectivity of science in general, which works by a different logic than synecdoche. Instead of metaphor, science works by universalizing its claims and often denying difference and the role language has in achieving perception and thus objectivity. In her account of the rise of metonymic modes of thought in the seventeenth century, Hejinian writes that "[u]ltimately, conditions are incomprehensible without the use of analytical conceptual structures, but an initial, essential recognition of difference—of strangeness—develops only with attention to single objects, while others are temporarily held in abeyance" ("Strangeness" 43). In this context, Hejinian's phenomenology of perception asks the question, how does sex come to mean?—which requires dissolving the illusion of objective universals and looking at particular contexts, frames, or language games:

> I'm looking, prematurely, for a
>   particular point of view—that
>   of one who has already
>   achieved objectivity
> Objectivities and metonymies
> But one can't die
> Sex sexes scale and flies
>   faithful to the ground (*The Cell* 9–10)

To reduce "objectivity" to a point of view already denies its objectivity by relativizing it as one perspective among many. In fact, Hejinian pluralizes the word and places it in a coordinating construction with "metonymies," in effect equating it with the type of snobbish logic that denies the importance of sex in its language. However, sex does affect measurement—it "sexes scale"—and remains perhaps more "faithful to the ground" of perception, that is, language. Language, as the particularizing of point of view, imbues "objectivities" with meaning, via figures of speech and structures like metonymy. More importantly, in this passage metonymy serves not an exclusively feminist, utopian logic, but is itself co-optable by any powerful ideology, such as universalizing scientism. As Shoptaw puts it, "Hejinian knows well the heritage of making women into metonymic part-objects."

Connotation and Coincidence

Unlike metonymy, Hejinian's mode of composition often attempts dissonant associations, augmenting discontinuity,[12] which can be seen in the above passage. Not only do the four last lines of the above poem, moving from poetic form to death and sex, have a determinable metonymic relationship, but the last line, personifying "sex" as an agent of scale and then a bird of faith, is internally dissonant. None of those elements, tested against the logic of metonymy, are intimately or even remotely associated with each other in American culture. Another example overtly exposes the difference between the logic of metonymy and the logic of the poem. In the line, "The rapist was seeking a / vegetable kingdom" (*The Cell* 131), the vegetable does not serve as a metonym in our current time and culture for any type of rape victim because there is no existing frame of reference that portrays women (or men) as vegetables in their sexuality.[13] An earlier line with "meat fruit"— a virgin is a "cherry" and her desired, passive body is "meat"—does invoke metonymies that refer to the sexual object as vulnerable to violation. And although "vegetable" can imply an involuntary static state, it hardly connotes the forced passivity of victimization. But the coincidence of rape and vegetable only calls attention to such logic by substituting conventionally unrelated terms into the metonymic chain.

The term *coincidence,* especially in the sense of accident, seems to describe the syntactic, syllogistic structure of *The Cell* better than the connotative logic of metonymy. Such a metonymic structure more closely resembles the conscious control of Silliman's "New Sentence," in which he gives polysemy and ambiguity mere lip service compared to Hejinian's surreal sentences that fully enact those two qualities. In her journals from June 1985, this seeming confusion of continuity and discontinuity becomes clearer in entries such as this one, which comes in the "*ars legendi*" under the heading "Elements in the Contents of My Work": "The discontinuity of consciousness is set against the continuity of reality" (Lyn Hejinian Papers, UCSD 74.47.6). What is more, in *The Cell* you have the added problem of line breaks and the lack of sentence punctuation, through which Hejinian seems to be rejecting any kind of conventional order that might draw traces of patriarchy, like a virus, into her sentences, her cells.

But *The Cell* resists such infections of order at the level of diction, semantics, and association, which opens the poem to anarchy, to the Other (writer/reader). In her essay "Smatter," Hejinian proposes a poetics of "putting things together in such a way as to enable them to coincide," which might better give insight into her formal structures (17). As Douglas Messerli points out, this coinciding is about opening up the subject: "For Hejinian, this co-incidence produces a new relationship, which is at once the heart of communal sharing and a movement toward the centric; by giving up the self *to* language, one discovers in the language of the community a new self . . ." (*"Language" Poetries* 7). This "new" self, an accident I might add, comes not from conscious effort, but from a relationship with others, a community, and ultimately, the Other. "Centric" order, like that of time or poetic measure, does exist in the poem but reveals its arbitrariness, as in the dating of the poems in *The Cell*.[14] Much of Hejinian's syntax seems chaotic or disordered, on the brink of not making sense, but that is because, in part, the "making sense" is the responsibility of the reader. He/she must make meaning out of what appears, from the perspective of coherent discourse, to be mere accidents and coincidences. Both coincidence and metonymy create continuity by being discontinuous, but the continuities of coincidence are not provided by the poem or by any socially constructed frame of meaning but must be offered by the reader. A collaboration. An openness.

Consider the following example, which is only one among hundreds:

> The driver in the car
> > ahead on a sunny day
> > hung his arm out, his
> > cruelty (*The Cell* 166)

The arm functions as synecdoche for the driver in the same way that the idea of hanging one's arm out the window is a metonymy for the pleasures of driving. But the figure's meaning does not stop there. Because of the apparent appositive created by the comma, the reader is forced to decide how "his arm" relates to "his cruelty." Unfortunately, no logic of homology connects these terms nor is there a context or syntax in which they could conceivably be related; this comma creates what appears to be an accident, which is what we call "a coincidence," an event to which we cannot assign any logical cause. Elsewhere, Hejinian calls such accidents the "inadvertence of what appears" ("Strangeness" 32). So, the reader must come up with those frames on her or his own. One could surmise that the cruelty is the obscene gesture of the middle finger, which American drivers often give to each other out of anger. However, one must make this leap of linguistic faith out of personal associations, not conventionally held ones.

In this collaboration between poet and reader, invited by the gap in meaning unfilled by any existing literary figure of speech, emerges an ethics of form. A nearing of self and Other. Such collaboration constitutes a perfect formal device for Hejinian's discourse on sexual difference in which self and Other are drawn together, by accident perhaps, and are forced into a choice: choose preexisting frames from which to define the relationship (e.g., gender roles) or devise a new meaning collaboratively from the proximity of two disparate and radically other words, cells, persons.

To encourage us to choose the latter, Hejinian's poetics of coincidence foregrounds the *contingency* of the relation between sex and identity. Sex, as a seemingly inescapable biological factor, does have an effect on (that is, it coincides with) the way we perceive and thus represent the world, but that effect does not come about in any determined way. The effects sexual difference will have on a particular body depend mostly on interpretation and inflection. Moreover, sex is not just a personal effect but also dependent on social modes of interpretation. "Sex," Hejinian writes, "is not an abbreviation/nor are the sexes abbreviation" (*The Cell* 169). The effect of sex must be rigorously analyzed, on the subjective and social scale, to begin to see its working in a particular person's situation, and thus the coincidence of the prior line: "We keep ourselves tenacious with / the grip of our lessons." The rigor of our inquiry into our bodies and perception, Hejinian implies, will allow us to begin defining our sex and sexuality for ourselves, through which we will be able to "keep ourselves," that is, to remain true and sincere to what is as well as to what is other.

Hejinian plays up the *accidental* connotations of "coincidence," inserting play into the rigid correspondence between sex and identity. For example, in one poem in *The Cell* the cyclops is a figure of the penis (57), and in another it is a vaginal or feminine figure (170). The trope shows that words have no inherent gender, no matter how powerful the syntactic frame in which the figure appears, but such tropes also show how context can control meaning. If "reality is simply that which is accessible to reason," the poem on page 57 begins, then sexuality is "optimistic," a "cyclops." The poem critiques this cyclopic view of sex and sexuality as providing only "undivided situations" that, without difference, would totalize and homogenize experience. Discontinuity, in the form of coincidence, allows for beauty, which "is divided somewhat," for difference ("The naked breasts we call night and day or me and not-me"). The poem explicitly embodies this coincidence:

> The boundaries between me and
> the rosey cobblestones and leaves
> are nowhere parallel (57)

Does this passage assert that if the boundaries are not parallel, then there must be some point of contact? Or does it mean that the boundaries are discontinuous? Or both? This poem does not necessarily "make sense" in terms of coherent, paraphrasable discourse, but the syntax of coincidence—here juxtaposing the subject to leaves and cobblestones and boundaries, which are usually considered rigid and separate—allows for the proliferation of meaning and, more importantly, for influence from the outside, the Other: "Inseparable from exposure, inspiration is what the ghost contained or could supply" (57–58). The ghost, as in Oppen and Howe, evokes otherness and provides inspiration in an otherwise undifferentiated context in which sexuality is controlled by phallocentric reason.[15] Much like Howe's notion of proximity but much more random and accidental, this loose affiliation, or process, provided by coincidence remains much more open to the possibility of a relation to the Other outside the logic of metonymy, text/context, part/whole, or specific/general.

Syntax: The Body's Time

In *Total Syntax,* Hejinian's fellow Language poet Barrett Watten defines syntax partially as "the way words make sense by means of their sequence in time" (65). This statement, as her journals in the time leading up to her conception of *The Cell* show, had a terrific impact on Hejinian and helped to focus her attention on the issue of time in poetry (Lyn Hejinian Papers, UCSD 74.47.6–7). By being outside of syntactic logic, these formal structures, like metonymy that I described earlier, are also out of time, at least the conventional notions of time as the passing of moments from a future into a past.

Perhaps one of the most salient features of this long poem is its dating, which provides a syntax of "sequence in time." Writing a section supposedly every few days over a period of almost three and a half years, Hejinian makes the passage of a subject through time and language the subject of her poem, which is confirmed by the mention of this passage of the subject at many points (see *The Cell* 85). Owing precedence to Stein's *Stanzas in Meditation, The Cell* explores the relations of mental faculties over a period of time with the writing unfolding (mutating) states of perception and their linguistic manifestation (which is redundant for Hejinian). Like a cell, which has finite components, *The Cell* puts certain signifiers into circulation at times working with and against the logic of syntax (the linguistic equivalent of time) and often stressing/stretching out a word's referential possibilities.

This stretching, according to Hejinian's papers, results from temporization and bears an inherent moral weight (Lyn Hejinian Papers, UCSD 74.47.6: 23 Apr 85). Consequently, the poem exposes how words in English bearing certain gendered connotations (or directly related to sex as division and as act) work *over time* to limit perception, action, and expression.

In addition to its temporality, *The Cell*'s syntax can reveal aspects of an ethics of sexual alterity. In *Total Syntax,* Watten claims that syntax has a spatial element, which for him includes "cultural and linguistic" spaces, and for Hejinian these spaces of syntax include the body and its social meanings. Because it consists literally as a syntax of cells, the body often serves in *The Cell* as syntax itself. One particular lyric from the series stands as a perfect illustration. Perhaps the most subjective of the entire series, in terms of a coherent, lyrical "I," this poem begins with a theme usually opposed to the body: mental anxiety: "This is my fortress consciousness, / *that* is anxiety." But the poem dissolves the distinction between mind and body:

> The time out of which
> > I'll never drop is a
> > skin
> It's fate to be personal
> > and wide awake (76)

The poem suggests here that the syntax (of) time is literally "a skin," which I read to be the same as "one's skin" or "my skin," and that the closest and most "personal" fate is that of embodiment—or, to reduce this poem to a platitude, we can never in life escape our skin. As she writes later in the poem, "Everything is that which is close to the body" (136). Embodiment in *The Cell,* obviously influenced by her reading of Merleau-Ponty, is so crucial to her ideas of perception because perception, an event that occurs in and through time, is also the problem with the discourse of the body. "Where do sounds entering your /ears meet?" (77) is a question that cleverly involves a Merleau-Pontian rejection of the mind/body split. The simple answer to the question of where they meet is, of course, in your brain, or better yet, your mind or consciousness. But Hejinian does not separate the sense from the conscious perception: "Imagine that all experience can be divided into parts but with the body and the mind always on the same side" (175). As in Duncan's work, we have here a perfect statement of Merleau-Ponty's notion of embodiment, and it can facilitate an analysis, like Beauvoir's, of sexual difference by looking at the *situation,* the divisibility, of experience.

The syntax of the body is the way cells are organized—bone cells bond with bone cells, blood cells flow together through the veins, brain cells connect electrochemically across synapses, and all these tissues connected by fascia—and in some ways, Hejinian organizes the poem like the body in its continuity. The cell then can serve as a metonymy and synecdoche for body:

Do you patrol? outside the
    self? around a body and
    the follicle in which it
    stands?
Or cell?
Request?
Have you reverted? (55)

Deeply troubled by the problems and questions of perception, Hejinian knows that consciousness is not capable of mapping the continuity found in nature (Lyn Hejinian Papers, UCSD 74.47.7: Mar–Sep 87). Therefore, the poem relies on the discontinuity of perception, signaled formally by the lack of parallel construction between the elements with question marks, through which solely the body is known. Continuity and totality of the body and perception would require the regulation implied in patrolling, which Hejinian is literally interrogating. The poem's form mimics this interrogation, and thus we have an attempt in the poem to balance the continuity and discontinuity that, albeit contradictory, comprise the "whole" body and poem.

Just as there is a syntax of the body, there is a body of syntax that produces the body. As works from the 1970s such as Michel Foucault's *History of Sexuality* maintain, discourse produces the body, and these various syntactic frames, manifestly social in nature (institutions, communities, disciplines), change through time as does the subject's embodied consciousness. Hejinian understands similarly a feedback loop in the production of the body: Discourse, as interpretations of the body, changes the way we perceive and live in our bodies, more specifically, sexed bodies. As the body changes (in and through) consciousness, the desire to know prompts changes in discourses about the body. Hejinian writes in her journals during January 1985 that "[c]hange is the nature of meaning," so she might concur that change in the body also produces changes in the way language comes to mean (Lyn Hejinian Papers, UCSD 74.47.6). This exchange is an endless process, but one that demands intervention. The poem engages the body as a theme only to dismantle it as the "material" on which sexual difference is inscribed. Hejinian thereby makes us aware of the sociolinguistic frames that make the meanings of sexual difference possible. Thus the body as "body," as subject and object of study, is a production of syntax, in both senses of the term. Both a producer and produced by syntax.

As within Duncan's writing, the body in *The Cell* reciprocates with poetry, not because one knows the world through a body (of poetry) but because the body is a product like a poem:

> The driver in the car
>> ahead on a sunny day
>> hung his arm out, his
>> cruelty
> It is a variable
> Productive with half a genital
> A part, and a body
>> particle to which we've deduced
>> poetry (166)

The first line, which I use above to show Hejinian's mode of coincidence over metonymy, is ironically contextualized in commentary about metonymy and synecdoche. An example of Hejinian's self-reflexive mode in *The Cell*, this passage not only calls attention to the frames the poem is exploring but also to the way the poem itself is framing the material. In talking about the construction of the body out of parts, Hejinian highlights the construction, or the ongoing constructing, of the poem in time both by the author and then by the reader's participation. Also, she connects this mode of production to sex ("half a genital") and thus connects sex to poetry, which in this particular poem is linguistically made out of parts of the body such as "arm" and "genital." The parts, in reality, do not exist apart from their signifiers. So, if the body and poetry are products, then how is "sex" produced in the poem?

Almost a quarter of the pages in this long poem display words relevant to the notion of "sex" as a situation, which includes but is not limited to gender roles/expectations. In addition, some of the individual lyrics seem to employ the signifier "sex" to mean the act of physical lovemaking, but I will restrict discussion to matters of sexual difference rather than sexuality. Although a pervasive trope in *The Cell*, the synonymous terms *sex* and *gender* hardly exist independent of context within and without the poem. Nor do they function as preexisting categories on which Hejinian fixes a certain ideology. Instead, she breaks the words open to ferret out their possible meanings and to de-form the syntagmatic relationships that make those meanings possible. As such, the terms of sexual difference proliferate and become anything but closed to question. In fact, meaning is opened up to the unexpected.

One of the many "points" Hejinian makes again and again about the reality of sexual difference is that it is not separate from thought or perception. In "The Person," we read the line "The head is a case with genitals" (*Cold* 176), and in *The Cell*, "the head with genitals" (166). Such lines demonstrate the way Hejinian regards thinking as gendered and gender as a thinking. The head, site of thought and only area of the body containing all five senses, becomes as well the site of gender. For Hejinian, this metonymy arises mainly because gender, something only contingently related but related nonetheless to the biological discourse of sex, exists primarily in the mind as meaning from specific interpretative practices. The fact that sex, in the way Beauvoir first pointed out, is open to interpretation—and not a determining prison, even in its materiality—makes it a textual practice and open territory for the poem. I base this hypothesis on the fact that sexual difference for Hejinian is inscribed in language itself:

> A phrase jumps to its
>   continuation—it is oblong like
>   a person
> And it has rather than
>   sweet reason sexual difference (*The Cell* 137)

Like many of the poems I have looked at throughout this project, interpretation of this passage hinges on an ambiguity, here, pronoun reference. On first reading, the second "it," appearing in the second stanza, might appear to refer to "A phrase," which seems to be the main subject of this stanza and thus the referent of "it." "A phrase," metaphor (synecdoche) of language itself, has "sexual difference" instead of reason like a person. But if the second "it" refers to "person," as we have seen that it often does, then the poem is suggesting that sexual difference matters more to a person's continuation than reason. The "sweet," which could be read as ironic or satiric, puts into question the credibility of this opposition of reason and sexual difference. At any rate, the passage places the emphasis on sexual difference in language and human being in the context of its (supposed) incompatibility with reason. "Sex," after all, "is the pleasure of inexactitude" (140).

Furthermore, sex for Hejinian is not, unlike Watten's definition of syntax, a complete or total notion. It is open-ended, as this poem from "The Person" suggests:

But I exaggerate
The great sequences of incompleteness flutter
many standards in nature crimp
Ego, Body, Position
I went to see
I rode a kind of engine of gender, a motive for bonding (*Cold* 178)

This "crimp" and "incompleteness" in "many standards," such as "Ego, Body, Position," are arrived at metaphorically by riding "a kind of engine of gender," which as a mode of thinking and analysis, can lead us to an appreciation of the differences in language that comprise sexual difference. The discontinuous form of the passage underscores such content by making all standards of sense cramped because of the lack of syntactic clues for monological meaning. This kind of crimping must occur, too, when sex-based standards are placed on discrete, unique, and indefinable human beings. Furthermore, "gender" acts here (if the comma can be taken as signaling an appositive) and in the rest of *The Cell* as "a motive for bonding," be it between women writers, between lovers, or between writer and text. Gender can lead us to "see" the bonds of obligation and response that underpin all social relations. Such "respect" can lead, for Hejinian, to a state of "androgyny" in poetry that would be the mark of an open text. As in Susan Howe's poetry, I understand this openness, in the context of "gender," as the possibility of sexual alterity, as distinct from sexual difference.

Sexual Alterity

Because sex is not total and not exact, potential lacunae exist in both our understanding of it and in its function in sociality. As she is reading Watten's essay, she writes in her journal: "quoting Smithson in Watten's *Total Syntax*: "'My memory becomes a wilderness of elsewheres . . .'" (p 42) (Lyn Hejinian Papers, UCSD 74.47.6: Dec 84). In this gap, "a wilderness of elsewheres," which Hejinian encourages in her poetry, surfaces the trace of a radical alterity, signaled by such phrases as "The authority of the unspeakable" (*The Cell* 133). Although this phrase cannot be singled out and privileged as a guiding trope of the poem due to Hejinian's open form, I think it still brings up a constellation of signifiers in the poem that signal a particular problem, that of the relation of otherness to the language (of the sexed body). In fact, many tropes in the poem can be read as drawing off the diction of the ethical turn after 1960: otherness (164, 175), the incommensurate, unknown (20–21, 60, 133, 148), ghosts (57, 100), and the trace (90). Alterity as a thematic and formal element clearly forms part of her theoretical thinking, too. In "Rejection of Closure," Hejinian quotes a passage in which Irigaray says that a woman's body is always other to itself, so not to this part of Irigaray's thinking does Hejinian ultimately object. In fact, I think Hejinian chooses this particular quote to shift the sensation of otherness from the subject to language (283). In *The Cell*, we also see Hejinian evoking the kind of ontological otherness operative in Irigaray's philosophy in such lines as "The object is itself but always ceasing to be itself" (175) because objects always retain a trace of otherness.

But even more than diction, this alterity is evoked by the form of the poem:

> The object is itself but
> > always ceasing to be itself
> So space has its sensualists
> Boom: soap: a fountain in
> > a potato (133)

The line break between "but" and "always" introduces a discontinuity between Being ("itself") and otherness ("ceasing to be itself"). This uncertainty and discontinuity are essential, especially when you are thematizing otherness into language, which in essence brings the Other into being. When Hejinian states in another poem that "saying so makes it meditation," she demonstrates her awareness of the way language can totalize as well as invite otherness. In this poem, she again invokes otherness by self-reflexively thematizing the space as tactile, sensual, material, and then by giving us examples. The spaces provided by the colons, which usually express continuity, become palpable gaps of otherness because there is no inherent relationship between the items of the list. This thwarting of sense, even on the level of coherent syntax, "a fountain in a potato," calls attention to the discontinuity that marks otherness in language. It is only a small step from this revelation to that of an absolute otherness evading all logic and language:

> The authority of the unspeakable
> The authority with no equal
> The appetite is a pleasant
> > duty
> Someone must be feeling it
> There's no equivalence, and nothing
> > can replace a blue
> Saying so makes it meditation

The word in a flow
  is the metonym
* * *

"Saying so," not just pure saying but making the unspeakable into a said, turns it into a "meditation," a mental or psychical inquiry into language. Obviously referring to Stein's *Stanzas in Meditation,* Hejinian spells out clearly her difference from Stein (and the logic of the metonym) later in this lyric by saying that language is not purely internal or self-contained but "reflects" a social reality:

But this procedure is exhausting
  in that it reflects
We can say "his penis
  escaped from his pants" but
  we can't say so of
  "her vagina"
It's unspeakable (*The Cell* 133–34)

This particular poem ends with the suggestion that emphasizing "constant changing / human life" in language is a "better," or "possible," alternative to the problem of sexual difference than accepting the anatomical binary of vagina-in/penis-out that statically structures discourse on sexual difference. In other words, Hejinian does not conflate sexual difference with the absolute difference of alterity. Rather, sexual difference is produced in language, which can tend then, through judgment, toward continuity and totality. The alterity comes in the "unspeakable" gap between the two terms of sexual difference even as they stand in coordination. Sexual difference arises and is produced, then, even in the very metaphors we use in everyday speech. In this syntactic shift, the poem critiques normative frames that regulate the meaning of sex, but Hejinian is not interested in doing away with these frames altogether, even if it were possible, because as she suggests in the poem, syntax is a measure of identity, of "position," her "female opinion," her "pleasure," and most of all her self and social "containment."

Other poems in *The Cell* series, as I have said, put gender in the context of scientific discourses, like biology or anatomy, while one poem reveals the social context of sexual difference, even if it is dismissed using derogatory terms:

This egg is an emotion
The sensing of a large
  amorous aptness

It is putting us in
            mind of the other things
            of most thoughts
Is "it" pleasure?
Endless it
And in defense of our
            sex

"But my darling," we said
            straddling the line between the
            artificial and the natural
If lust and narcissism are
            evil they must belong to
            social relations
Nothing economizes more than the
            economy itself
This is conduct
And in the example before
            us it exhibits lust and
            narcissism

Meanwhile, everyday life requires common
            sense insatiability
A disappearance from history
Thus the breasts are two
            entirely different thoughts
One is of tropical birds
            and the other of the
            Fire Department
Or one is of self-portraiture
            and the other of new
            tires
Thinking is a pleasant incorporation
It is an emotion of
            sex where it resembles the
            patience in travel

May 3, 1988 (141–42)

The first stanza begins by tracking how sexual difference ("egg") and the pleasure it brings not only defends "our sex" but also keys an epistemological and phenomenological mind-set "of the other things of most thoughts." But if "Endless" pleasure (and endless "it," I might add) is used as a defense of women's pleasure, then it, along with sexual difference, can be degraded as "evil," especially in our still-Puritan historical context that outlaws "lust and narcissism." But the poem points out the underside to this process of exclusion: "If lust and narcissism are evil they must belong to social relations." That is, the very process of moral judgment is always already grounded in various social relations, not the least of which is the face-to-face between two persons. This social grounding extends the process to gender, and thus the poem can define sexuality and sexual difference as a relation to alterity. As affect, "the egg" and its concomitant pleasures put us in touch with "other things," even as it functions in the "economy" that economizes sexual relations and differences.[16] This relation to what is other—which breaks with economy as "endless" pleasure and "insatiable" sense because of its "incorporation" of thought into body—is why the "breasts are two / entirely different thoughts / One is of tropical birds / and the other of the / Fire Department." None of these things has to do explicitly with sexual difference, of which breasts serve as a marker, but they figure metonymically the absolute difference arising from but not limited to contextual or social regulation.

As we have seen in other experimental American poems, such alterity usually works to simply say the obligation to the Other that inhabits language. But with Hejinian's poem, alterity works slightly differently. Obligation comes to mean for Hejinian that we keep using language, even in its contiguous and logical manifestations because those total aspects of language are also permeated with an otherness that obligates. It obligates us to keep saying. And to keep saying is ethical itself:

> For me too, the desire that is stirred by language seems to be located more interestingly within language, and hence it is androgynous. It is a desire to say, a desire to create the subject by saying, and even a feeling of doubt very much like jealousy that springs from the impossibility of satisfying this desire. ("Rejection" 283)

Desire, defined here as insatiable, very much in the sense that Levinas gives, motivates the very saying of language itself that moves out toward the Other and creates the subject in the process. Thus, this desire filled with doubt transfers us from sexual difference to a precinct that is "androgynous." This androgynous realm of the poem, in addition to the retention of sexual difference as a powerful category of analysis, gives us the possibility of a sexual alterity.

Hejinian's poetry offers us glimpses of what I would call a *genderless text,* a text in which gender is not a material force, or a world in which relations are not saturated and dominated by sexual difference. In fact, Hejinian's co-incidences lead to a proximity, much like that of Howe, that actually makes the identity and judgment of sex and gender impossible, or at best, difficult. One is left to relate ethically with the Other, outside the known and often exclusionary or hierarchical frames of reference, including most of all, sexual difference. An extended explication of one particular poem might exemplify this ethical potential in the larger text. Let us explore perhaps the most explicit exploration in the poem of this sexual alterity.

Employing again the metonymic figure of sand, Hejinian leaves us a minute but discernible trace to follow through the shifting linguistic and thus ideological frames of the poem. This trace allows us to see both the change in the perspective and the change in the subject/object of the poem. The object "sand" parallels in this poem, as in others, the phrase "sexual difference," and like sand in the poem, sexual difference loses its stable markers of meaning and drifts toward the void that surrounds it. The first stanza of the June 13, 1988, entry explicitly tracks this move from sexual difference to the uncertainty of alterity:

> We move roughly from sex
> >to uncertainty
> My meditation is a silica (*The Cell* 163)

This transition is, like sandpaper, a rough one, no matter what the contextual frame, from feminism to colloquial usage to science. Sexual difference has been such a prominent mode of exclusion or hierarchy in history, that it is difficult to think outside those frames and to find an alternative. But like the silica of sand in a clam, the possibility of such thinking can, over time, produce pearls, which could be either the words themselves or the unexpected relations they set up:

> Sands abob in the waters
> >between inevitability
> Or they are tuna with
> >spiders astride
>
> Writing in mobs
> Soaking

The elliptical nature of the sentence of the first two lines, which does not say what those pearlized sands are between, demonstrates formally how radically other any thing or idea would be (as "tuna with / spiders astride") that might provide an alternative to the "inevitability" of the cultural formations of sexual difference. No shift from existing frame to existing frame will do the trick. The potential pearl must come from a different approach, perhaps a kind of hit-and-miss bobbing[17] for meaning, perhaps a collaborative "writing in mobs" (not excluding the mobbing of sound in the repetition of -ob). This collaboration not only conveys a social vision of writing practice but also aptly describes the very form of this particular poem—which is itself a concatenation of six stanzas, themselves an anarchic mob in their juxtaposition of sounds, structures, and senses. These mobs might have to endure soaking—both perhaps the soaking some mobs encounter by police water cannon or the soaking that clams and other shellfish often require—in order to be, like the poem, cracked open and employed (albeit violently) toward sense and order. Likewise, the hegemony of normative modes of gender identity will indeed be a tough clam to crack, a verb that explicitly becomes a mode of interpretation:

> And isn't this itself the
>> endless triangulation: water, thing, and
>> nearing
> It seems the only backlit
>> method

Not a process of breaking into a hidden truth, interpretation is described as a "nearing," perhaps the same proximity that Howe uses so deftly to overcome imposed sexual difference in her poetry. Nor is this approach the approach of the illuminating light of reason from a higher, more privileged position from which the reader or writer might pass moral judgment; it is rather "backlit" like a screen or a slide. But in making "nearing" the very relation between things and element ("water"), an object in the triangulation, Hejinian opens the poem to that which cannot be brought into the poem except as a trace, the very saying of language. Such cultivation of traces yields no object but the pearl of the ethical saying of language, which is itself not a matter, literally, of being. This saying of alterity opens a future and ends this particular section of *The Cell*:

> Then going back to the
>> sex forgotten, the one directly
>> ahead
> Smaller than gravel, more coarse
>> than silt

The future is dying
But tomorrow is that to
　　which the future is unequal
June 13, 1988

The future—as a category of certainty or of thought, like the categories of history and past that have left women "forgotten"—is in this poem "dying." That is, no grand vision or plan would bring about a new sex, "the one directly ahead," which is the size of sand and as irritating and common. With each grain of sand in time, or each particular poem in a series, the futurist moment of totalization shrinks away from our present predicament. But one possibility remains: that "tomorrow is that to which the future is unequal," a sense of time employed throughout the entire poem and continually reinforced in the gaps between syntax and sense. The asymmetrical, diachronous notion of time opens the future to what cannot be anticipated, to what cannot even be hoped for, to what is unknowably other, to the Other (person). "[T]he future," she writes elsewhere in *The Cell*, "It isn't a verification" (67). In the poem "The Person," Hejinian explicates this kind of ethical openness in the context of time as fate:

> Kindness and worry, haste and interpretation
> here I translate my thought
> into language—to doubled fate
>
> But fate imposes its very interesting exercise: select
> You yourself could generate the aesthetic heat
> of globes and stops, of shore and drone
> This makes for altruism—
> the generosity of the poem
> If you know what to want you will be free (*Cold* 177)

Fate for Hejinian, whether it be one's sex or one's social position, does not determine the future but instead opens up the present, the poem, in "generosity" and "altruism." In such a rift in time lies the possibility for a relationship in sexual difference that is not mired in forgetting or dis-/re-membering, but instead seeks to put the alterity of the Other before definition according to genitals, a sexual alterity. In such an open fate lies freedom. But to protect this freedom, the process of interpretation, particularly within a feminist ethics, must always return to "the sex forgotten," and it must always continue to trace the potential opening toward the Other in a time out of joint.

Conclusion
What Difference Does Poetic Obligation Make?

Not marble, nor the gilded monuments
Of princes shall outlive this powerful rhyme,
But you shall shine more bright in these contents
Than unswept stone, besmeared with sluttish time.
When wasteful war shall statues overturn,
And broils root out the work of masonry,
Nor Mars his sword, nor war's quick fire shall burn:
The living record of your memory.
'Gainst death, and all-oblivious enmity
Shall you pace forth, your praise shall still find room,
Even in the eyes of all posterity
That wear this world out to the ending doom.
So till the judgment that your self arise,
You live in this, and dwell in lovers' eyes. (Shakespeare, *Sonnet 55*)

With any intellectual study, the question arises as to what difference it makes, in this case, reading experimental American poetry as an ethical poetics. This is a difficult question to answer, especially in the context of the current debate on the importance of poetry in general. As W. H. Auden famously quipped, poetry makes nothing happen, and, as others have more recently argued, nobody reads it, so how can it matter? But one could equally argue that popular reading does not translate into ethical action either. After all, many have read the major sacred ethical texts of humanity—the Bible, the Koran, the Vedas, and the Sutras, and so forth—without understanding their full ethical demands and without applying the precepts to their daily lives. Because the poetics of this avant-garde avoids moral pronouncement in favor of a more oblique formal approach to ethical issues and demands, it is even less suitable to understanding and application. But as I have attempted to show, this experimental poetry remains not merely arcane and hard to understand; indeed, it straightforwardly and sincerely addresses ethical situations, themes, and language. This thematic component carries with it the same kind of moral and political ramifications that any rules-based, logical, or self-directed ethics does. Allow me to draw out some of those ethical implications, which, because they mirror the format of traditional moral documents, may be more recognizable to contemporary readers.

For George Oppen, inviting otherness into his poetry allows him to recast the theme of obligation to others that was a major concern in both his biography and in his politics. Rather than take the activist, polemical, or propagandistic approach of many of the social realist writers of his time, Oppen evinces a passivity in his poetics that favors vulnerability. That vulnerability allows alterity (and therefore the obligation he believes accompanies it) to deform his poetry. The result reveals a primordial ethics that comes before the duty inherent in law, religion, morality, or self-discipline. Any moral system that assumes it has fully met its obligation to the Other, Oppen's poetry shows us, is fooling itself and may fall prey to violence. His indictment of U.S. foreign policy in Vietnam during the 1960s is a perfect example. Oppen's poetry demonstrates most imperatively the need in our postmodern world to seriously reconsider our moral systems and principles. "[R]everse ourselves regions of the mind," Oppen writes in "The Speech at Soli" (1975):

> alter
> mad kings
>
> gone raving
>
> war in incoherent
> sunlight it will not
>
> cohere it will N O T that
> other
>
> desertion
> of the total we discover (*New Collected* 239)

Unlike Ezra Pound's admission toward the end of *The Cantos* that its goal to make coherent and new the chaos of the modern world was a failed project (822), Oppen sees such incoherence as an ethical opportunity. By "reversing" our reliance on moral or political systems (capitalism, democracy, Christianity, patriarchy, oligarchy), we can "alter" the madness of kings and their wars and embrace the Other in the totality. "[I]t will not / cohere it will NOT," Oppen repeats for emphasis and seems to speak reassuringly to Yeats's disillusionment that the "center will not hold." No matter how much we *will* it, the world will not cohere into our rational systems.

But Oppen presents an alternative to the despair over the failure of moral systems. Ten years earlier in his poem "Rationality," (1965) Oppen had stated that there is no "'cure'" of modernity, "no reversal / Of some wrong decision." And this acceptance of the present does not signal resignation to a defeated past but a gesture of love in "the massive heart / Of the present, the presence / Of the machine tools." Notably, this gesture moves beyond Good and Evil to an awareness of others, "the young workman / Elated among the men" who is created new like the part manufactured in "the shock / Of the press" (*New Collected* 136). What is central in "Rationality" is not the mode of production, but its relevance to humanity and the signature of the Other that it bears simply in its saying. In Oppen's revision of "O Western Wind" (1962), the presence of the subway does not signal an advance or decline in the civilization that has produced one thousand years of poetry in English. It serves rather to frame what poetry always returns to, as Oppen suggests in his own return to poetry after his twenty-five-year hiatus:

After these years
I write again
Naturally, about your face (*New Collected* 74)

Coherent rationality cannot equally welcome that part of consciousness attuned to what gets left out, in this case, the face of the lover whom the poet longs for as in the ancient ballad. But in this poem, she is present, occupying and opening a space, a face, as the Other. The possibility of ethics itself arises in community because as the poet writes in "Myself I Sing," a revision of/ collaboration with Whitman, "Two. / He finds himself by two" (56). Not by his own cognizance does he achieve the identity necessary for moral judgment, but only in the presence of the language of another. Perhaps poetry, Oppen suggests, is capable of capturing nothing but the remaining traces of what escapes us. Such poetry gives us a model of how to ethically position ourselves, not as judges or decision makers, but as passive witnesses. His figure of the sea anemone in "Route" from *Of Being Numerous* models how we can filter from vast language the smallest words filled with infinity:

Words cannot be wholly transparent. Ant that is the
     'heartlessness' of words

Neither friends nor lovers are coeval . . .

as for a long time we have abandoned those in
     extremity and we find it unbearable that we should
     do so . . .

The sea anemone dreamed of something, filtering the sea
water thru its body (*New Collected* 194)

In one sense, Oppen's project revises American literary history by allowing
us to understand the Objectivist tradition of American poetry not only in
terms of clarity and sincerity but also to see the failure of such a project. By
recasting this poetry in terms of failure, *Poetic Obligation* also seeks a new
vision of poetry's relation to ethics. In the failure of the modern eye, we may
begin to feel the workings of ethics defined as something other than rules,
laws, or codes. The feeling is the opening of the self to a welcoming of the
Other in and through language, even if we cannot ever fully bear the "ex-
tremity" of the suffering of the Other. The practical stakes then become,
like the poetry itself, much more modest, humble, and obtainable. By self-
consciously exploring language via an Objectivist poetics, we become not
the arbiters of culture but anemones filtering the sea of language. In doing
so themselves, George Oppen and Charles Reznikoff show that the poem
can return us to what gives all interpersonal relations, and thus all ethics,
shape—the obligation that the alterity of the Other desires of me. In this
return, we may find that our view of poetry, poetics, politics, and personal
living has completely shifted outward and owned up to what has always
already been the other-orientation of human life.

For Reznikoff, responsibility to the Other, even the persecutor, gives his
poetry the ability to phenomenologically reduce the act of judgment itself.
By taking a step back from judgment within the context of the most egre-
gious atrocity of the twentieth century, the Holocaust, one that demands
moral judgment and denunciation from the world, Reznikoff's poetry shows
that an inescapable complicity and ethical substitution respond most foundationally to violence. Furthermore, this response does not perpetuate the
cycle of violence but instead takes responsibility for it. Counterintuitively,
Reznikoff takes responsibility himself for the six million Jews killed during
the Shoah in a way that ends the cycle of blame and challenges the naiveté
of the motto, "never again." Made more poignant because of his own Judaism, Reznikoff's response to the Nazi genocide shows the power of taking
on the burden of guilt of the perpetrator himself. In other words, by taking
"responsibility for the devil," Reznikoff's poem *Holocaust* effects a kind of
truth-and-reconciliation of an event that seems to be inconsolable. Like the
poet, we need to take responsibility for violence because it is always a threat,
always possible, even by the most banal of figures, namely, ourselves. Not
only does Reznikoff's posture in this poem complicate representations of

the Holocaust where Jews are victims and Nazi's are guilty, it also suggests humble new nonviolent and nonjudgmental ways to respond to atrocity that take responsibility for the Other. Because Reznikoff is an American and not a German, this response becomes not just a personal but a national endeavor. As Charles Bernstein claims, Reznikoff's poetry means to "acknowledge [America's] roots in violence" and to "giv[e] witness to what is denied at the expense of the possibility of America" ("Nearness" 30). If Reznikoff can stoop to acknowledge his own complicity in the Holocaust, then we can do the same. As Americans, then, rather than merely celebrating ourselves as liberators and judging the shortcomings of others in terms of human rights violations, we can also take responsibility for our history—slavery, racial injustice of segregation, the eradication of Native Americans, the oppression of women, and so forth—even as we learn to lessen, if we can never fully eradicate, violence.

A far cry from Reznikoff's restrained tone, the exceeding of moral duty by an ethics of excess arise as the common legacy that Edward Dorn and Robert Duncan leave to the experimental strain of American poetry. Because their careers peaked during the middle of the twentieth century, their emphasis on excess provides a metonym for the social experimentation and upheaval after World War II that included challenges to the racial apartheid of segregation, drug use as a means of expanding consciousness, emergent alternatives to familial units, transformation of gender roles, proliferation of sexual lifestyles, radical changes in electronic production of art—from TV to rock and roll—and the increasing importance of the body in all of these contexts. For Dorn, strangeness breaks through the boundaries of both the Enlightenment self and the immanent community that is formed through exclusion and domination. In this break, Dorn challenges the authority/authorship of both the self and society. In *Gunslinger*, the (literal) deconstruction of the subject in the form of the first-person narrator has a purpose: the alteration of community from an immanent and closed society in which profit and paranoia rule to an open, eclectic community of possibility where the unknowable and unanticipatable Other is welcome among fellow outcasts and characters. For Duncan, exploring the otherness within the body of the subject leads to a reconsideration of the way sexuality and sexual orientation come to mean within language and culture. Obligation to that otherness—what has yet to be fully understood or can never be understood—allows for change in the body of the subject as well as the body politic.

Both Dorn and Duncan enact and embody in their poetry the spirit of such opening and burgeoning. Dorn's unique brand of satire, which does not rely on judgment or idealism, posits a multifarious subjectivity that works from identity based not on *what is* but on what *could be*. In this ethics resides a certain freedom that, even in its implied debt to the otherness of the unknowable *could be,* liberates us from self-centered, and thus profit-driven, concerns. This model provides a revolutionary alternative to the individual of all-encompassing capitalism. Much in the way Dorn endorses ecstatic modes of being in the world, Duncan gives substance to the much-maligned notion of free love that our current media has given the air of a joke as if it were a nostalgic fad. Instead, the "love poetry" of Robert Duncan incessantly insinuates the inescapable responsibility toward the Other in the acts and atmosphere of love. In this context, the final quip of a 1997 cinematic spoof on the 1960s, *Austin Powers,* takes on an undeniable gravity. The main character, Austin Powers—created by Mike Meyers as a cross between a member of the 1960s pop group The Monkees and action-adventure spy James Bond—tells his nemesis, Dr. Evil, that what the kids of the 1960s were rebelling against was "squares like you who are into world domination." What we have at the beginning of the new millennium, Austin Powers promises, is "freedom with responsibility," which is a "very groovy thing" (*Austin Powers*). Free love, for Duncan, rather than simply being an excuse to fornicate with whomever one wishes, is inextricable from responsibility. In fact, love only occurs when it is given away freely from body to body without expectation—a paradoxical process without return that eternally returns. In such a formulation of ethics, as *bound love,* we not only can begin revising our skewed interpretations of the ideas and ideologies of the 1950s and 1960s but also revise our own notions of ethics as exclusively a limiting and austere morality. Duncan's ethics of excess does not repress but gives permission to embrace obligation, to live in one's body, to accept what one is, and to love others. Most important, poetry initiates this renaissance.

This ethics of excess and eros, though, does not simply involve the actions of an individual either. Both writers envision an ethical community based on sharing not only a common humanity, as Duncan claims in such works as "The Homosexual in Society" and "The Soldiers, *Passages* 26," but on sharing an invitation to an otherness-in-common. Dorn's emphasis on our obligation to the otherness that inhabits a community, as opposed to the sameness and conformity that inhibits it, creates a dreamworld in which anything is possible as long as we can envision it. As a result, we remain open to an Other whom we can never anticipate, be that Other one of an unknowable race, sex, class, orientation, or appearance. In a community that is founded on a groundless ground, a social form is not predetermined but is opened to what is to come, the Other. This lack of predestination means that our particular and unique historical situation—our bodies-as-situation, our interpretations of the meanings our bodies, and the relationship of our bodies to others—dictates organically what our communities will look like. The most important implications of such a relation between social structure and poetic form is that the community is always under construction, being composed, in the process of being written. In such a tentative environment, we may be freer to give love without fear of punitive responses from authorities and social norms. In more historically specific terms, Duncan shows us that we can and do love regardless of what the Other does in return. The implications of this idea in our world struck by an epidemic becomes plain: Love means loving the Other even with a communicable disease like AIDS. Community, then, mutates and opens to the flux of life's circumstance. What is more, the meaning of community is not predetermined but is our responsibility. And love is our obligation. Focused on the particular, that is, the bodies that make up a community, Duncan and Dorn help us to envision new cities, new families, new governments, and new wonders that we will always already have yet to create.

For Susan Howe and Lyn Hejinian, creating a poetics that is susceptible to the Other, in both form and content, takes poststructuralist and phenomenological critiques of gender one step further by addressing a *sexual alterity* that inhabits each sexed body (or alters the way that gender can come to mean, as Duncan did for sexuality).

What seems to happen over and over again in Hejinian's poetics of coincidence is a proximity to the Other, as in Howe's work, that reveals the social, thus ethical, bond of language. This language is still perhaps framed by oppressive orders, but a frame constructed of and through the cracked frames of culture and history. The realization that social power frames meaning through language is the first step toward changing frames. For Hejinian and Howe, that first step allows for responding to the Other in ways otherwise than through cultural definitions of sex, the very definitions that to older women like Lorine Niedecker and Simone de Beauvoir seemed almost insurmountable. Not only must institutions be changed, implies Hejinian, but the language framing those bodies must also self-consciously be changed. But do not get me wrong. Hejinian is no Luddite intent on smashing the frames she so brilliantly exposes; she is a crazy weaver with independent loom whose shuttle is at the service of no one but herself. Not that she isn't informed, negotiating cultural limitations and barriers; they just do not enter her work without being woven into her poetry's disruptive patterns. Hejinian joins with Howe as a maker of machines and textiles (words as technologies) that do nothing except, like a cubist painting, make us aware of our own technologies of judgment and gender.[1] In this way, the poetry of these two women can be said to have no gender in an ordinary sense, because the writing calls cultural figurations of gender into question and reformulates them in view of the ethical Other. They simply do not accept impositions of identity because their poetry is more interested in the workings of nonidentity in the poem. In other words, they do not rely on a necessary relationship between gender and the possibilities of expression.

For Howe, as for Hejinian, writing as a woman is beyond, or otherwise, than the question of gender, which is made up of writing, its syntax and paradigms. Or, more precisely, the question of gender cannot be applied to the poem from the outside since it is already part of the poem's warp. But the body in its sexual difference, as Howe's poetry demonstrates, exists not as something *more* real outside the poem; indeed, the poem is where the important stuff, the making of meaning and the interpretation of material, takes place. No body of "Christ" or "Mary Magdalene" are found outside the poem because through writing both these words have come to mean. For Howe, the traditional meanings of those words, as for women's bodies in general, have been irreparably damaging, and she aims to rewrite them. As these poets write the body and sex into the poem—and each of these poets writes in order to "become" a woman poet—they redefine in the process what the body means and how gender functions in writing. This process of redefinition, however, does not take place simply out of the poet's will to identify herself or to transcend unjust systems. It occurs within the precinct of the Other, the saying in language of nonidentity, the ineffable, and the incommensurate. The threads with which they weave the poems are not the writings' most important element; instead, the empty spaces in between, full of nothing, full of otherness, take precedence over what is said. By experiencing sexuality and gender as alterity, these women make possible an infinite variety of ways a woman can live and choose her identity. In this poetry of sexual alterity, one—naked, or at least hyperaware that one is covered in cloth—must face the Other without the ready-made of gender frames. In this uneasy welcome extended by the poem is the beginning of ethics.

In addition to these thematic lessons, the difficult form of innovative poetics, which *enacts* an ethics of obligation to the Other and doesn't just describe it, proves precisely the strength of this kind of writing. Understanding the formal experiments of American poetry during the ethical and linguistic turns of the mid-twentieth century gives us a way of reading all language for the alterity, or *saying*, that inhabits/inhibits it and gives it ethical force. Therefore, such a poethics can have a major impact on reading practices.

For one, the formal experiments of this group of poets change the reader's role in the production of meaning. Rather than treating the reader as passive receptor of ethical pronouncement, this poetics demands a more active role. Notably, this poetics does not pretend to have all of the right answers to ethical dilemmas or to even know the Other. That means that readers must be aware of their own moral judgments, particularly the language with which that judgment is executed. Next, experimental, open-ended form, which is in many ways beyond the control of the poet, creates an environment in which the reader is faced with the experience of alterity the poet encountered. In fact, the poet is an Other to whom the reader must respond as well (and vice versa). If reading is writing and writing is reading, as writers such as Hejinian believe, then experimental American poetry presents us with a unique ethical opportunity. Just as these poets thematically address and then formally enact their obligation to the Other, we as readers are afforded the chance to face the Other. Through the incommensurate form of the experimental long poem, the obligation to the Other happens to us, beyond our choosing. Regardless of *how* we respond, *that* we must respond does not change. At the same time, we can welcome the experience of confusion, doubt, indeterminacy, and obligation by altering our reading practices. Outlined below are some of the reading and interpretive strategies that the poethics of experimental American poetry teaches us.

First and foremost, this reading, which amounts to a kind of ethical criticism, does not merely pay attention to what poetry is or says (ontology) or what the poet does or intends (politics) but instead to what cannot be said in the poetry or its context (ethics). Of course, elements such as theme or pronouncement are still an important aspect of the ethical power of poetry —as I've shown, almost all of our experimental writers make straightforward statements with a moral tone. But because they also encourage the fragile trace of alterity in their poetry, they model for us the ways that reading form can reveal what is foundationally ethical about all language, in any kind of poetry or any kind of discourse. Ethical criticism inspired by experimental poetry, then, may:

Focus on ethical themes, which will, of course, change with the times at
    hand, but that are marked by an inescapable obligation to the Other;

Expose where those themes fall back on themselves and deconstruct; assess whether the poet is aware of such complicity even though control of such lacunae is beyond the poet's power;

Attend to accidents and other open-ended aspects of language that "catch" the trace of the Other for brief moments;

Be sensitive to identities and social positions (Jews, women, homosexuals, etc.) that have been othered by a dominant culture in a discourse of a particular place and time, acknowledge where language gives voice to the voiceless and takes responsibility for rather than condemning the oppressors;

Explore where identity breaks down or is underwritten by an "older" alterity; show where responsibility (in the form of a response to ineffable, unknowable alterity) presupposes and problematizes identification;

Notice where poetry breaks laws, either formally or thematically (but also in rare cases, legally—for example, it was only in the 1960s that poets such as Allen Ginsberg and LeRoi Jones were prosecuted for their poems. In Ginsberg's case, it was pornography laws and for Jones it was inciting a riot);

Acknowledge the linguistic frames used to construct and enforce conventional morals, whether in terms of social morays, gender norms, control of bodies, and so forth, and assess how poetry engages those frames *as language;*

Consider for itself new forms of "argument" and "exposition." Employing formal experiments like the ones in this poetry, ethical criticism can welcome alterity even while it "makes a point." By drawing on the formal wisdom of poetry, an ethical criticism can be more vulnerable, open-ended, self-questioning, and humble. Susan Howe's *My Emily Dickinson,* though it doesn't label itself "ethical," might be the best example of this kind of criticism.

Of course, this list is not complete—more principles will emerge from each rereading as well as from new poethical experiments in new times. This list serves merely as an opening gesture in a never-ending obligation to find meaning and respond to the Other.

For these poets, their poetry is their ethics. That is why close reading is the most appropriate method to trace this ethics, even if that tracking is an impossibility. We must recognize the limits that reading—which is, after all, a form of *identification*—poses for ethics. The main one is the risk of totalizing and thus violating the Other all over again. But ethical responsibility involves already a difficult subjection and calls for risks that do not guarantee success. One is always already responsible to the Other, so one must attempt to do what is (im)possible—fulfill obligation through a close reading of radical alterity in a text. In this study, I have advocated and followed a two-sided path to that close reading:

The first track is general and pertinent to all of the poets I read, namely, to look for any manifestation of radical alterity in language: indeterminacy, aporia, contradiction, irony, deixis, multiple meanings, variation, disruption, parataxis, mistake, accident, chance, ambiguous pronoun reference, paradox, equivocation, framing, and so on. Even if the various techniques the poets use change over time, the common thread is the (tentative) invocation/ invitation of what cannot be identified, the Other, in the poetry. Like looking at an eclipse indirectly through a pinhole camera, we can track in poetry the trace of the Other that motivates all ethics.

The second track is more specific to each poet. Taking cues from the poets' themes and forms themselves, we can see how the poetics raises various issues relevant to the ethical relation to the Other as they are conditioned by (and condition) a historical moment. For instance, Duncan's homosexuality and Howe's gender are ethically volatile issues at the time they are writing— Duncan writes at the beginning of the sexual revolution, while Howe's career takes flight at the height of the women's movement—even if we might not recognize some of their themes as ethically challenging now as they were then. For example, although homosexuals do not at this moment have equal protection under the law, it is at least legal to be gay in America, which it wasn't for Duncan in the 1960s. The point is that the way their ethics was conditioned by their time, being, and personal lives is instructive. It follows too that each poet's work must be approached in a different way with various ethical angles and issues. Dorn's speculative and futurist ethics of the *could be,* for instance, is best interpreted through a Heideggerian refraction of Levinas, rather than Levinas's work itself. As readers therefore, it is incumbent on us to find ethical theories that best resonate with the ethics of the poetry and poetics.

In certain ways, however, this avant-garde poethics is not historical, even if a particular poetics/ethics is historically conditioned. It responds to something universal, timeless—no, those are the words of an Arnoldian humanism—instead, this poethics responds to something elsewhere, out of time, of an "immemorial past," to use one of Levinas's favorite phrases, and is therefore (at) the limit of history. Levinas and the other philosophers of the ethical turn return us, unwittingly perhaps, to a new kind of universalism because the Other is *the* Other, no matter when or where. Experimental American poets during the ethical turn understood this, too. Their poetics responds to alterity beyond control because alterity limits power itself. That is why their project is so important—it returns us to the ethical foundations of poetics and the poetic foundation of ethics.

Another principle that arises out of this relinquishing of power in the poetry and that can be applied in other contexts is the abandonment of intent as the main mechanism of ethics. Although I find all of these poets to be exceptional human beings, they are all human beings nonetheless with the fears and follies that entail, and their ethics is not best measured by their actions. Having said that, though, each one of these poets has led an "ethical" life, being for others and making the world a better place with their actions and words. But that does not mean that they intentionally "craft" an ethics through their poetic art. Yes, all of the poets I include in this study deal with ethical issues thematically, but that is true of almost all poetry dating back to Homer. But these poets write in such a way that the demand of the Other obliges them and us through language. Since their poetry does not depend on the poets' intentions or on history or politics or action, then one could argue that this ethics can be found in any type of poetry or in any manifestation of language. And that would be true. Even the most violent and degrading language cannot rid itself of the trace of the Other and therefore what binds the subject of the enunciation to the interlocutor. The particular choices these poets made, regardless of whether they intended it or not, have the effect of exposing the way alterity inhabits/inhibits language itself as a scrape across the pavement exposes the nerves.

Can this experience of alterity, to which we are obligated to respond in the poem, transfer to our daily lives outside of poetic activity? That question is, of course, impossible to answer definitively because it would require us to assert a Logos once again and to therefore assume we know the Other. However, it is not unfair to conclude that if one becomes accustom to encountering alterity in the reading/writing of a poem, then one would be less likely to respond to alterity in other contexts with the same disdain for, distrust of, and discrimination against the Other that has marked the history of Western thought and civilization. Will reading experimental poetry make us better people? That is the wrong question, in my opinion. Instead, we should be asking what does the Other in the poem demand of us. Where shall we find the trace of the Other in a poem that we may not be able to adequately read or understand? Finally, we must continually ask ourselves as readers and writers how we can face the demands of obligation in every aspect of our situated lives.

A way of reading/writing that puts alterity first can, however, have important implications on how we relate to others. Although this poetry may not tell us how to be better people, it does provide a model of ethical interaction. Nonjudgment, passivity, vulnerability, openness, embodiment, emphasis on other people, preference for ambiguity, indeterminacy, and multiplicity—these qualities we find in the poetry and poetics of these American authors can change our way of being in the world. Without asserting too much, I believe that our systems of morality and justice, infallible though they are, would look much different if they took as their founding assumptions the inviolability and ineffability of the Other rather than the sanctity and self-possession of the subject, if they took inescapable responsibility as their starting point rather than a false sense of freedom. These different structures, which are also structures of difference, are implied in the poetry.

Ultimately, what we find when we read poetry this way—for the strange and the unknowable—we find that, despite more than 2,500 years of discrediting, poetry is the most ethical of all discourse because it unabashedly welcomes the Other. By welcoming poetic obligation, by welcoming new ways of writing/thinking/seeing/hearing, by welcoming what cannot be placed into the propositional language of logic and philosophy, poetry is able to get at the ethics of ethics itself. This origin, though unknowable, is not un-sing-able, un-verse-able, un-form-able. It is response-able. It is poetic.

Notes

Preface

1 See Baker, *Obdurate Brilliance,* for a summary of how phenomenological philosophy since Nietzsche has been dedicated to subsuming philosophy, along with all human sciences, under the rubric of language or discourse theory (1–7).

2 See Plato, *Republic,* Book II, 85; Book IX, 270; Book X, 300ff.

3 See Fischer, *Does Deconstruction Make Any Difference?,* as one of the first book-length works to engage this trend.

4 J. Hillis Miller's 1981 essay, "The Ethics of Reading" was one of the first to apply poststructuralist ethical theory to literature (in Culler and Konigsberg). Because the translation of these French philosophers in English does not really happen until the 1980s, I am not making an argument for direct "influence."

5 For another historical approach to experimental American poetry, see McGann.

Introduction

1 See also Pound, *Guide to Kulchur* and *ABC of Reading.*

2 I continue the convention of capitalizing "Other" when it refers to a person. See Alphonso Lingis's translator's note in Levinas, *Totality and Infinity* 24n.

3 See Kenner, *Homemade World* 163–76, Mary Oppen's *Meaning: A Life;* Quartermain's *Disjunctive Poetics;* Perloff, *Poetics of Indeterminacy;* Altieri, *Enlarging the Temple;* Sharp, "Objectivists 1927–1934"; Fredman, *A Menorah for Athena;* Dembo, "Four Interviews"; and Heller, *Conviction's Net of Branches* for histories of the Objectivists. The information in the next few paragraphs comes from these sources.

4 See Quartermain, *Disjunctive,* and Fredman, *Menorah,* for the importance of these historical and cultural conditions in Objectivist poetics.

5 See also Attridge on this distinction, 23–24.

6 See Hegel, *Phenomenology of Spirit,* chapter 4, for the entire discussion of this process.

7 For the use and germination of the term *poethics,* see Bruns, "Poethics" 206–25, and Retallack *Poethical Wager* 9–12, 196–222.

8 For more on this emphasis on the means of production in Language poetry, see McGann 213–20.

9 See Krzysztof Ziarek, *Inflected Language,* for more on the relationship between the work of Heidegger and Levinas on language.

10 A good discussion of these terms may be found in Krzysztof Ziarek's "Semantics of Proximity" 231–33.

11 See *Otherwise Than Being* and "The Trace of the Other," where Levinas teases out the linguistic workings of responsibility. See also Derrida, *Of Grammatology,* 65–73, 100–105, and "Différance" *Margins* 20–27 where he discusses the ethical importance of this concept for language. Kristeva's *chora* and Irigaray's *semiotic* may also fit into this notion of a saying before language.

12 The French reads, "Recherche se dédiant en poème a l'autre: un chant monte dans le donner, dans l'un pour l'autre, dans la signifiance même de la signification." *Recherche* here may be translated as a very ("seek," "desire," "to pry into," "research") or a noun ("desire," "search," "studied elegance"). *Se dédiant* also has the suggestion of "to retract."

13 Cf. Levinas, *Totality and Infinity* 83–85.

14 Discovery of the work of Levinas by literary critics has been a major motivating force in this new dialogue. See Altieri, *Canons and Consequences;* Attridge, "Innovation" 20–31; Daly, *Swallowing The Scroll;* Docherty, *Alterities;* Eaglestone, *Ethical Criticism;* McCaffery, "The Scandal of Sincerity" 167–90; Newton, *Narrative;* Robbins, *Altered Readings;* Ewa Plonowska Ziarek, *Rhetoric;* and Krzysztof Ziarek, *Inflected Language.*

15 In *Alterities,* Thomas Docherty calls for a criticism that, with an attitude of humility, locates difficulty and alterity in art rather than reducing it to identity with the Same, 7–12.

Part 1

1 Williams is quoted in Brogan 239. Pound's three dicta, which he dates in "A Retrospect" from a 1912 agreement with Richard Addington and HD, are "(1) Direct treatment of the 'thing,' whether subjective or objective, (2) To use absolutely no word that does not contribute to the presentation, and (3) As regarding rhythm: to compose in the sequence of the musical phrase, not in the sequence of the metronome" (*Literary Essays* 3). The preface to the 1915 anthology *Some Imagist Poets,* which did not include Pound, adds six more principles, including the following: "(1) To use the language of common speech, but to employ always the exact word, not the nearly-exact, nor the merely decorative word. (2) To create new rhythms—as the expression of new moods—and not to copy old rhythms, which merely echo old moods ... (3) Absolute freedom in the choice of subject."

2 For an incisive reading of the differences between the three versions, see Fredman, *A Menorah for Athena* 125–43.

3 Critics who focus on Zukofsky's valuation of totality are Palmer, "On Objectivism" 122; Altieri, "Objectivist" 14–15; and DuPlessis and Quartermain, *Nexus.* Even Heller, although he introduces the notions of "conviction" and "desire," still relies heavily on the notion of objective truth and sincere accuracy in *Conviction's Net of Branches* 2–9.

4 Altieri, Palmer, Quartermain, and Perloff concentrate mainly on recharting the aesthetic aspects of Objectivism. See also Woods, Peterson, Silliman, and Palmer

("On Objectivism") on the ethics behind that aesthetics. Davidson (*Ghostlier*), Finkelstein, Heller, Byrd, Hatlen, and DuPlessis who address the social and political engagement of these poets. Heller, Naylor, Feld, Fredman, Parlej, Ma, Hirsch, and Chilton focus on the ontological in Objectivist poetics, mostly through the philosophy of Heidegger.

5 The warrant for my argument is that closure induces violence. As argued succinctly by Krzysztof Ziarek in *Inflected Language,* resemblance equals identity and the closure of tautology leaves no room for the difference or alterity of otherness 10–19, 89–93.

6 Most criticism on Objectivism focuses exclusively on the ontological understanding of desire (as a desire to *think with things as they exist*). See Altieri, "The Objectivist Tradition" 7, 14–5; Heller, *Conviction's Net of Branches* 11, 105; and Palmer, "On Objectivism" 122.

7 Oddly enough, this insistence that even the infinite has a referent, that it is a word, seems to foreground the preeminence of language in Zukofsky's thinking. Such textuality deconstructs his "faith" that every signifier has a signified outside the text. Cf. Steve McCaffery's argument against Zukofsky in *North of Intention* 120.

1. Saying Obligation

1 For explicit discussion of Oppen's ethics and/or morality, see Berry 305–22; Chilton 89–112; Corman 116–45; Finkelstein, "Syntax" 429–43; Hatlen, "Opening" 263–95; Heller, "Conviction's Net"; Hirsch 169–80; Hooker 81–103; Mottram 149–76; Nicholls 240–53; Peterson 101–3; Silliman 85–92; Bernstein 6–40; Nicholls 251; and Woods 215–33.

2 While Nicholls's essay sets the terms for a reading of Oppen informed by Levinas's work and provides a necessary starting point, Nicholls's argument, only a few paragraphs of which are devoted to this connection, extends little beyond a proposal and does not actually give a detailed analysis. Picking up where Nicholls leaves off, Tim Woods in *The Poetics of the Limit* gives a more thorough argument for the connection between Levinas's thought and Oppen's poetics but does not examine closely enough how "ethical responsibility" actually manifests in Oppen's poetic form.

3 See DuPlessis ("When" 23), Hooker, and Nicholls.

4 See also Levinas, "Trace of the Other" 353 and *Totality and Infinity* 194, 289.

5 See also Feld 13–32.

6 See also McCaffery, "Scandal" 171–73, on Levinas's critique of intention.

7 A major weakness in Woods's work is the absence of a discussion of Levinas's scepticism toward poetry, which can most readily by seen in "Reality and Its Shadow." See Robbins, *Altered* 139 and McCaffery, "Scandal" 175. See also Llewelyn, Wyschogrod, and Blanchot, *Infinite* 53.

8 See also Krzysztof Ziarek, "Language" 102–5 and Libertson 336.

9 In earlier work, before *Otherwise than Being,* Levinas clearly distinguishes certain forms as more attuned to ethics than others: "Not every discourse is a relation with exteriority" (*Totality* 64–77).

10 In "The Servant and Her Master" the poetic does not seem to be tied necessarily to any genre or medium of poetry. This is evident in the final footnote of the piece that states:

> We said earlier that the word poetry referred to the disruption of immanence to which language is condemned in becoming its own prisoner. There is no question of considering this disruption as a purely aesthetic event. But the word poetry does not after all name a species whose genus is referred to by the word art. Inseparable from speech (*le verbe*), it overflows with prophetic meanings. (159)

11 Simon Critchley rightly identifies this as the key tension in Levinas's metaethics (19).

12 For more discussion on the ethics of this kind of reading, which he calls *clôtural,* see Critchley 14–31, 59–106.

13 For discussion of the uniqueness of Oppen's formal choices see DuPlessis for Oppen's emphasis on white page space ("When" 28–29); Berry for the ambiguous syntactical effects (305–6); and Finkelstein for form in context ("Syntax"). Woods mentions several of these formal elements in Oppen's work but does not unpack them to show how they explicitly reveal a prior ethical obligation (231). Krzysztof Ziarek in *Inflected Language* gives a more theoretical argument for why such "poetic strategies" are ethical (135).

14 Although Woods acknowledges this failure that "preserves the alterity of the other," his analysis of Oppen attempts again and again to portray him as the one "aware" of or "allowing" ethics into the poetry.

15 In Hatlen and Mandel, "Poetry and Politics," Oppen explains that one of his reservations about Zukofsky's poetry was that "he used obscurity in the writing as a tactic" (45). See also the interview with Schiffer in which Oppen admits that "understanding" has always been an issue in his poetry, but he rejects "any policy of obscureness" (15).

16 See also Berry 310.

17 Oppen metonymizes singularity using the figure of the eye and numerousness through representations of buildings, cars, waves, islands, helicopters, and so on. In relation to Reznikoff's poetry, Bernstein in "Reznikoff's Nearness" defines metonymy as "the fragment as substitute for, hinting at, something else, something that only it can stand for, is an instance of—a manifestation or emanation. The part for the (w)holy. *Witness of the detail understood as metonymic*" (20). See also DuPlessis, "When" 23 and Peterson 101–3.

18 See Hatlen, "Opening" 263–95; DuPlessis "When" 28; and Brogan 127.

19 See also Oppen's comment on this poem in an interview with Power: ". . . it defi-
    nitely rejects that inner space. It says no to it except where the spirit moves out to
    infinity, or at least to the given which I take to be infinite" (199).
20 Chilton says that adequation of signifier with signified accounts for the ungram-
    maticality of Oppen's poetry. Chilton dismisses ambiguity and "metaphorical
    complexity" in favor of the typical Objectivist "directness" (91). The failure of
    directness, I say, allows Oppen's poetry to multiply.
21 See Peterson on the way these formal elements disrupt dependence on a singular
    subjectivity in Oppen (97).

2. A Phenomenology of Judgment

1 Laws against sodomy existed in New York from its founding as a Dutch settle-
   ment to 1980 with many revisions and challenges in between. The laws operative
   at the time Reznikoff was writing this poem dated back to 1892: "Another criminal
   law revision in 1892 retained the 20-year maximum for sodomy, but eliminated
   the 5-year minimum, and limited the scope of the prohibited acts to 'by the anus
   or by or with the mouth[.]'" (See also Laws of New York 1892, Vol. 1, page 681,
   ch. 325, enacted 18 Apr 1892). The state's psychopathic offender law of 1950 excluded private, consensual activity from its scope, and accompanying that new
   law was a reduction of the penalty for sodomy from a felony to a misdemeanor,
   the first such action in the country. Although some court cases began to throw
   out the bases for enforcement of New York's sodomy laws, sodomy was still ille-
   gal and used to entrap and arrest mostly men engaged in consensual anal and
   oral sex. The New York legislature attempted to rewrite the law in 1965 but eventually reinstated most of the anti-sodomy laws for same-sex acts. It wasn't until
   1980 in *People v. Onofre et al.* that the New York Court of Appeals ruled the laws
   unconstitutional (Painter).
2 Woods addresses this charge and attempts to save Zukofsky's poetry from "and
   imperialistic ontologization of the world" (131). The beginning of his chapter 5
   addresses this problem of objectification, as does page 5 ("without any interference from the imperialist ego") and page 68 ("without appropriating the 'otherness' of an object").
3 A note on the first page of the poem states, "All that follows is based on a United
   States government publication, *Trials of the Criminals before the Nuernberg* [sic]
   Military Tribunal and the records of the Eichmann trial in Jerusalem." See Fredman, *Menorah* 171 fn 20. See also Ezrahi, Shevelow, and Davidson, *Ghostlier*
   149–70.
4 For one account of the role of complicity in the Holocaust, see Daniel Jonah
   Goldhagen's *Hitler's Willing Executioners.*
5 Studies like Paul Chodoff's "Late Effects of the Concentration Camp Syndrome"
   (1963) and *Psychiatric Aspects of the Nazi Persecution* (1964) describe "a special

case of 'survivor guilt'" and would have been available to both Levinas and Reznikoff (Chodoff. "Late" 154).

6 The most explicit reference in Levinas's philosophical writings comes on the dedication page of *Otherwise Than Being:* "To the memory of those who were closest among the six million assassinated by the National Socialists, and of the millions on millions of all confessions and all nations, victims of the same hatred of the other man, the same anti-semitism [*sic*]." Another dedication on the same page is written in Hebrew and left untranslated. It is an acronym meaning, "May his [their] soul be preserved among the living." I thank Ranen Omer-Sherman for the translation.

7 Coming the closest to an indictment of Reznikoff, Ezrahi, soon after the poem was published, descries that any irony in *Holocaust* "must be read into the text" causing Nazi and Jew to appear "as two facets, that is, of the human condition" (37).

8 Oppen's poetics is very similar to Reznikoff's in *Holocaust,* but it has drawn more fire. Perloff sees the lack of commentary on Oppen's part as an almost silent approval of the atrocity because he is not overtly emotional about it ("Shipwreck" 199). See also Berry 312 and Parlej 71. In addition to the discussion of atrocity in the criticism, others have elaborated Oppen's relation to totalitarian and violent political systems. Hooker 92–93, Feld 66–68, and Naylor 102n provide the main critique of Oppen on this point.

9 Hooker does talk about the complicity of this passage in relation to its difference from "Language of New York" section 5 (100).

10 Fredman discusses the role of ethnic difference in Reznikoff's view of himself as poet (*Menorah* 6–11), while Quartermain discusses immigration and class (9–15).

11 See also Corman for a reading of Oppen's poetry as a facing-the-world, especially its horror (130).

Part 2

1 See Fredman's discussion of containment in Olson's poetry in *Grounding* 35–46.

3. The Ethics of Excess

1 Wesling discusses the complex role of morals in Dorn's satire and its ability to deal with contradiction, but Wesling seems too ready to call him didactic and to capitulate to Dorn's detractors: "though Dorn's moral positions may well be right, they are righteously and simplistically expressed. Such issues eventually get raised about Dorn, and properly so" (4).

2 Cf. Wesling 5–6, 16; von Hallberg, who sees the poem as "severe" and "vivacious" in the vein of *The Dunciad* (66); Davidson, "To Eliminate" 116–17; and Bollobás, who sees Dorn as providing a "corrective" to society (49).

3 Both von Hallberg 78–79, and Dewey 59 paint Dorn satire as one of existential clarification, rather than utopian vision.

4 The claims for Dorn's didacticism are extensive: Wesling speaks of Dorn's "didactic, polemical purpose" (5–7); although von Hallberg states that *Slinger* is less didactic than some of his other poetry, Dorn "deals in explanations"—this is discursiveness (65)—and in judgment not emotion or prophesy (84–86).

5 Perloff and Davidson both cite the critique of reason in the poem. As Davidson points out, "By disavowing laws of sequence and causality, the Slinger may eliminate the contingent nature of times and places and thus penetrate time and space" ("To Eliminate" 124). Cf. Perloff ("Introduction" x, xii).

6 Despite Lockwood's claim that his passage is parody of Henry David Thoreau (174), it seems clear that there is a straight edge to this appropriation that endorses Thoreau's satire. See Fredman, "Annotations" 97.3–6.

7 For a general discussion of Dorn's dealings with subjectivity, see Wesling 6–7; Davidson, "To Eliminate" 137; Dorn, *Interviews* 100; Dewey 48–50; Trotter 165–76; and McPhilney 351–89.

8 On the aptness of the Horse's names, see Davidson, "To Eliminate" 119–20 and Perloff, "Introduction" xi.

9 See *Poet's Prose* for Fredman's discussion of the relation of conjecture to being (58–96).

10 As Blanchot would say, in the eternal return of subjectivity, the subject always returns to itself other than itself. This difference that prevents complete identity of the self with self, or totality, occurs in the relation with the Other. See *Infinite Conversation* for his reading of the eternal return.

11 The final form of the Gunslinger's name could be either a registering of the slurring effects of the character's drug use throughout the story or a reference to the Dolly Madison rip-off (the "Zinger") of the famous 1960's American "Twinkie" snack cake.

12 See also Lockwood on the significance of the Horse's name and its relation to resistance of authority (169). He also points out Slinger's name change (157).

13 See also Perloff "Introduction," x–xi, and Davidson when he writes that I "is able to live according to celebrations rather than schedules" ("To Eliminate" 121–23).

14 Although Dorn rejects the importance of Heidegger's philosophical system to the poem (*Interviews* 50, see also Davidson's discussion in "To Eliminate" 119–20), certain tropes of Heidegger's are useful in understanding certain aspects of the poem. See also Lockwood's description of ecstasy in the poem (152, 154, 199).

15 See also von Hallberg 78–79 on Olson's "self-acts" in *Slinger*, which are closely related to proprioception because perception is the becoming-itself of the body.

16 See Dresman on the relation of Dorn to Olson in terms of geography (91–94).

17 Davidson has an excellent discussion of the draw in "To Eliminate" 128–29.

18 Cf. Dorn in *Interviews* where he speaks of the "shared mind" (26, 67) and *Gunslinger*, which speaks of "this group in which our brain / is contained" (116); see also Wesling's discussion (20) and Davidson's, "To Eliminate" 122.

19 They allegorically are one subject—multiple, diverse, complex, mutable, and often at odds with itself. As Perloff says, "selves collide, merge, and take on each other's identity; indeed, the group supercedes the individual" ("Introduction" xi). On the collective subject in *Slinger* see also Davidson, "To Eliminate" 122–23; Dewey 48–59; Gery 48–51; and McPhilney 351–89.

20 Lockwood on the Horse: "energized by a kind of Blakean vision of the universe, he becomes an evangelist and clever practitioner of the art of subverting external authority" (169).

21 See Blanchot's *The Unavowable Community,* which was written in response to Nancy's *Inoperable Community.*

22 Wesling argues that Dorn's morality is speculative in that attention brings in a return on the investment (13, 22, 41). See Dorn's use of the word in the context of "The Cycle" as "a big speculation about [Robart's/Hughes's] habits" (*Interviews* 33).

23 The line from Blake is: "Every thing possible to be believ'd is an image of truth" (37).

24 Cf. Pound's judgment of capitalism in *The Cantos.* See Fredman, "Annotations" 100.14.

25 See Lockwood, who elaborates on the problems Al et al. have with their "ambiguous roles" (178–79).

26 See "Différance" 20–27 and *Of Grammatology* 65–73.

27 Davidson wants to retain sight as the ethical lynchpin in Slinger's world: "Sight becomes the dominant argument against the 'Vicious Isolation' of the local citizenry" ("To Eliminate" 130–31). As Davidson points out, however, vision as a sense is totalizing (138).

28 Davidson's reading of "selvedge" as "self-edge" is instructive, especially in the context of subjectivity ("To Eliminate" 130). According to Lockwood, a "selvedge" is the border of a fabric, "and the word reminds us of Dorn's elaborated conception of the poem now—as a kind of tapestry of moving figures" (167).

29 See Olson in "Projective Verse" (148). Anne Dewey's article is an excellent study of the relation to open form and political openness.

30 See Fredman, "Annotations" 170.7–8.

31 See Davidson, "To Eliminate" 138–39 and Perloff, "Introduction" x–xi.

32 Also see Wesling 4, 7 and von Hallberg 60–61 for admissions of such problems and defenses against such allegations. Their answer to this ethical dilemma is to say that Dorn is "moral without being prescriptive. Rather, he understands how difficult it is to exist ethically in a society in which all systems are severely mediated" (Wesling 7).

33 This simile does not mean "that Information is poured straight in; it is no longer mediated," as Davidson suggests ("To Eliminate" 145); it means that because of the slipperiness of the signifier, ethics cannot be a matter of the *letter* of the law. Blanchot's work illuminates the kind of situation here at issue in his description of the 1968 Paris strike. In the unavowable community of May 68, "Everyone had

something to say, and, at times, to write (on the walls); what exactly mattered little. Saying it was more important that what was said. Poetry was an everyday affair. 'Spontaneous' communication, in the sense that it seemed to hold back nothing, was nothing else than communication communicating with its transparent, immediate self . . ." (*Unavowable* 30).

34 Von Hallberg states that Dorn's satire is unique because his verse is "sensitive to wide complicity" in the things he is satirizing (81).

4. The Body Ethical

1 See Johnson: "The book's title establishes the contrasts of bow and lyre, war and music, Apollo and Hermes, whose tension generates this book's field" (99).

2 Davidson shares this sentiment that Duncan has been mistakenly read as "irresponsible" for his reticence to condemnation and to certain ideas of "what a poet should be" ("Cave" 36–37). John Crowe Ransom rejected Duncan's poetry from the *Kenyon Review* by calling it an "obvious homosexual advertisement" (Ray 286–88). Yvor Winters rejected his lack of "moral fiber" (Christensen).

3 Levinas in particular was skeptical of "love." In 1961, Levinas writes, "The metaphysical event of transcendence—the welcome of the Other, hospitality—Desire and language—is not accomplished as love. But the transcendence of discourse is bound to love. We shall show how in love transcendence goes both further and less far than language" (*Totality* 254).

4 See also Bollobás 50–51; Davidson, "First" 60; and Burnett 96 for more discussion of Duncan's notion of law.

5 For a rejection of Duncan as postmodern, see Taggart, "Of the Power."

6 For other readings of Duncan's ethics in Objectivist or ontological terms, see Davidson "Caves," 35; Molesworth 91; Altieri, *Enlarging* 153; and Schiffer, "Robert Duncan" 162.

7 See Altieri who claims that Duncan and Olson wish to, in T. E. Hulme's words, "hand sensations over bodily," and that poets such as Duncan "seek meaning not in systems but in existential contexts or 'situations'" (*Enlarging* 44–46). This explains Duncan's lifelong emphasis on breath, rhythm, spacing, and typography.

8 Duncan's early illnesses and accidents—he fell as a child, which resulted in permanent crossed-eyes—play a role in the importance of his body throughout his career. See O'Leary and Christensen.

9 Johnson conversely wants to curtail reading Duncan in terms of otherness: "Too many readers are misled by Duncan's eclecticism, abstraction, and allusiveness, reading him as a poet of otherness rather than of the here and now" (177), but this is because Johnson does not see otherness as integral to presence; Bollobás despite her insistence on Duncan's judgmental ethics, does claim for his poetry a "humility, tolerance and openness to the other" (50); John Taggart's reading of Duncan in "Of the Power of the Word" is the one exception that hypothesizes the workings of otherness in the poetry as an ethical event.

10 See "Strife," where Duncan says that a poem should speak for itself and that poetry "catches" him (*Fictive* 124) and is again echoed in "Shadows, *Passages* 11":
"For poetry / is a contagion" (*Bending* 32).

11 Duncan's view of the body even changes over time, fulfilling his oscillating
process, but making it difficult to define. "Poetry before the Body" (1978) gives a
very strong picture of Duncan's view of the role of the body in poetry during the
last few years of his career. In it, he wants to return to a time before language was
seen as a mental operation, a "self-function," and was grounded in the body, as in
the poetry of dance. "Immediate. No mediators" (*Fictive* 62). From this immediate and embodied Poetry arises "poetry that begins as the admonition of realities
begins and the Word begins. The reality of the mountain first was without "being,"
for "being" is the primary appreciation of self-consciousness" (*Fictive* 62). However, the essay's rejection of consciousness completely reverses his views during the
1950s and 1960s (esp. in *Writing Writing* and *Letters*) that the poet must remain
conscious of the writing process at all times. Regardless, the more immediate
contradiction here is that even Duncan himself must practice "poetry" rather than
"Poetry" even if his aim is an unmediated conduit or passage to the body, which
by this point he seems to be deeming an impossibility.

12 Derrida in *Of Grammatology* writes both of "the navel" and "the hinge" which, in
their spacing, signal the absence that is *différance* and thus the trace of the Other
(xlix, 65–73, 216–29).

13 As Taggart points out, most other postmodern poetry employs silence to invoke
the uncertainty of otherness, but he complains that the excess of Duncan's voice
overshadows the postmodern search for silence as an ethical gesture: "These
techniques acknowledge silence through the contrived failure or frustration of
statement . . . This is not to be confused with what we hear in Robert Duncan's
poetry and poetics. That voice is radically present, non-stop, insistent to the
point of irritation for the reader accustomed to both modernist and postmodernist not-saying; it is the voice of a believer for whom none of the gods—and
none of the words—is dead" ("Of the Power" 197). I think Taggart mistakenly
separates Duncan from this postmodern tendency to "acknowledge silence," particularly in the realm of form.

14 There are many discussions of Christian love in Duncan's work: see particularly
Altieri, *Enlarging* 159 and Fredman *Grounding* 121–22.

15 The woman's body as a cross is a pun on which Luce Irigaray also plays in *Ethics
of Sexual Difference* 5–19.

16 See the preface to *Ground Work: Before the War* called "Some Notes on Notation."

Part 3

1 The only exceptions are in the special issue's introduction by editor Lawrence
Buell, where in passing he mentions Teresa L. Eberts's "dismissal of 'ethical feminism'" and Luce Irigaray's critique of Levinas (12, 16). But this can hardly be called

an adequate discussion, at least what this dimension deserves. Feminist ethics should be added to the five currents that Buell mentions.

2 There are some notable exceptions to the lack of feminist-ethical literary criticism, particularly Ewa Ziarek's *Rhetoric of Failure.*

3 Woods seems to not get the importance of his own pun when he writes, "A poem like *The Cell* is thus a phenomenological exploration of the texture of everyday experiences and of how language contains and *engenders* experiences" (253 emphasis mine).

4 For a reading of the sexual ethics in Niedecker's poetry, see my essay on her, which places Niedecker's writing in the context of Simone de Beauvoir's notion of sex and lived experience.

5 See DuPlessis's formulation of this ideal in *Pink Guitar* 152–53.

6 I agree with both Janet Lyon's and Lisa Tickner's analyses of the common goals as well as the beneficial, mutual influence of female avant-garde artists on their so-called misogynistic male counterparts. Tickner shows that the relation between the sexes and the difficulties of feminism are at the heart of Modernism (22–23). See also DuPlessis, *Pink Guitar,* for the relation of feminist practice to women's avant-garde poetry in which she asks the question why is there the divide between experimental and "humanist" feminist poetry (152–53).

7 See Marjorie Perloff, "Canon and the Loaded Gun," in which, as the first critic to yoke Lorine Niedecker and Howe analytically in a feminist context, she describes them as heavily influenced by male writers—a fact that makes them, like Emily Dickinson, unattractive to feminist critics who insist a poem must have a gyno-centric content or particularly female-influenced lineage. Susan Rubin Suleiman discusses the idea of *écriture féminine* in *Subversive Intent* (125). She argues that the avant-garde engendered the possibility of Kristeva and Hélène Cixous's work (*Subversive Intent* 11–32). See also Kristeva, "Women's Time" 483, and Felski.

8 See my essay on Simone de Beauvoir and Lorine Niedecker for more on the emergence of feminist poethics in the 1960s. See also chapter 4 for my discussion of the terms *lived experience* and *body-as-situation* in the context of Duncan's poetry.

5. The Nearness of Poetry

1 The title of the book and poem comes from Edward Calamy's *The nonconformist's memorial: Being an account of the lives, sufferings, and printed works, of the two thousand ministers ejected from the Church of England, . . . by the Act of uniformity, Aug. 24, 1666.* First written in the early eighteenth century, it was later edited, revised, and expanded by Samuel Palmer in 1775 and again for a second edition in 1802. The Act was also referred to as "The Great Ejection" (Seed).

2 This theme of rescue recurs in Howe's criticism: See Freitag; Davidson, *Ghostlier* 81; Keller, *Expansion* 201; Back 11; and particularly Simpson, and Reinfeld. DuPlessis, *Pink Guitar* 144; Vickery 14; and Perelman 132 take a dissenting view.

3 By categories, I mean a reliance on categories of identity such as "middle class, white, Irish, feminine," and so forth. See also Peter Middleton's essay on Howe and Kristeva concerning their use of language.

4 See also Hartley for a list of such subversive devices, borrowed from Dickinson, that further Howe's opening to, as she says in *My Emily Dickinson*, "the trace of the holy" (2–3).

5 Hear Simone de Beauvoir's echoes of Hegel's master-slave dialectic in the Introduction of Part 3 in *Second Sex* (139).

6 If the notion of nearness, especially in the context of the body, is not grounded in presence, then we are presented with a phenomenological problem of how the Other appears bodily and to the body of the subject. I think Howe's response to this problem in her poetry is the notion of the trace. Pervading her poems (*Europe* 56, 59, 119, 125, 145, 162, 177; *Singularities* 44–7; *Nonconformist's* 52, 79, 82), this notion of the trace functions, as it does for Derrida and Levinas, as the trace of the Other in the text. See *My Emily,* in which Howe discusses it explicitly as "the trace of the holy" (35), and Hartley's reading of this passage (2–3). On the notion of trace in Howe's work, see Perelman 133 and 136, who sees it also in the context of Derrida's problematic that dis-covery of the Other is also a "covery" and erasure. See also Davidson, *Ghostlier* 81.

7 On the presence and influence of Duncan in Howe's poetry see Daly 43, as well as her tribute to Duncan (Susan Howe Papers, UCSD 201.9.18).

6. Permeable Ethics

1 In her journals, Hejinian denounces feminisms that simply want to wrest power from men without changing the patriarchal structure of power; among them she places Robert Duncan, whom she feels fetishizes the power of the poetic word. "I'm just not interested in power," she writes. See Howe's interview in *Birth-Mark:* "I am troubled by some feminist criticism because in its stridency is only another bias. And in a strange sense it's still a male bias. Instead of questioning the idea of power itself, many women want to assume power" (169–70). I think the two poets share a desire to redefine or disperse power. See also Hartley at the end of his chapter 4.

2 In the journals, Hejinian claims that *The Cell* is a moral poem in conjunction with another long poem she was writing at the time, "The Person" (Lyn Hejinian Papers, UCSD 74.47.6–7: 23–25 April 1985 and 17 Mar 1987).

3 Robbins discusses Levinas's use of Dostoevsky in depth (*Altered* 147–50). See also Levinas's citation of *Crime and Punishment* ("Trace" 351).

4 DuPlessis gives a good definition, although not exactly a French definition, of "female aesthetic" or *écriture féminine:*

> To define then. "Female aesthetic": the production of formal, epistemological, and thematic strategies by members of the group Woman, strategies born in struggle with much of already existing culture, and overdetermined by two

elements of sexual difference—by women's psychosocial experiences of gender asymmetry and by women's historical status in an (ambiguously) non-hegemonic group. (*Pink Guitar* 5)

5 See Shoptaw's discussion of the form of *The Cell* in "Hejinian Meditations."
6 I am indebted to Deborah Mix's work and discussions with me on the subject of metonymy in Hejinian. See her 'A vulnerable known not sure' in *How2*.
7 Hejinian is not exaggerating that claim of totality. The *Oxford English Dictionary*'s slogan in 2004, according to its website <http://www.oed.com/>, was "The definitive record of the English language," while Simon Winchester's book on the first 1928 edition of the dictionary is tellingly titled, *The Meaning of Everything*. It's not just modern culture that is infatuated with totality; postmodern culture continues it.
8 In her discussion of Jakobson in "Strangeness," Hejinian theorizes metonymy as operating "within several simultaneous but not necessarily congruent logics . . . Metonymy moves attention from thing to thing; its principle is combination rather than selection" (38). See also Mix's discussion and Conte's definition of metonymy as poetic structure (55, 71, 78, 125–59). Shoptaw also discusses the use of discontinuity in Hejinian's metonymy.
9 See Dickinson in a letter to T. W. Higginson, cited in Howe's *My Emily Dickinson* (132–33).
10 For example, in the context of meteorology, which Hejinian brings up in the poem, the sex of the subject does not matter unless (1) the metaphors used in its discourse are gendered or (2) there is something about having a particular set of genitals or hormones that helps one predict the weather. The latter is ludicrous.
11 Cp. when Hejinian refers to William James's discussion of how the psychologist objectifies his own mind ("Strangeness" 37).
12 Hejinian's essay "Strangeness" I think misses the structural continuity of metonymy because she is concerned with the way that metonymy preserves particulars and the difference between them, as well as many other manifestations of discontinuity: "arbitrariness, unpredictability, and inadvertence" (32); "disjuncture or discontinuity between the spatial existence and the temporal existence of a person" (37); "the metonymic world is unstable" (38); "While metonymy maintains the intactness and discreteness of particulars, its paratactic perspective gives it multiple vanishing points" (38); and she wrongly argues that science privileges the forms of aphorisms and parataxis (42). Cp. Conte who defines metonymy as contiguity, "a syntagmatic chain of particulars—details directed along a line," in *Unending Design* 143. One could say that Hejinian's understanding of metonymy is not exactly "wrong"; instead she is looking for the discontinuous in the continuous. See also Shoptaw.
13 With the possible exception, of course, of Ginsberg's "Howl": "Who cooked rotten animals lung heart feet tail borsht & tortillas/ dreaming of the pure vegetable

kingdom," which is reference still to consumption of food, even if the poem is also much about sexuality (129).

14 The dates at the bottom of each poem, which, as Hejinian's journals show, correspond to the date she drafted the poem, but they are still arbitrary in that the day is not specifically significant within the content of the poem. That is, a poem does not necessarily reflect autobiographical suggestions in contextual parts of the journal that she was, say, having a good or bad day.

15 In a draft of this poem in her journals, it is clear than "cyclops" modifies "penis," which in the published version is replaced with the pronoun, "it" (Lyn Hejinian Papers, UCSD 74.47.7: 16 Jan 87).

16 There is a funny side note to how the metonymic chain of cell—egg—head—eye happened for Hejinian in this poem. In the journal where she was drafting *The Cell*, Hejinian glosses the stanza numbered 54, which turns out to be the poem titled "March 3, 1987" in *The Cell* (78), with a parenthetical aside. The stanza reads: "My head, it is a threaded egg / All those wide heads of egg are female / New again—." The gloss reads, with line breaks preserved:

(In basic Elements yesterday Grant Fisher mentioned
Pound's comment—belief?—that the brain was a
mass of sperm ejaculated up the spine. Certainly
this is not true of the brains of women, which
must consist, then, of eggs.)
Egg, eye, + cell (Lyn Hejinian Papers, UCSD 74.47.7: 3 Mar 1987)

17 *Abob* is a word that appears often in Hejinian's corpus ("Rejection"; Messerli, *Other Side* 591).

Conclusion

1 Cf. Teresa de Lauretis's *Technologies of Gender*.

Bibliography

Ahearn, Barry. "Zukofsky, Marxism, and American Handicraft." In Scroggins, *Upper Limit*, 80–93.

———. *Zukofsky's "A": An Introduction*. Berkeley: U of California P, 1983.

Allen, Donald and George F. Butterick, eds. *The Postmoderns: The New American Poetry Revised*. New York: Grove, 1982.

Altieri, Charles. *Canons and Consequences: Reflections of the Ethical Force of Imaginative Ideals*. Chicago: Northwestern UP, 1990.

———. *Enlarging the Temple: New Directions in American Poetry during the 1960s*. Lewisburg, PA: Bucknell UP, 1979.

———. "The Objectivist Tradition." *Chicago Review* 30 (1979): 5–22.

Andrews, Bruce. *Paradise and Method: Poetics and Praxis*. Evanston, IL: Northwestern UP, 1995.

Arendt, Hannah. *Eichmann in Jerusalem: A Report on the Banality of Evil*. Revised and enlarged edition. New York: Penguin, 1994.

Armantrout, Rae. "Poetic Silence." *Writing/Talks*. Ed. Bob Perelman. Carbondale: Southern Illinois UP, 1985. 31–47.

Attridge, Derek. "Innovation, Literature, Ethics: Relating to the Other." *PMLA* 114.1 (1999): 20–31.

Augustine, Jane. "'What's Wrong with Marriage': Lorine Niedecker's Struggle with Gender Roles." In Penberthy, 139–156.

Austin Powers. Dir. Jay Roach. Wr. by Michael Meyers. Perf. Michael Meyers, Elizabeth Hurley, Michael York. New Line Cinema, 1997.

Back, Rachel Tzvia. *Led by Language: The Poetry and Poetics of Susan Howe*. Tuscaloosa: U of Alabama P, 2002.

Baker, Peter. *Deconstruction and the Ethical Turn*. Gainesville: U of Florida P, 1995.

———. *Obdurate Brilliance: Exteriority and the Modern Long Poem*. Tallahassee: U of Florida P, 1991.

Baraka, Amiri. *The Baraka Reader*. New York: Thunder's Mouth, 1991.

Beauvoir, Simone de. *The Second Sex*. Trans. H. M. Parshley. New York: Vintage Books, 1989.

Bernstein, Charles. "Reznikoff's Nearness." *Sulfur* 32 (1993): 6–40.

Berry, Eleanor. "Language Made Fluid: The Grammetrics of George Oppen's Recent Poetry." *Contemporary Literature* 25.3 (1984): 305–322.

———. "The Oppen-Williams Connection." *Sagetrieb* 3 (1984): 99–116.

Bertholf, Robert J. *Robert Duncan: A Descriptive Bibliography*. Eds. Robert Creeley and Black Sparrow Press. Santa Rosa, CA: Black Sparrow, 1986.

Blake, William. *The Complete Poetry and Prose of William Blake*. Ed. David V. Erdman. Commentary by Harold Bloom. Newly Revised Edition. New York: Anchor Books, 1988.

Blanchot, Maurice. *The Infinite Conversation*. Trans. Susan Hanson. Minneapolis: U of Minnesota P, 1993.

———. *The Space of Literature*. Trans. Ann Smock. Lincoln: U of Nebraska P, 1982.

———. *The Step Not Beyond*. Trans. Lycette Nelson. Albany: State U of New York, 1992.

———. *The Unavowable Community*. Trans. Pierre Joris. Barrytown, NY: Station Hill, 1988.

———. *The Writing of the Disaster*. Trans. Ann Smock. Lincoln: U of Nebraska P, 1995.

Bollobás, Enikő. "Versions of the *Whole Earth Catalogue*: On the Poetry of Robert Duncan and Ed Dorn." *High and Low in American Culture*. Ed. Charlotte Kretzoi. Budapest: L. Eötvös University, Department of English, 1987.

Boone, Bruce. "Robert Duncan and the Gay Community: A Reflection." *Ironwood* 22 (1983): 66–82.

Boughn, Michael. <mboughn@epas.utoronto.ca> "Re: Slinger." 19 Dec 1995. UB Poetics Listserv group <poetics@ubvm.cc.buffalo.edu> via archive at <http://listserv.acsu.buffalo.edu/archives/poetics.html> Accessed 26 March 1997.

Breslin, Glenna. "Lorine Niedecker: Composing a Life." *Revealing Lives: Autobiography, Biography, and Gender*. Eds. Susan Groag Bell and Marilyn Yalom. Albany: State U of New York P, 1990: 141–153.

Brogan, Jacqueline Vaught. *Part of the Climate: American Cubist Poetry*. Berkeley: U of California P, 1991.

———. "Planets on the Table: From Wallace Stevens and Elizabeth Bishop to Adrienne Rich and June Jordan." *The Wallace Stevens Journal* 19.2 (1995): 255–278.

———. "ta(l)king eyes." *Joyful Wisdom: a journal for postmodern ethics* 2.1 (1995): 71–88.

Bronk, William. *Life Supports: New and Collected Poems*. San Francisco: North Point, 1981.

———. *Vectors and Smoothable Curves: Collected Essays*. San Francisco: North Point, 1985.

Bruns, Gerald. *Heidegger's Estrangements: Language, Truth, and Poetry in the Later Writings*. New Haven: Yale UP, 1989.

———. "'Poethics': Or John Cage and Stanley Cavell at the Crossroads of Ethical Theory." In Perloff and Junkerman, 206–225.

Buell, Lawrence. "Introduction: In Pursuit of Ethics," *PMLA* 114.1 (1999): 7–19.

Burnett, Gary. "Introduction to Robert Duncan's Letters." *Ironwood* 22 (1983): 96–97.

Butler, Judith. "Performative Acts and Gender Constitution: An Essay in Phenomenology and Feminist Theory." *Writing on the Body: Female*

Embodiment and Feminist Theory. Eds. Katie Conboy, Nadia Medina, and Sarah Stanbury. New York: Columbia UP, 1997. 401–417.

Byrd, Don. "The Poetry of Production." *Sagetrieb* 2 (1983): 7–43.

Caputo, John. *Against Ethics: Contributions to a Poetics of Obligation with Constant Reference to Deconstruction.* Bloomington: Indiana UP, 1993.

Chanter, Tina. *Ethics of Eros: Irigaray's Rewriting of the Philosophers.* New York: Routledge, 1995.

———. *Time, Death, and the Feminine: Levinas with Heidegger.* Stanford, CA: Stanford UP, 2001.

Chilton, Randolph. "The Place of Being in the Poetry of George Oppen." In Hatlen, 89–120.

Chodoff, Paul. "The Holocaust and Its Effects on Survivors: An Overview." *Political Psychology* 18.1 (1997): 147–157.

———. "Psychiatric Effects of the Nazi Oppression." Presented at the American Psychiatric Association Divisional Meeting, Philadelphia—Saturday, Nov. 21, 1965.

Christensen, Paul. "Robert Duncan." *American National Biography.* New York: Oxford UP, 1999.

Cixous, Hélène. "The Laugh of the Medusa." *Critical Theory Since 1965.* Eds. Hazard Adams and Leroy Searle. Tallahassee: Florida State UP, 1986.

Committee of Public Safety. "'My Place in the Sun': Reflections on the Thought of Emmanuel Levinas." *diacritics* 26 (1997): 3–10.

Conte, Joseph. *Unending Design: The Forms of Post-Modern Poetry.* Ithaca: Cornell UP, 1991.

Corman, Cid. "To Each Other We Will Speak." *Ironwood* 13 (1985): 116–145.

Cornell, Drucilla. *The Philosophy of the Limit.* New York: Routledge, 1992.

Critchley, Simon. *Ethics of Deconstruction: Derrida and Levinas.* Oxford: Blackwell, 1992.

Culler, Jonathan D., and Ira Konigsberg, eds. *American Criticism in the Poststructuralist Age.* Ann Arbor: U of Michigan P, 1981.

Culler, Jonathan. Lecture at the School of Criticism and Theory at Cornell, July 1997.

Cushman, Steven. *William Carlos Williams and the Meanings of Measure.* New Haven: Yale UP, 1985.

Daly, Lew. *Swallowing the Scroll: Late in a Prophetic Tradition with the Poetry of Susan Howe and John Taggart.* Buffalo, NY: Apex of the M, 1994.

Davenport, Guy. *Cities on Hills.* New York: UMI, 1983.

Davidson, Michael. "A Book of First Things: *The Opening of the Field.*" *Robert Duncan: Scales of the Marvelous.* New York: New Directions, 1979. 56–84.

———. "Cave of Resemblances, Caves of Rime: Tradition and Repetition in Robert Duncan." *Ironwood* 22 (1983): 33–46.

———. "'To Eliminate the Draw': Narrative and Language in Slinger." *Internal Resistances: The Poetry of Edward Dorn.* Berkeley: U of California P, 1985. 113–149.

——. *Ghostlier Demarcations: Modern Poetry and the Material World.* Berkeley: U of California P, 1997.

Davie, Donald. "Niedecker and Historicity." In Penberthy, 361–376.

Dembo, L. S. "The 'Objectivist' Poet: Four Interviews." *Contemporary Literature* 10 (1969): 155–219.

Derrida, Jacques. "Che cos'è la poesia?" *Between the Blinds: A Derrida Reader.* Ed. Peggy Kamuf. New York: Columbia UP, 1991. 221–237.

——. *Dissemination.* Trans. B. Johnson. Chicago: U of Chicago P, 1981.

——. "Force of Law: The Mystical Foundations of Authority." *Cardozo Law Review* 11.5–6 (1990): 940–960.

——. *Of Grammatology.* Trans. Gayatri Spivak. Baltimore: Johns Hopkins UP, 1974.

——. *Margins of Philosophy.* Trans. Alan Bass. Chicago: U of Chicago P, 1982.

——. *Writing and Difference.* Trans. Alan Bass. Chicago: U of Chicago P, 1978.

Dewey, Anne. "The Relation between Open Form and Collective Voice: The Social Origin of Processual Form in John Ashbery's *Three Poems* and Ed Dorn's *Gunslinger.*" *Sagetrieb* 11 (1992): 47–66.

Docherty, Thomas. *Alterities: Criticism, History, Representation.* Oxford: Clarendon, 1996.

Dorn, Edward. *Gunslinger.* Durham, NC: Duke UP, 1989.

——. *Interviews.* Ed. Donald Allen. Bolinas, CA: Four Seasons Foundation, 1980.

Dresman, Paul. "Internal Resistances: Edward Dorn on the American Indians." In Wesling, 87–112.

Duncan, Robert. *Bending the Bow.* New York: New Directions, 1968.

——. *Caesar's Gate: Poems, 1949–50.* Berkeley: Sand Dollar, 1972.

——. *Fictive Certainties: Essays.* New York: New Directions, 1985.

——. *Ground Work: Before the War.* New York: New Directions, 1984.

——. *Ground Work II: In the Dark.* New York: New Directions, 1987.

——. *Letters.* Highlands, NC: J. Williams, 1958.

——. "Letters on Poetry and Poetics." *Ironwood* 22 (1983): 97–133.

——. *The Opening of the Field.* New York: Grove, 1960.

——. *Play Time: Pseudo Stein.* Privately printed, 1969.

——. *Roots and Branches.* New York: Scribner, 1964.

——. *Selected Poems.* Ed. Robert J. Bertholf. New York: New Directions, 1993.

——. *A Selected Prose.* New York: New Directions, 1995.

——. *Writing Writing: A Composition Book for Madison, 1953.* Portland, OR: C. Reyes, 1971.

——. *The Years as Catches: First Poems, 1939–1946.* Berkeley: Oyez, 1966.

DuPlessis, Rachel Blau. "A Bibliography of Interviews of George and Mary Oppen Chronologically Arranged." *Sagetrieb* 6.1 (1987): 137–139.

——. "The Circumstances: A Selection from George Oppen's Uncollected Writing." *Sulfur* 10 (1987): 10–43.

———. "Lorine Niedecker, the Anonymous: Gender, Class, Genre and Resistances." In Penberthy, 113–138.

———. "Objectivist Poetics and Political Vision: A Study of Oppen and Pound." In Hatlen, 123–148.

———. *The Pink Guitar*. New York: Routledge, 1990.

———. "'When the familiar becomes extreme': George Oppen and Silence." *North Dakota Quarterly* 55 (1987 Fall): 18–36.

DuPlessis, Rachel Blau, and Peter Quartermain, eds. *The Objectivist Nexus.* Tuscaloosa and London: U of Alabama P, 1999.

Ezrahi, Sidra DeKoven. *By Words Alone: The Holocaust in Literature.* Chicago: U of Chicago P, 1980.

Feld, Ross. "Some Thoughts on Objectivism." *Sagetrieb* 12 (1993): 13–32.

Felski, Rita. *Beyond Feminist Aesthetics: Feminist Literature and Social Change.* Cambridge: Harvard UP, 1989.

Finkelstein, Norman. "The Dialectic of *This In Which.*" In Hatlen, 359–373.

———. "Syntax and Tradition: George Oppen's *Primitive.*" In Hatlen, 429–443.

———. *The Utopian Moment in American Poetry.* Rev. ed. London: Associated UP, 1993.

Fischer, Michael. *Does Deconstruction Make Any Difference? Poststructuralism and the Defense of Poetry in Modern Criticism.* Bloomington: Indiana UP, 1985.

Foster, Edward, ed. *Postmodern Poetry: The Talisman Interviews.* Hoboken, NJ: Talisman House, 1994.

Foucault, Michel. *The History of Sexuality: Vol. 1: An Introduction.* Trans. Robert Hurley. New York: Vintage, 1990.

Franciosi, Robert. "'Detailing the Facts': Charles Reznikoff's Response to the Holocaust." *Contemporary Literature* 29.2 (1988): 241–264.

Fredman, Stephen. "All Is Now War: Oppen, Olson, and the Problem of Literary Generations." Paper delivered at the 1995 Modern Language Association Convention.

———. *The Grounding of American Poetry: Charles Olson and the Emersonian Tradition.* Cambridge: Cambridge UP, 1993.

———. *A Menorah for Athena: Charles Reznikoff and the Jewish Dilemmas of Objectivist Poetry.* Chicago: U of Chicago P, 2001.

———. *Poet's Prose: The Crisis In American Verse.* 2nd ed. Cambridge: Cambridge UP, 1990.

Fredman, Stephen, and Grant Jenkins. "First Annotations towards Ed Dorn's *Gunslinger.*" *Sagetrieb* 16 (1996): 57–177.

Freitag, Kornelia. "Writing Language Poetry as a Woman: Susan Howe's Feminist Project in *A Bibliography of the King's Book, or, Eikon Basilike.*" *Amerikastudien/American Studies* 40:1 (1995): 45–57.

Friedrich, Hugo. *The Structure of Modern Poetry: From the Mid-Nineteenth to the Mid-Twentieth Century.* Evanston, IL: Northwestern UP, 1974.

Frost, Elisabeth A. *The Feminist Avant-Garde in American Poetry.* Iowa City: U of Iowa P, 2003.

Gallop, Jane. *Thinking through the Body.* New York: Columbia UP, 1988.

Gans, Steven. "Lacan and Levinas: Towards and Ethical Psychoanalysis." *Journal of the British Society for Phenomenology* 28 (1997): 30–48.

Gery, John. "Edward Dorn, Community Poet." *Occident* 101.1 (1981): 48–51.

Ginsberg, Allen. *Collected Poems: 1947–1980.* New York: Harper & Row, 1984.

Goldhagen, Daniel Jonah. *Hitler's Willing Executioners: Ordinary Germans and the Holocaust.* New York: Knopf/Random House, 1996.

Golding, Alan. "George Oppen's Serial Poems." In DuPlessis and Quartermain, 84–106.

Haney, David P. "Aesthetics and Ethics in Gadamer, Levinas, and Romanticism: Problems of Phronesis and Techne." *PMLA* 114.1 (1999): 32–45.

Hartley, George. *Textual Politics and the Language Poets.* Bloomington: Indiana UP, 1989.

Hatlen, Burton, ed. *George Oppen: Man and Poet.* Orono, ME: National Poetry Foundation, 1981.

Hatlen, Burton. "'Not Altogether Lone in a Lone Universe': George Oppen's *The Materials.*" In Hatlen, 325–357.

———. "Opening Up the Text: George Oppen's 'Of Being Numerous.'" *Ironwood* 26 (1985): 263–295.

———. "A Poetics of Marginality and Resistance: The 'Objectivist' Poets in Context." In DuPlessis and Quartermain, 37–55.

Hatlen, Burton, and Tom Mandel. "Poetry and Politics: A Conversation with George and Mary Oppen." In Hatlen, 23–50.

Hegel, Georg Wilhelm Friedrich. *The Phenomenology of Spirit Reader: Critical and Interpretive Essays.* Ed. Jon Stewart. Albany: State U of New York, 1998.

Heidegger, Martin. "Letter on Humanism." *Basic Writings: from Being and Time (1927) to The Task of Thinking (1964).* New York: Harper & Row, 1977.

———. "The Nature of Language." *Poetry, Language, Thought.* Ed. Harper Colophon. New York: Harper & Row, 1975.

———. *On the Way to Language.* New York: Harper & Row, 1971.

———. "The Origin of the Work of Art." *Poetry, Language, Thought.* Ed. Harper Colophon. New York: Harper & Row, 1975.

Hejinian, Lyn. *The Cell.* Los Angeles: Sun & Moon, 1992.

———. *The Cold of Poetry.* Los Angeles: Sun & Moon, 1994.

———. *Lyn Hejinian Papers.* MSS 74. University Library, Mandeville Department of Special Collections, U of California, San Diego—abbreviated UCSD, followed by numbers representing collection, box, and folder.

———. *My Life.* Los Angeles: Sun & Moon, 1987.

———. "The Rejection of Closure." *Writing/Talks.* Ed. Bob Perelman. Carbondale: Southern Illinois UP, 1985. 270–291.

————. "Smatter." *L=A=N=G=U=A=G=E* 8 (June 1979): 17.

————. "Some Notes toward a Poetics." In *American Women Poets in the 21st Century: Where Lyric Meets Language.* Eds. Claudia Rankine and Juliana Spahr. Middletown, CT: Wesleyan UP, 2002.

————. "Strangeness." *Poetics Journal* 8 (1989): 32–45.

————. "Two Stein Talks: Language and Realism; Grammar and Landscape." *Temblor* 3 (1986): 128–139.

Heller, Michael. *Conviction's Net of Branches: Essays on the Objectivist Poets and Poetry.* Carbondale: Southern Illinois UP, 1985.

————. "Conviction's Net of Branches." In Hatlen, 417–28.

————. "A Mimetics of Humanity: George Oppen's *Of Being Numerous.*" *American Poetry* 4 (1987): 19–33.

Hewett, Greg. "Revealing 'The Torso': Robert Duncan and the Process of Signifying Male Homosexuality." *Contemporary Literature* 35.3 (1994): 522–546.

Hindus, Milton. *Charles Reznikoff: A Critical Essay.* Santa Barbara: Black Sparrow, 1977.

Hirsch, Edward. "'Out There Is the World': The Visual Imperatives in the Poetry of George Oppen and Charles Tomlinson." In Hatlen, 169–180.

Holveck, Eleanore. "The Blood of Others: A Novel Approach to the Ethics of Ambiguity." *Hypatia* 14.4 (Fall 1999): 3–17.

Hooker, Jeremy. "'The Boundaries of Our Distances': On 'Of Being Numerous.'" *Ironwood* 26 (1985): 81–103.

Howe, Susan. *The Birth-Mark: Unsettling the Wilderness in American Literary History.* Hanover, NH: Wesleyan UP, 1993.

————. *The Europe of Trusts.* Los Angeles: Sun & Moon, 1990.

————. *My Emily Dickinson.* Berkeley: North Atlantic, 1985.

————. *The Nonconformist's Memorial.* New York: New Directions, 1993.

————. *Singularities.* Middletown, CT: Wesleyan UP, 1990.

————. Susan Howe Papers. MSS 201. University Library, Mandeville Department of Special Collections, U of California, San Diego—abbreviated UCSD, followed by numbers representing collection, box, and folder.

Irigaray, Luce. *An Ethics of Sexual Difference.* Ithaca: Cornell UP, 1993.

————. "Questions to Emmanuel Levinas." *The Irigaray Reader.* Ed. Margaret Whitford. Oxford: Basil Blackwell, 1991. 178–190.

————. *Speculum of the Other Woman.* Ithaca: Cornell UP, 1985.

————. *This Sex Which Is Not One.* Trans. C. Porter and C. Burke. Ithaca: Cornell UP, 1985.

————. "Volume without Contours." *The Irigaray Reader.* Ed. Margaret Whitford. Oxford: Basil Blackwell, 1991. 53–68.

Jenkins, G. Matthew. "Lorine Niedecker, Simone de Beauvoir, and the Sexual Ethics of Experience." *Tulsa Studies in Women's Literature* 23.2 (2004): 311–337.

Johnson, Mark. *Robert Duncan.* Boston: Twayne, 1988.

Keller, Lynn. *Forms of Expansion: Recent Long Poems by Women*. Chicago: U of Chicago P, 1997.

———. "Interview with Susan Howe." *Contemporary Literature* 36 (1995 Spring): 1–34.

Kenner, Hugh. "Disconnected Numerousness." *Ironwood* 26 (1985): 205–211.

———. *A Homemade World: The American Modernist Writers*. New York: Knopf, 1975.

———. *The Pound Era*. Berkeley: U of California P, 1971.

Kinnahan, Linda A. *Lyric Interventions: Feminism, Experimental Poetry, and Contemporary Discourse*. Iowa City: U of Iowa P, 2004.

Kitch, Sally L. "Gender and Language: Dialect, Silence, and the Disruption of Discourse." *Women's Studies* 14 (1987): 65–78.

Kristeva, Julia. *Desire in Language: A Semiotic Approach to Literature and Art*. New York: Columbia UP, 1980.

———. *The Powers of Horror: An Essay on Abjection*. New York: Columbia UP, 1982.

———. *Revolution in Poetic Language*. New York: Columbia UP, 1984.

———. "Women's Time." *Critical Theory Since 1965*. Eds. Hazard Adams and Leroy Searle. Tallahassee: Florida State UP, 1986.

Lacan, Jacques. *The Ethics of Psychoanalysis, 1959–1960*. Trans. Denis Porter. New York: Norton, 1992.

———. "The Mirror Stage as Formative of the Function of the I as Revealed in Psychoanalytic Experience." In *Jacques Lacan. Ecrits: A Selection*. Trans. A. Sheridan. New York: Norton, 1977. 1–7.

———. "The Signification of the Phallus." In *Jacques Lacan. Ecrits: A Selection*. Trans. A. Sheridan. New York: Norton, 1977. 280–291.

———. "The Subversion of the Subject and the Dialectic of Desire in the Freudian Unconscious." In *Jacques Lacan. Ecrits: A Selection*. Trans. A. Sheridan. New York: Norton, 1977. 292–325.

Lauretis, Teresa de. *Technologies of Gender: Essays on Theory, Film, Fiction*. Bloomington: Indiana UP, 1987.

Levinas, Emmanuel. *Ethics and Infinity: Conversations with Philip Nemo*. Trans. Richard A. Cohen. Pittsburgh: Duquesne UP, 1985.

———. *Existence and Existents*. Pittsburgh: Duquesne UP, 2001.

———. "Le regarde du poete." *Monde Nouveau* 98 (1956).

———. *Noms Propres*. Paris: Editions Fata Morgana, 1975.

———. *Otherwise Than Being or Beyond Essence*. Trans. Alphonso Lingis. Dordrecht: Kluwer Academic Publishers, 1991.

———. *Outside the Subject*. Trans. Michael B. Smith. Stanford, CA: Stanford UP, 1994.

———. *Proper Names*. Trans. Michael B. Smith. Stanford, CA: Stanford UP, 1996.

———. "Reality and Its Shadow." *The Levinas Reader*. Trans. Sean Hand. Oxford: Basil Blackwell, 1989. 100–116.

————. "The Servant and Her Master." *The Levinas Reader.* Trans. Sean Hand. Oxford: Basil Blackwell, 1989. 150–159.

————. *Sur Maurice Blanchot.* Paris: Editions Fata Morgana, 1975.

————. *Totality and Infinity.* Trans. Alphonso Lingis. Pittsburgh: Duquesne UP, 1969.

————. "The Trace of the Other." Trans. Alphonso Lingis. In *Deconstruction in Context.* Ed. Mark Taylor. Chicago: U of Chicago, 1986. 350–353.

Libertson, Joseph. *Proximity: Levinas, Blanchot, Bataille and Communication.* The Hague: Martinus Nijhoff, 1982.

Llewelyn, John. *The Middle Voice of Ecological Conscience: A Chiasmic Reading of Responsibility in the Neighborhood of Levinas, Heidegger, and Others.* New York: St. Martin's, 1991.

Lockwood, William J. "Art Rising to Clarity: Edward Dorn's Compleat Slinger." In Wesling, 150–207.

"Louis Zukofsky." Electronic Poetry Center. 3 May 2006 <http://wings.buffalo.edu/epc/authors/zukofsky/zuk.pub.html>.

Lyons, Janet. "Militant Discourse, Strange Bedfellows: Suffragettes and Vorticists before the War." *differences* 4 (1992): 100–133.

Lyotard, Jean-François. *The Post-Modern Condition: A Report on Knowledge.* Minneapolis: U of Minnesota P, 1984.

Ma, Ming-Qian. "A 'Seeing' through Refraction: The Rear-View Mirror Image in George Oppen's *Collected Poems.*" *Sagetrieb* 10 (1991): 83–98.

Madison, Gary B., and Marty Fairbairn, eds. *The Ethics of Postmodernity: Current Trends in Continental Thought.* Evanston, IL: U of Northwestern P, 1999.

Martone, John. "The Psalmic Poetics of George Oppen." *Poesis* 6.1 (1984): 40–50.

Matthias, John. "Robert Duncan and David Jones: Some Affinities." *Ironwood* 22 (1983): 140–157.

McAleavey, David. "Clarity and Process: Oppen's *Of Being Numerous.*" In Hatlen, 381–406.

McCaffery, Steve. *North of Intention: Critical Writings 1973–1986.* New York: Roof Books, 1986.

————. "The Scandal of Sincerity: Towards a Levinasian poetics." *Pretexts: Studies in Culture and Writing* 6 (1997): 167–190.

McGann, Jerome J. "Contemporary Poetry, Alternate Routes." In *Social Values and Poetic Acts.* Cambridge: Harvard UP, 1988. 197–220.

McPhilmey, Kathleen. "Towards Open Form: A Study of Process Poetics in Relation to Four Long Poems." PhD diss., University of Edinburgh, 1980.

Melnick, David. "A Short Word on My Work." *L=A=N=G=U=A=G=E* (Feb 1978): 12–13. 13 Nov 2006 <http://english.utah.edu/eclipse/projects/LANGUAGEn1/>.

————. *Pcoet.* San Francisco: G. A. W. K., 1975. 10 Jan 2007 <http://english.utah.edu/eclipse/projects/PCOET/pcoet.html>.

Merleau-Ponty, Maurice. *The Phenomenology of Perception.* London: Routledge, 1962.

Meschonnic, Henri. *Le langue Heidegger.* Paris: Presses Universitaires de France, 1990.

Messerli, Douglas. *From the Other Side of the Century: A New American Poetry 1960–1990.* Sun & Moon, 1994.

———. *"Language" Poetries: An Anthology.* New York: New Directions, 1987.

Michael, Walter Benn. *Our America: Nativism, Modernism, and Pluralism.* Durham, NC: Duke UP, 1995.

Middleton, Peter. "On Ice: Julia Kristeva, Susan Howe and Avant Garde Poetics." *Contemporary Poetry Meets Modern Theory.* Eds. Anthony Easthope and John Thompson. Toronto: U of Toronto P, 1991. 81–95.

Mix, Deborah. "'A vulnerable known not sure': Metonymy as/and Transformation." *How2* 1.3 (2000). <http://www.asu.edu/pipercwcenter/how2journal/archive/online_archive/v1_3_2000/current/readings/mix.html> Accessed 15 Aug 2007.

Moi, Toril. *Feminist Theory and Simone de Beauvoir.* Oxford: Blackwell, 1990.

———. *Sexual/Textual Politics: Feminist Literary Theory.* London: Methuen, 1985.

———. *Simone de Beauvoir: The Making of an Intellectual Woman.* Oxford: Blackwell, 1994.

———. *What Is a Woman? and Other Essays.* Oxford: Oxford UP, 1999.

Molesworth, Charles. "Truth and Life and Robert Duncan." *Ironwood* 22 (1983): 83–94.

Mottram, Eric. "The Political Responsibilities of the Poet: George Oppen." In Hatlen, 149–176.

Nancy, Jean-Luc. *The Inoperative Community.* Trans. Peter Conor, et al. Minneapolis: U of Minnesota P, 1991.

Naylor, Paul. "The Pre-Position 'Of': Being, Seeing, and Knowing in George Oppen's Poetry." *Contemporary Literature* 32.1 (1991): 100–115.

Newton, Adam Zachary. *Narrative Ethics.* Cambridge: Harvard UP, 1995.

Nicholls, Peter. "Of Being Ethical: Reflections on George Oppen." In DuPlessis and Quartermain, 240–253.

Niedecker, Lorine. *"Between Your House and Mine": The Letters of Lorine Niedecker and Cid Corman, 1960–1970.* Ed. Lisa Pater Faranda. Durham, NC: Duke UP, 1986.

———. *From This Condensery: The Complete Writing of Lorine Niedecker.* Ed. Robert J. Bertholf. Highlands, NC: The Jargon Society, 1985.

———. *The Granite Pail: The Selected Poems of Lorine Niedecker.* Frankfort, KY: Gnomen, 1996.

———. *Harpsicord & Saltfish.* Ed. Jenny Penberthy. Durham, NC: Pig, 1991.

———. "Lake Superior Country." In Penberthy, 311–326.

———. *Lorine Niedecker: Complete Works.* Ed. Jenny Penberthy. Berkeley: U of California P, 2002.

————. *New Goose.* Prairie City, IL: The Press of J. A. Decker, 1946.

————. *North Central.* London: Fulcrum, 1968.

Oderman, Kevin. "Earth and Awe: The One Poetry of George Oppen." *Sagetrieb* 3.1 (1984): 63–75.

O'Leary, Peter. *Gnostic Contagion: Robert Duncan and the Poetry of Illness.* Middletown, CT: Wesleyan UP, 2002.

Oliver, Kelly. *Reading Kristeva: Unraveling the Double-bind.* Bloomington: Indiana UP, 1993.

Olson, Charles. "Human Universe." *Human Universe and Other Essays.* Ed. Donald Allen. San Francisco: Auerhan Society, 1965.

————. *The Maximus Poems.* Berkeley: U of California P, 1983.

————. "Proprioception." *Additional Prose.* Ed. George F. Butterick. Bolinas, CA: Four Seasons Foundation, 1974.

————. "Projective Verse." *Poetics of the New American Poetry.* Eds. Donald Allen and Warren Tallman. New York: Grove, 1973. 147–158.

Oppen, George. "An Adequate Vision: A George Oppen Daybook." Ed. Michael Davidson. *Ironwood* 26 (1985): 5–31.

————. The George Oppen Papers. MSS 16. University Library, Mandeville Department of Special Collections, U of California, San Diego—abbreviated UCSD, followed by numbers representing collection, box, and folder.

————. "Mind's Own Place." *Kulchur* 10 (Summer 1963): 3–8.

————. *New Collected Poems.* Ed. Michael Davidson. New York: New Directions, 2002.

————. *Primitive.* Santa Barbara: Black Sparrow, 1978.

————. *The Selected Letters of George Oppen.* Ed. Rachel Blau DuPlessis. Durham, NC: Duke UP, 1990.

————. "Statement on Poetics." *Sagetrieb* 3.3 (1984): 25–27.

Oppen, Mary. *Meaning: A Life.* Santa Barbara: Black Sparrow, 1978.

Painter, George. "The Sensibilities of Our Forefathers: The History of Sodomy Laws in the United States: New York." 2001. Bob Summersgill. <http://www .sodomylaws.org/sensibilities/new_york.htm>. Accessed 11 March 2005.

Palmer, Michael. *First Figure.* San Francisco: North Point, 1984.

————. "On Objectivism." *Sulfur* 10 (1987): 117–126.

————. *Sun.* San Francisco: North Point, 1988.

Parlej, Piotr. "Testing the Image: The Double Interrogative in the Poetry of George Oppen." *Sagetrieb* 10.1 (1991): 67–82.

Paul, Sherman. *The Lost America of Love: Re-reading Robert Creeley, Ed Dorn, and Robert Duncan.* Baton Rouge: Louisiana State UP, 1981.

Penberthy, Jenny, ed. *Lorine Niedecker: Woman and Poet.* Orono, ME: National Poetry Foundation, 1996.

Peperzak, A., ed. *Ethics as First Philosophy: The Significance of Emmanuel Levinas for Philosophy, Literature, and Religion.* New York: Routledge, 1995.

———. *To the Other: An Introduction to the Philosophy of Emmanuel Levinas.* West Lafayette, IN: Purdue UP, 1993.

Perelman, Bob. *Marginalization of Poetry: Language Writing, and Literary History.* Princeton, NJ: Princeton UP, 1996.

Perloff, Marjorie. "Canon and Loaded Gun: Feminist Poetics and the Avant-Garde." *Stanford Literature Review* 4 (1987): 23–45.

———. *The Dance of the Intellect: Studies in the Poetry of the Pound Tradition.* Cambridge: Cambridge UP, 1985.

———. "Introduction." *Gunslinger.* Durham, NC: Duke UP, 1989.

———. *Poetic License: Essays on Modernist and Postmodernist Lyric.* Evanston, IL: Northwestern UP, 1990.

———. *The Poetics of Indeterminacy: Rimbaud to Cage.* Princeton, NJ: Princeton UP, 1981.

———. *Radical Artifice: Writing Poetry in the Age of the Media.* Chicago: U of Chicago P, 1991.

———. "'The Shape of the Lines': Oppen and the Metric of Difference." In Hatlen, 215–229.

———. "The Shipwreck of the Singular: George Oppen's 'Of Being Numerous.'" *Ironwood* 26 (1985): 193–204.

Perloff, Marjorie, and Charles Junkerman, eds. *John Cage: Composed in America.* Chicago: Chicago UP, 1994.

Peterson, Jeffrey. "The Siren Song of the Singular: Armantrout, Oppen, and the Ethics of Representation." *Sagetrieb* 12.3 (1993): 89–104.

Pierce, Harvey. *The Continuity of American Poetry.* Middletown, CT: Wesleyan UP, 1987.

Plath, Sylvia. *The Collected Poems.* Ed. Ted Hughes. New York: Harper & Row, 1981.

Plato. *The Republic of Plato.* Ed. and trans. Benjamin Jowett. New York: P. F. Collier & Son, The Colonial Press, 1901. Project Gutenberg. <http://www.gutenberg.org/dirs/etext94/repub13.txt>. Accessed 15 August 2007.

Pollet, Sylvester. "Oppen's 'Return.'" *Sagetrieb* 2.2 (1983): 123–127.

Pound, Ezra. *ABC of Reading.* New York: New Directions, 1934.

———. *The Cantos of Ezra Pound.* New York: New Directions, 1971.

———. *A Draft of XXX Cantos.* New York: New Directions, 1990.

———. *Guide to Kulchur.* London: Faber and Faber, 1938.

———. *The Literary Essays of Ezra Pound.* Ed. T. S. Eliot. London: Faber 1954.

Power, Kevin. "Conversation with George and Mary Oppen, May 25, 1975." *Texas Quarterly* 21 (1978): 46–50.

Quartermain, Peter. *Disjunctive Poetics: From Gertrude Stein and Louis Zukofsky to Susan Howe.* Cambridge: Cambridge UP, 1992.

Rabaté, Jean-Michele. *Language, Sexuality, and Ideology in Ezra Pound's Cantos.* Albany: State U of New York, 1986.

Ray, Kevin. "Obvious Advertisement: Robert Duncan and the Kenyon Review." *Fiction International* 22 (1992): 286–291.

Reinfeld, Linda. *Language Poetry: Writing as Rescue.* Baton Rouge: Louisiana State UP, 1981.

Reisman, Jerry. "Lorine: Some Memories of a Friend." In Penberthy, 35–38.

Retallack, Joan. *The Poethical Wager.* Berkeley: U of California P, 2003.

———. "Poethics of a Complex Realism." In Perloff and Junkerman, 242–273.

Reznikoff, Charles. *Poems 1918–1975: The Complete Poems of Charles Reznikoff.* E. Seamus Cooney. 2 vols. Los Angeles: Black Sparrow, 1989.

———. *Holocaust.* Los Angeles: Black Sparrow, 1975.

———. *Testimony: The United States (1885–1915) Recitative.* Vol. I. Santa Barbara: Black Sparrow, 1978.

———. *Testimony: The United States (1885–1915) Recitative.* Vol. II. Santa Barbara: Black Sparrow, 1979.

Rieke, Alison. "Words' Context, Contexts' Nouns: Zukofsky's Objectivist Quotations." *Contemporary Literature* 33 (1992): 113–134.

Robbins, Jill. *Altered Reading: Levinas and Literature.* Chicago: U of Chicago P, 1999.

———. "*Visage, Figure:* Reading Levinas's *Totality and Infinity*." *Yale French Studies* 79 (1991): 135–149.

Rorty, Richard, ed. *The Linguistic Turn: Recent Essays in Philosophical Method.* Chicago: U of Chicago P, 1967.

Rothenberg, Jerome, and Pierre Joris, eds. *Poems for the Millennium.* Vol. 1. Berkeley: U of California P, 1995.

Rudman, Jack. "Sometimes a Painful Existing." *Ironwood* 22 (1983): 159–172.

Said, Edward W. *Orientalism.* New York: Pantheon, 1978.

———. *The World, the Text, and the Critic.* Cambridge: Harvard UP, 1983.

Sartre, Jean-Paul. *Being and Nothingness.* Trans. Hazel E. Barnes. New York: Washington Square, 1992.

Savage, Elizabeth. "Innovation as Interrogation in American Poetics (Frances Sargeant Osgood, Lucy Larcom, Adah Menken, Lizette Reese, Nineteenth Century, Twentieth Century, Truth, Cultural Narratives, Women Writers)." *Dissertation Abstracts International.* Vol. 59–05A, 1998: 1575.

Schiffer, Reinhold. "Interview with George Oppen." *Sagetrieb* (1984): 9–23.

———. "Robert Duncan: The Poetics and Poetry of Syncretic Hermeticism." *Poetic Knowledge: Circumference and Center.* Eds. Roland Hagenbüchle and Joseph T. Swann. Bonn: Bouvier, 1980.

Scott, Charles. *The Question of Ethics: Nietzsche, Foucault, and Hiedegger.* Bloomington: Indiana UP, 1990.

Scott, Joan. "Gender: A Useful Category of Historical Analysis." *Gender and the Politics of History.* New York: Columbia UP, 1988.

Scroggins, Mark. "The Revolutionary Word: Louis Zukofsky, *New Masses,* and Political Radicalism in the 1930s." In Scroggins, 44–64.

Scroggins, Mark, ed. *Upper Limit Music: The Writing of Louis Zukofsky.* Tuscaloosa and London: U of Alabama P, 1997.

Seed, John. "Remembering." 5 Jul 2005. Amazon Customer Review. <http://www .amazon.com/gp/product/0781206243/sr=8–2/qid=1148747019/ref=sr_1_2/ 103–3489529-9420638?%5Fencoding=UTF8>. Accessed 25 May 2006.

Sharp, Tom. "'Objectivists' 1927–1934: A Critical History of the Work and Association Of Louis Zukofsky, William Carlos Williams, Charles Reznikoff, Carl Rakosi, Ezra Pound, George Oppen. Volumes I And II." PhD diss., Stanford U, 1982.

———. "George Oppen: Discrete Series 1929–1934." In Hatlen, 271–292.

Sharpe, Charles H. "George Oppen: The World Intact." *Ironwood* 26 (1985): 114–115.

Shevelow, Kathryn. "History and Objectification in Charles Reznikoff's Documentary Poems, *Testimony* and *Holocaust*." *Sagetrieb* 1 (1982): 290–306.

Shoemaker, Steven. "Between Contact and Exile." In Scroggins, 23–43.

Shoptaw, John. "Hejinian Meditations: Lives of *The Cell*." *Journal X* 1.1 (1996). <http://www.olemiss.edu/depts/english/pubs/jx/1_1/shoptaw.html>. Accessed 17 February 2005.

Silliman, Ronald, ed. *In the American Tree.* Orono, ME: National Poetry Foundation, 1986.

———. "For Open Letter." *Open Letter* 7 (1977): 89–93.

———. "Third Phase Objectivism." *Paideuma* 10 (1981): 85–92.

Simpson, Megan. *Poetic Epistemologies: Gender and Knowing in Women's Language-Oriented Writing.* Albany: State U of New York, 2000.

———. *Some Imagist Poets: An Anthology.* Boston: Houghton Mifflin Company, 1915.

"Sonata form." *The Harvard Dictionary of Music* (2003). <http://0-www.xreferplus .com.library.utulsa.edu:80/entry/4665767>. Accessed 17 May 2006.

Stein, Gertrude. *Stanzas in Meditation.* Los Angeles: Sun & Moon, 1994.

———. *Tender Buttons.* Los Angeles: Sun & Moon, 1991.

Stewart, Jon, ed. *The Phenomenology of Spirit Reader: Critical and Interpretive Essays.* Suny Series in Hegelian Studies. Albany: State U of New York, 1998.

Suleiman, Susan Rubin. *Subversive Intent: Gender, Politics, and the Avant-Garde.* Cambridge: Harvard UP, 1990.

Taggart, John. "Of the Power of the Word." *Ironwood* 22 (1983): 192–198.

———. John Taggart Papers. MSS 11. University Library, Mandeville Department of Special Collections, U of California, San Diego—abbreviated UCSD, followed by numbers representing collection, box, and folder.

———. "To Go Down to Go Into." *Ironwood* 16 (1988): 270–285.

———. "Walk-out: Reading George Oppen." *Chicago Review* 44.2 (1998): 29–93.

Tickner, Lisa. "Men's Work? Masculinity and Modernism." *differences* (1992): 1–37.

Tidd, Ursula. "The Self-Other Relation in Beauvoir's Ethics and Autobiography." *Hypatia*, 14.4 (Fall 1999): 163–174.

Trotter, David. *The Making of the Reader: Language and Subjectivity in Modern American, English, and Irish Poetry.* New York: St. Martin's, 1984.

Vickery, Ann. *Leaving Lines of Gender: A Feminist Genealogy of Language Writing.* Hanover, NH: Wesleyan UP, 2000.

Vintges, Karen. "Simone de Beauvoir: A Feminist Thinker for Our Times." *Hypatia* 14.4 (Fall 1999): 133–144.

von Hallberg, Robert. "'This Marvelous Accidentalism.'" In Wesling, 45–86.

Wagner-Martin, Linda. *Sylvia Plath: A Literary Life.* New York: St. Martin's, 1999.

Watten, Barrett. *Total Syntax.* Carbondale: Southern Illinois UP, 1984.

Weisman, Karen A. "'The Most Beautiful Thing in the World'?: George Oppen's Quest for Clarity." *American Poetry* 7.3 (1990): 20–30.

Wesling, Donald, ed. *Internal Resistances: The Poetry of Edward Dorn.* Berkeley: U of California P, 1985.

Weinberger, Eliot, ed. *American Poetry Since 1950: Innovators and Outsiders.* New York: Marsilio, 1993.

———. "A Case of AIDS Hysteria." *Sulfur* 3.3 (1984): 170–172.

Willet, Cynthia. *Maternal Ethics and Other Slave Moralities.* New York: Routledge, 1995.

Williams, William Carlos. "The New Poetical Economy." In Hatlen, 267–270.

———. *Paterson.* Ed. Christopher J. MacGowan. Rev. ed. prepared by Christopher MacGowan, ed. New York: New Directions Pub. Corp., 1992.

———. *Selected Poems.* Ed. Charles Tomlinson. New York: New Directions, 1985.

Woods, Tim. *The Poetics of the Limit: Ethics and Politics in Modern and Contemporary American Poetry.* New York: Palgrave, 2002.

Wyschogrod, Edith. "The Art in Ethics: Aesthetics, Objectivity, and Alterity in the Philosophy of Emmanuel Levinas." *Ethics as First Philosophy: The Significance of Emmanuel Levinas for Philosophy, Literature, and Religion.* Ed. Adriaan Peperzak. New York: Routledge, 1995.

Ziarek, Ewa Plonowska. *The Rhetoric of Failure: Deconstruction of Skepticism, Reinvention of Modernism.* Buffalo: State U of New York, 1996.

Ziarek, Krzysztof. *Inflected Language: Toward a Hermeneutics of Nearness.* Albany: State U of New York, 1994.

———. "The Language of Praise: Levinas and Marion." *Religion and Literature* 22 (1990): 93–107.

———. "The Semantics of Proximity: Language and the Other in the Philosophy of Emmanuel Levinas." *Research in Phenomenology* 19 (1989): 213–247.

———. "Semiosis of Listening: The Other in Heidegger's Writings on Holderlin and Celan's 'The Meridian.'" Unpublished essay, 1992.

Zukofsky, Louis. *"A."* Berkeley: U of California P, 1978.

———. *All: The Collected Short Poems, 1923–1958.* New York: Norton, 1965.

———. *Bottom: On Shakespeare.* Austin, TX: The Ark, 1963.

———. *Prepositions: The Collected Critical Essays of Louis Zukofsky.* Berkeley: U of California P, 1981.

———. "Sincerity and Objectification: With Special Reference to the Work of Charles Reznkkoff" and "Program: Objectivist." *Poetry* 37 (1931): 268–285.

Index

Allen, Donald M., 5

alterity. *See* Other

Andrews, Bruce, 13, 102, 123, 188

Antin, David, 46

Arendt, Hannah, 72, 73

Armantrout, Rae, 155

art, 44, 45

Auden, W. H., 215

avant-garde poetry. *See* poetry

Baker, Peter, 20, 24, 159, 169

Baudrillard, Jean, 13

Beauvoir, Simone de, 9, 131, 148, 154, 156, 157, 167, 168, 202, 205, 221, 240n

Bernstein, Charles, 6, 74, 219, 232n

Bible. *See* religion

Blake, William, 101, 124, 129, 132, 236n

Blanchot, Maurice, 17, 19, 50, 64, 69–71, 101, 235n

Blaser, Robin, 5, 121, 123, 126, 131, 135

body, 28, 98, 118, 119, 120, 126, 128–131, 133, 134, 137–143, 147–149, 152, 153, 156–158, 162, 163, 168–170, 172, 173, 175, 176, 178, 180, 181, 186, 193–196, 200–204, 219–222, 227

Bronk, William, 5

Buber, Martin, 139

Bunting, Basil, 4

Caputo, John, 107

Cavel, Stanley, 13

Celan, Paul, 18, 47

Chanter, Tina, 154

Cixous, Hélène, 164, 239n

close reading, 19, 224–227

coincidence, 11, 198, 199, 200, 201, 221

community, 41, 91, 93, 99–102, 105, 109, 111–113, 117, 131, 139, 149, 152, 199, 203, 217, 219, 220, 221

complicity, 55, 56, 74–85, 116, 172, 192, 219, 224

content, 19, 34, 35, 37, 42, 43, 46, 48, 50, 55, 59–61, 85, 92, 105, 108, 116, 121, 124, 131, 140, 146, 157, 166, 170, 175, 184, 185, 215, 221, 223, 225

Coolidge, Clark, 6

Cornell, Drucilla, 154

Creeley, Robert, 5, 88

cultural studies, 9

Dante, 131, 143, 175

Davidson, Michael, 31, 93, 94, 130, 233–240n

Descartes, René, 94

Derrida, Jacques, 5, 10–12, 17, 78, 79, 94, 105, 165, 230n, 238n

desire, 27, 29, 30, 31, 37, 38, 55, 61, 63, 146, 148, 194, 218

Dickinson, Emily, 164, 166, 168, 170, 174, 181, 240–241n

Dienstfrey, Patricia, 156

dire. See the saying

dit. See the said

Dorn, Edward, 5, 9 14, 20, 88, 89, 91–117, 133, 140, 148, 172, 219, 221, 234–237n; *The Gunslinger*, 20, 91–117, 148, 172, 219, 221, 225, 235n, 236n

Dostoevsky, Fyodor, 187

double-double turn, 6

Duncan, Robert, 5, 6, 9, 14, 20, 28, 88, 89, 118–149, 152; *Bending the Bow,* 118, 120–126, 129, 131, 132, 136, 140, 142, 144, 147, 163, 170–173, 183–186, 202, 204, 219, 220, 225, 237–240n; *Groundwork: Before the War,* 120, 130, 141, 143; *Letters,* 121–122; *Opening of the Field,* 146; *Passages* poems, 20, 119–134, 138–145, 147–149, 157, 220, 238n; *Roots and Branches,* 146

DuPlessis, Rachel Blau, 5, 42, 153, 159, 160, 174, 231n, 232n, 239–240n

ecstatic. *See* ekstasis

ekstasis, 97, 99, 101, 102, 133

Eliot, T. S., 55

eros. *See* love

ethical turn, 7, 20, 31, 64, 68, 97, 120, 131, 133, 165, 206, 222, 226

ethical. *See* ethics

ethics, 1, 6, 7, 19, 20, 24–28, 31, 33, 35, 36, 38, 41–48, 51, 58, 60, 63, 65–79, 85, 88–94, 97, 99, 100, 102, 103, 107, 109, 110, 114, 116, 117, 119, 122–127, 131, 134, 135, 138–141, 144–149, 152–156, 159–164, 166, 169–175, 180, 183–189, 192, 193, 199, 202, 211, 212, 217–227

excess, 89, 92, 93, 95, 98–103, 105–111, 114, 115, 117, 119, 121, 122, 126, 138, 141, 219

existentialism, 8, 88, 143

experimental poetry. *See* poetry

failure, 10–14, 24, 25, 30–36, 47, 60–65, 89, 112, 184, 185, 216–218

Fanon, Frantz, 9

feminism, 8, 9, 152–168, 174, 181, 185, 212

form, 2, 18–21, 24, 25, 34, 38, 43, 44, 46, 50–60, 64–67, 72, 73, 76, 78, 84, 89, 92, 103, 105–110, 116–121, 124, 131, 138–141, 144, 146, 149, 153, 157, 160, 162, 165–167, 170–177, 180–213, 221–227

Foucault, Michel, 6, 12, 203

Fraser, Kathleen, 155

Fredman, Stephen, 66, 67, 74, 127, 235–236n

freedom, 9, 16, 88, 122, 146, 149, 163, 165, 168, 172, 176–178, 180, 213, 220, 227

gender. *See* sex

Gilligan, Carol, 154

Ginsberg, Allen, 224, 241n

Gleason, Madeline, 6

Grosz, Elizabeth, 154

H. D., 156, 230n

Harryman, Carla, 155

Hatlen, Burton, 44, 48, 59

Hegel, Georg Wilhelm Friedrich, 9, 36, 46, 95, 168, 229n, 240n

Heidegger, Martin, 12, 15, 20, 46, 53, 59, 96–98, 133, 166, 173, 181, 225, 229n, 231n, 235n

Hejinian, Lyn, 1–6, 8, 11, 15, 20, 152–158, 182–214, 221, 222, 239–240n; *The Cell,* 1, 3, 20, 155, 183–214, 239–242n; *My Life,* 182, 183

Holocaust, 7, 64–65, 68–74, 78–85, 117, 173, 218

homosexuality, 62, 63, 135, 148, 170, 220, 224, 225. *See also* sexual orientation

Howe, Fanny, 152

Howe, Susan, 6, 10, 15, 20, 28, 152, 155, 157, 159–185, 197, 201, 206, 212, 221–225, 239–241n; *Defenestration of Prague,* 167; *My Emily Dickinson,* 162, 165, 172–177, 180, 181, 183, 224; *The Liberties,* 162, 163, 180; *The Nonconformist's Memorial,* 20, 159, 162, 164, 166, 169–180; *Singularities,* 163, 166, 175

identity, 9, 10, 11, 24, 36, 59, 91–99, 102, 105, 110–113, 120, 121, 128, 129,

137, 139, 145–149, 153, 157, 160, 161,
163, 165, 166, 168, 169, 172–174, 177,
180, 183, 199–201, 207–212, 217–224,
227
Imagism, 4, 85, 143
innovative poetry. *See* poetry
Irigaray, Luce, 133, 154, 162, 163, 167–169,
171, 172, 189, 207, 238n

Jardine, Alice, 162
Jews. *See* Judaism
Jones, LeRoi, 224
Judaism, 4, 5, 7, 24, 40, 61, 64–73, 80, 81,
85, 218, 224
judgment, 3, 37–39, 42, 49–52, 59, 62–67,
73–85, 89, 107, 116, 128, 137, 145, 155,
162–164, 174, 185–188, 192, 195, 208–
212, 217–222, 227; phenomenology of,
77–84

Kant, Emmanuel, 7
Kristeva, Julia, 10, 12, 17, 148, 153, 154, 156,
161, 177, 230n, 239–240n

Lacan, Jacques, 13
Language poetry, 6, 8, 25, 49, 151–157,
160, 162, 182, 185
Levertov, Denise, 5, 88
Levinas, Emmanuel, 4, 7, 10–12, 15–20,
27, 28, 33, 36–38, 40, 43–46, 50, 52, 59,
60, 62, 63, 67–72, 78, 79, 105–117, 127,
133, 134, 146, 148, 156, 165, 166, 169,
172, 173, 187, 210, 225, 229n, 230–234n,
237n; *Ethics*, 36; *Existence & Existents*,
27; *Otherwise than Being*, 16, 67,
234n; *Totality and Infinity*, 7, 36, 44,
45, 106
Lévi-Strauss, Claude, 94, 96
Lewis, Wyndham, 41
linguistic turn, 6, 7, 89, 137, 165, 223
lived experience, 156, 197
long poem. *See* form

love, 89, 119, 120, 126–127, 137, 140, 141,
144, 146, 147, 149, 152, 173, 217, 221
Lyotard, Jean-François, 8, 13

Marxism, 8, 9
maternity, 68–71, 147
Mayer, Bernadette, 152
McCaffery, Steve, 46, 181, 183, 231n
Melnick, David, 151
Melville, Herman, 52
Merleau-Ponty, Maurice, 128, 129, 131,
133, 143, 148, 156, 157, 186, 187, 202
Messerli, Douglas, 152, 198
Mill, John Stuart, 7
Miller, Henry, 138
Modernism. *See* Modernist
Modernist, 3–5, 23, 29, 31, 35, 37, 41, 42,
45, 56, 65, 143, 153
Monroe, Harriet, 4
morality, 2, 4, 7, 9, 26, 40, 41, 44, 47, 52,
59, 63–67, 73, 76, 77, 79, 81–85, 89–93,
113, 114, 121–126, 135, 144, 153–156,
185–193, 202, 215–220, 223, 227
morals. *See* morality

Nancy, Jean-Luc, 9, 98, 99, 101
nearness. *See* proximity
New York, 4, 6, 43, 62, 64, 233n
Niedecker, Lorine, 4, 152, 156, 161, 164,
221, 239n
Nietzsche, Friedrich, 97, 116, 181, 229n
Notley, Alice, 152

objectification, 25, 29, 61, 63, 64, 67, 134
Objectivists, 3–5, 8, 12, 23–25, 28, 29, 34,
36, 38, 40, 44, 49, 53, 61, 64, 67, 73, 74,
78, 82, 84, 87, 88, 122, 123, 161, 187, 218,
229n, 230n, 231n, 233n
obligation, 11–21, 24, 25, 31, 34, 37–60,
63, 67–81, 84, 85, 89, 106, 107, 116–119,
126–128, 133, 137, 139, 141–148, 152, 165,

Sartre, Jean-Paul, 9, 156
satire, 91, 92, 101, 104, 108, 114, 115, 116,
    197, 219
the saying, 15, 16, 18, 34, 44, 46, 53–55, 59,
    60, 107, 116, 127, 140, 148, 151, 152, 157,
    165–167, 172, 174, 177, 183, 212, 217, 222,
    223
Scalapino, Leslie, 152
self. See identity
sex and gender, 41, 153–158, 161, 162,
    166, 169, 173, 175, 178, 180, 181, 184,
    188, 193–198, 200, 202–206, 209–213,
    219–225
sexual alterity, 15, 158, 169–173, 180, 181,
    206, 211, 213, 221, 222
sexual difference, 2, 152–165, 169, 177,
    180, 188, 189, 192, 196, 197, 200,
    204–208, 210–213, 222
sexual orientation, 157, 169. See also
    homosexuality
sexuality, 120, 131, 134–136, 138, 147,
    149, 157, 170, 200, 201, 204, 210, 219,
    221
Shoah. See Holocaust
silence, 28, 46, 50–52, 55, 57, 67, 73, 81,
    140–144, 149
Silliman, Ron, 6, 13, 188, 191, 192, 198
sincerity, 18, 25, 40, 79, 89, 122, 128, 187,
    218
Spicer, Jack, 5, 128
Stein, Gertrude, 49, 156, 164, 166, 184,
    186, 188, 189, 192, 201, 208
Stevens, Wallace, 106
subjectivity. See identity
substitution, 71, 79–80, 82
survivor guilt, 69, 70, 79
Swift, Jonathan, 96, 116, 163

Taggart, John, 140, 237–238n
Templeton, Fiona, 152
theme. See content
Thoreau, Henry David, 93, 101, 235n
totality, 8–11, 17, 18, 23–31, 35, 39, 47, 51,
    52, 53, 57, 61, 63–65, 88, 92, 94, 95, 100,
    102, 105, 112, 113, 119, 120, 133, 184, 193,
    195, 196, 200, 203, 205, 207, 208, 213,
    216, 224, 230n
the trace, 10, 11, 16, 18, 19, 46, 53, 95, 105,
    106, 109, 111, 113, 131, 145, 166, 178, 223,
    225, 226

universal, 3, 58, 69, 127, 132, 134, 165, 167,
    194, 197, 225

Vietnam, 6, 8, 48, 75, 114, 118, 124, 128,
    131, 132, 216
vulnerability, 41–47, 50, 52, 57, 60, 64, 85,
    118, 216, 227

Waldrop, Rosemary, 152, 155, 157
Watten, Barrett, 201, 202, 205
Weingberger, Eliot, 91
Wiesel, Elie, 82
the what is, 88, 89, 92, 95, 106, 109, 123,
    124, 125, 126, 128, 131, 132, 145, 220
Whitman, Walt, 48, 217
Williams, William Carlos, 4, 14, 20, 23,
    35, 43, 58, 63, 123, 130
Woods, Tim, 3, 24, 26, 34, 152, 155, 239n

Ziarek, Ewa P., 154, 230n, 239n
Ziarek, Krzyzstof, 229–232n
Zukofsky, Louis, 4, 5, 14, 23–28, 31, 34, 39,
    47, 61, 63, 88, 119, 124, 184, 232n, 233n;
    Prepositions, 25–28